F

Play Ball!

Doughboys and Baseball during the Great War

Barnes, Belmonte & Barnes

Schiffer Publishing Ltd
4880 Lower Valley Road • Atglen, PA 19310

Library of Congress Control Number: 2018956490

Edited by Ian Robertson
Designed by Jack Chappell
Cover design by Jack Chappell
Cover image courtesy of Library of Congress
Type set in Bosox/Sabon/Georgia

ISBN: 978-0-7643-5678-0
Printed in China

Published by Schiffer Publishing, Ltd.
4880 Lower Valley Road
Atglen, PA 19310
Phone: (610) 593-1777; Fax: (610) 593-2002
E-mail: Info@schifferbooks.com
Web: www.schifferbooks.com

Contents

This book is respectfully dedicated to all the Americans who put aside their daily work clothes for US Army khaki, US Navy blue, or US Marine Corps green in the Great War.

Casey Stengel, a renowned outfielder and US Navy sailor in 1918, once responded to a writer's question about playing baseball, saying:

> We're the hero today and the goat tomorrow. . . . It only goes to show you that good luck is as sure to stumble your way as bad luck. You've got to learn how to take both. You have to remember that nothing lasts—neither the good nor the bad.

Casey's words would have been easily understood by the Doughboys in the First World War and by all United States soldiers, sailors, airmen, coast guardsmen, and Marines in the period since.

Lest We Forget

Acknowledgments

As with all military history books, this project would never have been possible without the help of some truly good friends: Charles G. "Chuck" Thomas, Brennan Gauthier, Serge Kugener, Rogier VandeHoef, Col. (ret.) James "Sluggo" Ebertowski, the honorable Joan Shkane, Jesse Smith at the Virginia War Memorial, Christopher Garcia at the Virginia War Museum, Marvin-Alonzo Greer, and Maj. (ret.) Richard "Digger" Dell. All gave freely of their own time to ensure the accuracy and readability of the book you are holding. Brennan, Rogier, Serge, Marvin, and Chuck also contributed some extremely valuable pieces of their personal collections to ensure the completeness of this work.

Other important contributors were Maj. Gen. (ret.) Ken Bowra, Kevin Born, John Adams-Graf, Ed Loyd, Dr. Margaret McMahon, Sven (Ole) Jordan and the Walter Erickson Collection, Luther Hanson, Dr. John Metz, the National Guard Educational Foundation, the Canadian War Museum, the Kautz Family YMCA Archives at the University of Minnesota, the New York Department of Military and Naval Affairs, the Library of Virginia, the Library of Congress, the National Archives, the Robert Goodwin Collection, the US Army Quartermaster School and Museum, the Army Logistics University, the US Army Military History Institute, and the Virginia National Guard Archives.

We also wish to thank the management, staff, fans, and players of the Richmond Flying Squirrels for keeping the love of the game alive for all of us. Especially noteworthy are Ed Loyd, Charley and Steven Moore, Janice Tapia, Bonnie Siddons, Ray Edwards, Tom Schaefer, Allen Moser, Bill Anderson, Jeff O'Flaherty, Parney Parnell, and, of course, Nutzy.

Color photography of uniforms and artifacts is courtesy of Alison Hutton unless otherwise indicated.

We also received the help and encouragement of some truly fine soldiers: MG Timothy P. Williams, BG James Ring, BG Walt Mercer, BG Paul Griffin, Col. (ret.) Charles R. Brown, CW5 John L. Birkner, Col. Matthew

Hamilton, LTC Stephen Crow, and SGM Alan Ferris. Thanks are also owed to Josh VerStandig, Dylan Krupp, Bryan Hutton, Sam Glier, Michael Coddington, and Josh Lurier for their great support.

Many thanks are owed to Bob Biondi and Peter Schiffer for giving us the opportunity to tell this story. We would also like to thank Ian Robertson and Jack Chappell for bringing it to life.

And perhaps most of all, a sincere thank you to our wives—Michele Barnes, Pam Belmonte, and Emily Barnes—for their patience and sense of humor. In the dictionary, next to the phrase "long suffering, " are pictures of these three ladies.

Foreword: Batter Up

Baseball is the most American game. No other sporting contest so closely reflects the American psyche and culture. Its uniqueness is derived from the fact that part of the game is clearly defined and unchanged since play first began, and another part of the game fluctuates and changes constantly. Like the United States, the hard-and-fast rules are few in number, yet critical to the game: there must be a diamond-shaped infield with bases at each corner, each base is ninety feet apart from the center of the base to the center of the next base, the pitcher's mound is sixty feet six inches from home plate, each team is allowed three outs during their time at bat, etc.

Beyond these rules, the universe of play is wide open. The size, shape, and depth of the outfield are different in each ballpark. The outfield can be bounded by a brick wall, a wooden wall, an earthen berm, a fountain, or even a "Green Monster." The outfield walls can be painted, plain, padded, or covered with ivy. The composition of the infield can be grass, dirt, AstroTurf, or any combination thereof. Defensive players may be arrayed by their manager or position coaches in countless formations, requiring only that the pitcher be on the mound and the catcher behind the plate. This need for analysis and flexibility may be one of the reasons that the leader of a ball club is called a "manager" instead of "coach, " as with most other team sports. As a result, the game is constantly evolving and allows a freedom of innovation much like the United States itself.

Two other features of baseball make it a unique game for players and spectators alike. Baseball is the only game where there is a degree of danger for the fan on any given pitch. Anyone who does not believe that baseball can be a personally exciting experience is invited to sit directly behind the third-base dugout when a left-handed power hitter is at bat against a hard-throwing, right-handed pitcher. The second feature is even more important: baseball is timeless. Of all the major team sports, baseball is the only one not ruled by a clock. Recent attempts to speed up the game have added a clock to discourage pitchers from taking too long between pitches, but the game itself knows no time constraints. If the score is tied, the game continues until concluded.

So it is this set of strict rules for some aspects and the allowance of innovation for others that ties the game together. The nearly fanatical devotion the Doughboys of the Great War had for the game will be obvious as the reader moves through these pages. Whether they were in stateside training camps, just behind the front lines in France, or occupying the German Rhineland, the soldiers took advantage of every opportunity to play the game.

We three authors were drawn to the subject of Doughboys and the game of baseball. We are baseball fans as well as Great War historians, and being given the opportunity afforded by Schiffer Publishing to combine our two shared interests into one book is a dream come true.

The dream came with a price. We quickly realized that we would have to translate early-twentieth-century baseball terms into modern language. In most cases we relied on the participants to tell us about their baseball adventures through books, letters, and newspaper reports. Because we went directly to the source, we were confronted by words and phrases that were foreign to us, both as historians and ardent baseball fans. For example, the word "bingle" was often used as the term for a one-base hit that today we always call a "single." Pretty simple, right? How about referring to the pitcher in the pitcher/catcher "battery" as the "boxman"? How about calling errors "foozles"? Still simple? What was not nearly as

The love of baseball starts early. This prewar photograph shows a very small boy dressed and ready to play. In most American towns in the twentieth century, more boys would aspire to being a professional baseball player than to being the president of the United States.

simple were the references to the "Johnson League." Eventually we realized that this phrase referred to the American League, which was created and managed by Ban Johnson—hence the "Johnson League." When a modern-day baseball fan reads the box score for his team's game, one of the first things checked is the number of runs driven in by a player: the "runs batted in, " known as RBIs. Don't look for that number in the 1919 box scores from the Americans in France or Germany. Along with hits and runs, the scorekeepers were more likely to list the number of "put outs" and "assists" that were credited to a player than the RBIs.

Wherever possible, we searched the documents of the period to understand how soldiers viewed and talked about the game. At times, we wondered if they were speaking English. Read, for example, the following words from an April 1919 sports column in *The CRO* about the problems major league clubs were having while signing players for the 1919 season:

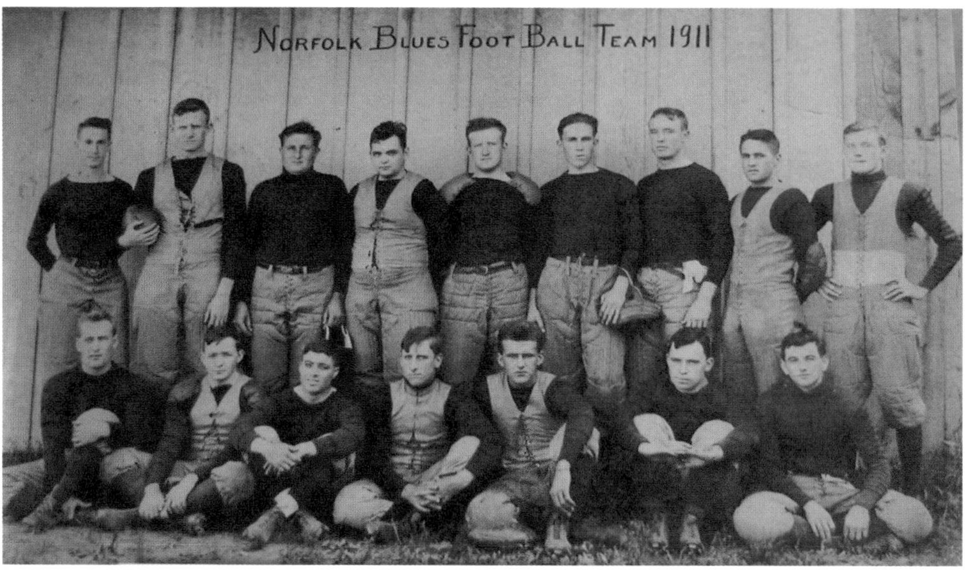

Even before the war began, soldiers were interested in team sports and were encouraged to serve on unit teams as a way to build unit cohesion and physical fitness. In 1911, the football team from the Virginia National Guard's Norfolk Light Artillery Blues poses for a group shot. By 1917, the Blues would be part of the 111th Field Artillery Regiment, 29th Division. *Courtesy of Virginia National Guard*

> New York is having a little trouble getting their new portsider, Dutch Leonard, into line. The raisin grower is obdurate and the officials the same. Like his colleagues, he is out of luck, and will probably affix his John Hancock to a document when he awakes to the fact that his holdup days in baseball are finis.[1]

We have also abstained from adding "[*sic*]" to quotes, preferring to let the Doughboys speak to you in their own words and with their own spelling without editorial comments. We have added brackets with some context in some quoted areas to give further explanation, or to clarify actions.

Another idiosyncrasy of the time was rooted in the fact that there were teams both from the American League and the National League in some cities: Boston, New York, St. Louis, Philadelphia, and Chicago. At times the Boston Braves were called the Boston Nationals and the Red Sox might be called the Boston Americans. Here is an example: "According to our friend, Hughey Fullerton, the New York Americans have a wonderful chance for the American League bunting."[2] Translation: Hughey thinks the Yankees will win the pennant. For a while the Yankees were also known as the Highlanders, due to the location of their playing field. The Cleveland Indians were often referred to as the "Cleveland Naps, " their earlier name in honor of their most famous prewar player and manager, Napoleon Lajoie (who was also known as ""Nap, " "Larry, " and "the Frenchman"). The Brooklyn Dodgers were also known as the Brooklyn Robins (in honor of their manager, Wilbert Robinson) or the Brooklyn Superbas or the Brooklyn Trolley Dodgers. More confusing were the myriad name changes among the many minor-league and Negro League teams. Nevertheless, we persevered, and we hope you will find the story that follows easily understood.

A few words about the Doughboys—the true subjects of the book. By the end of the war, there were over four million of them. More than two million were in France, fighting in the Meuse-Argonne Offensive, and another two million were in stateside training camps, awaiting their turn to cross the Atlantic to the western front. The ethnic and racial makeup of the soldiers in the US Army during the period is fascinating, and the subject of much research and discussion. Some argue that the

United States Army was the most diverse and integrated military force in the war—unless of course you happened to be African American or an immigrant from an African country. Of the four million men called Doughboys, approximately 800, 000 (almost 20 percent) were born outside the United States. Coming from Italy, Ireland, Poland, Latin America, Scandinavia, Liberia, Armenia, Holland, Russia, Greece, Iceland, Japan, China, and India, many men between ages eighteen and forty-five found themselves serving in the US military. Surprisingly, a large number also came from the enemy countries of Germany, Bulgaria, and Turkey and the Austro-Hungarian Empire; in many cases these men were also drafted, assigned to Army units, found to be trustworthy, and served honorably.

African Americans were not integrated into the main force, instead serving in segregated combat and logistics units. As one result, most baseball games in the Army were between soldiers from the same two racial categories that were on the service form: "White" or "Colored." Draft boards and Army personnel clerks struggled with the categorization for Asian men. Some would place them in the "white" category, while others would scratch out "White" and "Colored" and write in "Yellow" or "Japanese." Equally puzzling was the block on service forms for "Christian Name." With a good number of Jewish soldiers and a fair number of Islamic soldiers, the clerks made the best of the situation. They simply interpreted this as "First Name, " filled out the paperwork, and moved to the next soldier. Nevertheless, and in spite of this strange segregation of fighting forces, there were some integrated baseball games with teams from white units facing off against teams from African American units.

Before they became Doughboys, big-league and minor-league ballplayers were no more or no less patriotic than their fellow citizens. Some immediately rushed to join the Army after war was declared. Others did their very best to stay out of the Army by working in "war service" jobs in factories and shipyards. What no ballplayer—nor any US citizen of the period—wanted was to be considered a "slacker." This simple word carried so much more meaning in 1917 and 1918 than it does today. Sailors on shore leave after completing a transatlantic convoy would roam the streets and subways of New York City in "Slacker

Raids." They would arrest and turn in to local police stations the men they encountered without military identification or paperwork showing their exemption for war service work. As late as 1922, local newspapers would print the names of local men who had not registered for the draft, in what were known as "slacker" lists. As a result, most professional ballplayers chose either to enlist or find a job close to home in one of the many war industries.

Another important fact to keep in mind while reading this work is that while baseball is known as America's "National Pastime, " we share the North American continent with two other great countries. During the period before and during the Great War, many Canadians could be as fanatical in their love of baseball as citizens of the United States. A number of great ballplayers migrated southward to play in the American major leagues. Others remained in Canada to play on their many local minor-league teams in hopes of being traded or sold to the "big leagues." Regardless, as we shall see, the Canadian Army also brought baseball with them to France.

At times, it seemed to us that we were writing two different books on two different subjects. One book would be about the many professional baseball players who served in the US military in the Great War, and the other one about the Doughboys who maintained such a high enthusiasm for the game that they played even within range of enemy machine gun and artillery fire. This led us to ultimately realize that it truly is just one story, with the central theme being that the game and the players/soldiers are inseparable. If baseball truly is America's "National Pastime" and serves as a metaphor for the United States of the early twentieth century, the soldiers, sailors, and Marines of World War I were the all-American boys who made it so.

So with this modest introduction and explanation of some terms that will be encountered, it is time to roll the ball out to the pitching mound, get our "ball and strike" counter ready, nod to the waiting batter, and yell "Play Ball!"

1st Inning
I Don't Care If I Never Get Back

Famed American sportswriter Jimmy Cannon wrote, "It is part of our national history that all boys dream of being Babe Ruth before they are anyone else."[1] For the American men—and some women—serving in World War I, Ruth was already on his way to becoming an icon, but most of them had grown up with other baseball players as their heroes. Ty Cobb, Honus Wagner, Walter Johnson, "Home Run" Baker, and others filled their daydreams with baseball exploits for them to emulate. Other sports of the period drew an audience, but only baseball—and to a lesser degree boxing—truly had a grip on the average US sports fan during the period 1890 to 1916, the period during which most Doughboys were born or came of age.

Baseball of the prewar period was also a much-rougher game than it is today. Tommy Leach, a well-known infielder of the early-twentieth-century Pittsburgh Pirates, was recorded as saying:

> Baseball was a more exciting game back in those days. It was more rugged, first of all. Take the equipment. We had little gloves that would just fit over your hand. Now they have those big nets, and they catch the ball in the webbing. But we had to catch the ball with our hands.
>
> And the fields. Now the lowest minor leagues have better fields to play on than we had in the major leagues. You never knew how a ball was going to bounce in those days. Lots of times we'd get a rake and rake the ground around our own positions.[2]

A typical scene in any American town, city, or open field at the turn of the century: a group of boys playing a pickup game of baseball. The fact that these boys actually have a real catcher's mitt and a screen behind home plate sets them apart as being luckier than most of their contemporaries. *Courtesy of Library of Congress*

Edd Roush, another famous player from the period, agreed:

> Now they have infields and outfields that aren't full of rocks. . . . Back in the old days there were parks weren't much better than a cow pasture. Spring training was the worst. Some of these parks they'd want you to play exhibition games in had outfields like sand dunes and others were hard as a cement sidewalk.[3]

If these comments seem harsh and somewhat self-serving, they really aren't. Before the First World War, the United States was still essentially a frontier country populated by individuals who believed in setting their own paths, even if it meant raking your own part of the baseball diamond. One of the greatest prewar ballplayers was Howard "Smokey Joe" Wood. Wood recalled that in 1899, when his family moved from their home in the Midwest to Colorado, "they went by covered wagon

. . . [and] when he sat up on the front seat of the wagon next to his father he was wearing his baseball glove."[4]

During the first years of the twentieth century, many of the men who had fought in the Civil War were still alive. There were men in prison who had ridden with the Dalton and Doolin bank-robbing gangs. Oklahoma did not become a state until 1907, and it would not be until 1912 that Arizona and New Mexico were granted statehood. The American League did not begin play until 1901. The advent of Hollywood and the rapidly growing film industry advanced the national belief that anything was possible if you worked hard enough.

Another early ballplayer recalled that players of the time were "stupid guys, smart guys, tough guys, mild guys, crazy guys, college men, slickers

It was a natural progression from small boys playing baseball to soldiers playing on their unit's team. In this prewar picture, the "Indoor Baseball" team from Company C, 3rd New York Infantry Regiment—a National Guard unit, poses for their portrait. Turn-of-the-century National Guard armories had large-enough interiors to allow such sporting events. *Courtesy of NYDMNA*

from the city, and hicks from the country. Back then a country kid was likely to really be a country kid."[5] These same words could also be used to describe the American Doughboys of the Great War. It is small wonder that playing baseball had such an attraction to the soldiers and sailors during and after the war. They too were individualistic and were equally inclined to rake their own position, rather than expecting someone else to do it for them.

One of the biggest factors in baseball being such a large part of American life before the war was that there were ball teams everywhere. Most schools, towns, churches, colleges, Army units, Navy ships, and Marine Corps detachments, and many large or small businesses, fielded a team. Hans Lobert, a well-known Pittsburgh Pirate infielder, recalled that in "Williamsport, Pennsylvania, where I grew up, there was a team called the Demarest Sewing Machines that played only a few blocks from where we lived, and I used to sneak into the games all the time . . . so I wouldn't have to pay my ten cents."[6] Another prewar ballplayer recalled being on a team called the Hoegee Flags, a team sponsored by a sporting-goods store that provided uniforms showing flags of many nations on the back. The Flags became known for playing teams "all

Much farther to the west, in the Hawaiian Islands, the team from Company K, 2nd Infantry Regiment—a Regular Army unit, takes a break from practice to have their picture taken. Following the military tradition of "stacking arms," these ballplayers have used a catcher's mask to hold their bats in place and top off their stack with a brand-new, still-in-the-box baseball.

over Southern California, " where they even played against a very young but already dominating pitcher named Walter Johnson.[7]

It was the same all over the country and included all ethnic and religious groups and all neighborhoods. All fielded teams and supported their local heroes. In the countryside and in small towns, teams would borrow a horse-drawn wagon and travel to nearby towns looking for a game. Sam Crawford from Wahoo, Nebraska, a Hall of Fame outfielder and longtime teammate of Ty Cobb, later recalled his experience on such a trip:

> It was a lumber wagon, with four wheels, the kind they used to haul the grain to the elevator, and was pulled by a team of two horses. . . . I think there were eleven or twelve of us—and we just started out and went from town to town, playing their teams.
>
> One of the boys was a cornet player, and when we'd come to a town he'd whip out that cornet and sound off . . . and we'd announce that we were the Wahoo team and were ready for a ball game. . . . We didn't have any uniforms or anything, just baseball shoes maybe.[8]

Joe Wood recalled a similar enthusiasm in the town of

> Ouray, in western Colorado, nearly eight thousand feet above sea level . . . in 1903. Those people were crazy about baseball. They used to have town teams . . . and they'd cross the mountains to play each other. Everybody made a great hullabaloo out of those games.[9]

Another reason for baseball's popularity was that players of all body types and shapes could succeed if they had the talent and the personal drive to use it. Tall, lanky men with extremely long arms, such as Walter Johnson, could become great pitchers. Short, scrawny men, such as Wee Willie Keeler, could excel as infielders and hitters. Large, heavyset men, such as Babe Ruth, could become All Stars as both a pitcher and an outfielder while redefining the notion of power hitter. Jack-rabbit-fast men such as Hans Lobert could steal hundreds of bases and put on postgame exhibitions,

At the other, older end of the baseball spectrum, a group of Republican congressmen prepare for their annual baseball game against the Democrats—a tradition that began in 1909 and continues today. Since it would be fiscally irresponsible to have uniforms made each year, the ballplayers have borrowed uniforms from a number of local sources, including the United States Marine Corps and the Washington Senators. *Courtesy of Library of Congress*

racing against horses around the bases. Awkward looking, bow-legged men such as Honus Wagner could parlay their natural talent and toughness into a Hall of Fame career and a reputation as one of the greatest to ever play the game. Graceful Olympic gold-medal winners such as Jim Thorpe could showcase their talents on the diamond. Even deaf players such as William Hoy could display their outfield skills without hearing the crack of the bat or the shouted warnings of fellow outfielders.

It was a rougher period, with little or no regard for feelings, and a deaf player such as Hoy became "Dummy" Hoy to players and fans alike. For whatever reason, "Dummy" seems to have been the standard nickname for deaf players. Luther Haden Taylor of the New York Giants was also known as "Dummy, " and Dummy Deegan, Dummy

Leitner, and Dummy Stephenson all played in the big leagues, suffering with that nickname. Equally cruel was the nickname for Canadian-born Jay Justin Clarke. Due to his dark complexion he became known simply as "Nig" Clarke. (Clarke will reappear in later pages, and not because of his nickname; his service in the Marines in France will eventually persuade him to give up baseball for good and reenlist in the Marine Corps.) Hall of Fame pitcher Mordecai P. Brown had lost parts of two fingers in a childhood farm accident and therefore became known as "Three Finger" Brown. Ballplayers of Native American descent were invariably nicknamed "Chief." German Americans were often nicknamed "Dutch" or "Heinie, " and Jewish players were usually nicknamed "Moe." Other nicknames would be less cruel or ethnically driven, but still a sign of the times. Players who wore glasses became "Specs" or "Specks." Country boys joining a team were almost automatically nicknamed "Rube." In the early days of the century, big-league teams included Rube Marquard, Rube Waddell, and Rube Benton—all pitchers of some note.

In many ways, the makeup of the US military during the First World War mirrored the clubhouses of professional baseball. The Army, Navy, and Marine Corps were filled with country boys, city men, shop clerks, cowboys, coal miners, college kids, children of immigrants, and even recently arrived immigrants themselves. And like baseball, the military services were strictly segregated. African Americans were welcome to serve in the military, but only in the 9th and 10th Cavalry Regiments, the 23rd and 24th Infantry Regiments, or in one of the few Black National Guard units in Chicago, New York, Detroit, or Washington, DC. They were drafted in large numbers after the United States joined the war, but always only for service in segregated units, such as the 92nd and 93rd Divisions, one of the many pioneer infantry regiments, or one of the Services of Supply (SOS) logistical support units. Black baseball teams had existed as far back as 1859, and like many of the white minor leagues of the nineteenth century, their fortunes rose and fell with their ability to draw paying audiences to their games. In large eastern cities such as Philadelphia, Boston, and New York, the Negro Leagues tended to

Love of the game cut across all racial, country-of-origin, and economic boundaries. Here we have the well-dressed and most likely affluent Danbury (Connecticut) Men's Club; the man on the far left poses with his baseball bat. *Courtesy of Library of Congress*

flourish, but teams were also playing in Chicago and Kansas City. Some of the teams would have "Cubans" in their name to give the impression that the ballplayers had originated in the Caribbean.

Ultimately it did not matter; when universal military conscription was declared under the Selective Service Act of 1917, black ballplayers—Cuban or not—were subject to the same military draft as white ballplayers.[10]

It was the draft that had the greatest effect both on regular citizens and professional ballplayers alike as America entered the war. With speed of utmost importance in building the Army, the first step was to incorporate National Guard soldiers into the Regular Army forces. Under the provisions of the National Defense Act of 1916, the president had two choices for activating Guard units: He could either "call out" a Guard regiment for federal service, thereby allowing it to continue as a National Guard unit on active duty, or he could "draft" the unit into federal service, thus making it a federal unit. In most cases, the Guard units were activated under the first option as National Guard on active duty and a short while later were moved to the second category by presidential decree.[11]

In spite of patriotic fervor and bellicose prowar rhetoric, it was soon obvious that there were not enough volunteers rushing to the recruiting stations to build the US military to its required strength and size. More importantly, President Wilson believed that a nationally conscripted army would be more representative of true American ideals. It also supported his statements that America's entry into the war was not for national gain, but to establish a peaceful world. Therefore, all eligible men should take part in that vision. On the other hand, there was strong opposition by some congressmen from several southern states to the concept of universal drafting of men for the Army. These congressmen argued they were concerned that universal conscription would lead to a rise of militarism in the country and that it was un-American to force men into the US Army. However, their true motives became obvious. These congressmen disapproved of the draft because of their fear that it would provide military training to the African American men in their states, thus giving them the means to force racial equality. Assistant Army Chief of Staff Maj. Gen. Tasker H. Bliss saw through their subterfuge and wrote that the southerners did not like "the idea of looking forward five or six years by which time their entire male negro

Typical of the period, this Niagara Falls, New York, ballplayer gives a clear picture of the equipment and uniforms of the prewar period. Given the state of many of the fields on which they played, this rough-looking area could actually be one of the local baseball diamonds.

population will have been trained to arms."[12] Despite the objections of the southerners and some other antiwar congressmen, President Wilson and Secretary of War Newton Baker persevered and were able to pass the desired conscription legislation through Congress, making it strictly under civilian oversight.

The Selective Service Act of 1917 was designed to fix many of the problems that appeared during the Civil War, when a similar conscription act was established in the Northern states to provide soldiers for the Union Army. The Act of 1917 authorized a selective draft of all eligible males between ages twenty-one and thirty-one. It specifically prohibited any man selected from buying his way out of service by replacing himself with a paid "substitute." During the Civil War, the use of these substitutes had been one of the most despised features of the conscription act because it favored those with the money to pay their way out of serving by allowing them to provide someone else in their place.

The Act of 1917 allowed for some draft exemptions: family dependency, work in an occupation essential to the war effort, or personal religious beliefs. As we will see, some professional athletes, and in particular some major-league baseball players, sought exemption from the draft to continue their careers. Regardless of future intentions or desires, draft registration was required for all male citizens in the designated age group. Only after a man's registration was complete could any request for draft exemption be considered. Administration of the registration and subsequent draft was entrusted to local draft boards composed of civic leaders in each community or town. The country was divided into draft districts, with each district responsible for registering and managing approximately 2, 100 men. Large cities such as Philadelphia, Chicago, and New York would have more than fifty local "draft boards, " while smaller cities such as Baltimore would have only twenty-four. These boards registered the men and issued them draft cards, which included a draft number specific to that prospective draftee. The numbers were then drawn in a national lottery, and all men holding that number at each draft board were now considered to be "selected"—a much more palatable term than "drafted."

In 1917, almost ten million men registered for the draft. This number proved inadequate because a surprisingly large number of men either were exempted or were considered mentally or physically unfit to be soldiers. The War Department also recognized that the war in Europe was consuming vast quantities of manpower, and the government projected that the United States would require a massive Army to achieve victory. Therefore, in 1918, the age range for draft registration was expanded to include all males from eighteen to forty-five. At the beginning of the war, "the total male population of the country was about 54, 000, 000." By the end of 1918, under the new age guidelines, the total number of men registered for the draft had increased to twenty-six million.[13]

On 20 July 1917, Secretary of War Baker drew the first draft number out of a fishbowl with much ceremony and fanfare. Because the draft was universal, African-Americans and other minorities were included

And here the final step of the progression: being a professional baseball player was the dream that Americans of all shapes, sizes, and colors pursued in the early years of the twentieth century. In the days before the war, no numbers or names appeared on jerseys, and the mitt fit easily into a rear pocket. *Courtesy of Library of Congress*

on the same terms as whites. The irony was that the military force in which they would serve remained completely segregated as far as black and white soldiers were concerned. Of the more than three million men who were eventually drafted into the US Army, more than 300, 000 were African Americans. The remainder were white, Hispanic, Asian, or Native American. A large number of immigrants and foreign-born men working in the Unites States were also drafted. This was a consequence of their being in the United States when the draft was declared. Ultimately, approximately 800, 000 foreign-born men served in the US Army, making up almost 20 percent of the total force. Foreign-born men also served in the US Navy and Marine Corps. Some foreign-born women volunteers served in the Army Medical Corps as nurses and in the Army Signal Corps as telephone operators.[14]

As is the nature of all large organizations and bureaucracies, there were complaints about the draft system. Some alleged that draft boards were not completely impartial. Critics argued that some boards were rendering their decisions on exempting registrants more on the basis of their social class or community standing than the validity of their individual situation. In particular, farmers were more likely to be drafted than industrial workers. They based this fact solely on the "critical war effort" exemption, which tended to value factory work over farm labor. On the whole, the vast majority of US citizens found the entire draft system to be relatively fair.

In addition to understanding the draft and its consequences, it is also important to understand that the US Army of the period was actually three separate forces: The Regular Army, consisting of volunteers; the National Guard, a reserve force also made up of volunteers but closely tied to their states and local communities; and the National Army, which would be built from the many thousands of men being drafted. By 1918, of every hundred men in the Army, the draft had provided seventy-seven; the Regular Army, thirteen; and the National Guard, ten.

At first, National Army units also maintained a regional flavor similar to the National Guard, since the initial draftees from a region or city would be sent to train at the same location. Toward the end of the war, the distinctions among the Regular Army, the National Army, and the National

Guard had disappeared, since the Army made the decision to abandon this cumbersome "regional" concept. After that point, the Army would provide replacements from whichever source was most available. With combat losses—and in many divisions the heavy influx of replacements—whatever local character a division may have had in 1917 was gone by the end of 1918. In the beginning, it was the National Army into which most drafted professional ballplayers were assigned.

It is also important to understand a very significant difference between the Army of 1917 and the modern version. Today's US Army soldier receives his job-specific training at sites designated to provide that training. Quartermaster soldiers receive their specific job-related training at Fort Lee, while artillery soldiers receive theirs at Fort Sill, and so on. After completion of training, the modern-day soldier is then assigned to a unit and travels to where that unit is stationed. During World War I, each of the thirty-two major training camps set up for the National Guard and the National Army was expected to provide all of the training for a complete division. Certain skills, such as field artillery operations for officers or radio and telegraph repair or installation procedures, would be taught at other specialized training locations, but the soldier would almost always return to his original unit of assignment for the rest of his training. This separation of officers or enlisted men from a unit for periods of time for specialized training is considered the norm for today's soldier, but during the period in question there were some unexpected problems. In some cases, the officers or noncommissioned officers would be gone for considerable periods and would not train together with their soldiers until they reached France. After arrival in France, many officers would again be detached from their unit for even more specialized or tactical training. On completion of the training, they often returned to their home unit only to discover that many of the men under their command had been shipped out as replacements for other units.

And what of the soldiers themselves? The "average draftee of 1917 was five feet seven and a half inches in height and wore slightly over size seven shoes."[15] As a result of the first draft selecting men between ages twenty-one and thirty-one, the initial soldiers in the National Army were reasonably fit and mature. The later draft, which included men from age eighteen to forty-five, was considered by many to be less promising because of the large number of very young or much-older men. The expansion of the upper age limit from thirty-one to forty-five would also have a great effect on professional baseball because now many of the coaches, scouts, and even retired players were required to register and thus were eligible to be "selected." Before we can get to that point, it is necessary to understand the contentious relationship that developed between professional baseball, professional baseball players, the US government, and the Great War.

Tired of constant criticism from his political opponents about America's weak military forces, President Woodrow Wilson (*center*) leads a "preparedness" parade to showcase his support for a strong military. Unfortunately, when war is declared against Germany in April 1917, the Regular Army and National Guard are still woefully small in comparison to the force that will be needed. *Courtesy of Library of Congress*

2nd Inning
It's War! And the Game Goes On?

It may not have been a sign of things to come, but it was certainly a warning that life was about to change for the citizens of the United States. Francisco "Pancho" Villa's March 1916 raid on the small town of Columbus, New Mexico, set in motion a number of events that would greatly affect the citizens of the country and the game of baseball. While most of the Regular Army was hurriedly deployed to the Mexican border and then deep into Mexico itself, the National Guard units from all the states began to wonder what role they would play. They did not have long to wait, and their questions were soon answered. With Mexican cross-border attacks by other raider bands continuing, President Woodrow Wilson mobilized the National Guard units from Texas, Arizona, and New Mexico for service on the border. Unfortunately, these states could provide only a few thousand soldiers, and most of them were infantry. Many more soldiers, particularly cavalry, would be needed to secure the long US-Mexican border. Realizing this, Wilson then mobilized the National Guard from all the other states and ordered them to the border. This put another 100, 000 men in uniform and gave the country pause to reflect. While Europe was in flames, with the countries there fighting an increasingly deadly war using modern weapons such as gas, airplanes, and machine guns, the United States was quickly being dragged into a potential conflict on its southern border.

After many missteps and organizational problems mobilizing the Guard units in many states, some units began the long train ride to the border. Some of the first units to deploy came from Wyoming, Massachusetts,

Illinois, and California. For California, it proved to be a short trip, since the soldiers from that state directly sought to guard the state's southern border with Baja, California. Other states' units lagged behind, still trying to get the proper equipment and the right number of soldiers ready for duty. By the time most of the Guardsmen arrived and took up their positions on the US side of the border, the mission of the Punitive Expedition forces inside Mexico had changed. Instead of actively seeking out Pancho Villa, Brig. Gen. John J. Pershing's forces focused on patrolling and maintaining a defensive posture inside Mexico. With time, the Regular Army soldiers in Mexico and the National Guardsmen, now fully engaged in guarding the border, settled into their daily regimen of training and border patrol duty. Instead of the combat that many expected, they struggled to contend with the powerful combination of boredom, desert heat, dust storms, rattlesnakes, and stinging insects. To pass the time, the soldiers quickly learned to entertain themselves with baseball games,

A group of National Guard soldiers guarding the US-Mexico border gather around some of their baseball equipment. Baseball proved to be one of the healthier diversions for these Guard units, which spent almost eight months guarding the border. The campaign hats and canvas leggings so prominent in this photograph all would disappear, to be replaced with more-practical hats and puttees when the soldiers arrived in France.

boxing matches, sing-alongs, and endless poker games. One of the National Guard units serving to guard the Texas-Mexico border in the Brownsville area was Virginia's Battery B, Norfolk Light Artillery Blues. Justifiably proud of their athletic abilities in general, and their football skills in particular, they challenged the football team from nearby Texas A&M College to a game. In retrospect this was probably a bad decision, since they were beaten by the Texas college team 76 to 0. Nevertheless, it certainly gave the soldiers something to talk about besides the heat, dust, sunburns, and rattlesnake hunts. In many ways, the time on the border served as a preview for what many of them would encounter when they trained for another war in the not-too-distant future.

If the United States were to join in the European conflict, it was not going to be because the country had a great desire to fight in France. In many German American and Irish American communities, support was stronger for the German side than for the Allied countries. In the

A group of ballplayers from Troop C, 13th Cavalry Regiment, pose for a team picture while serving in the Punitive Expedition against Pancho Villa in 1916. The 13th was one of the Regular Army cavalry regiments that chased Villa and his men in the early days of the Mexican border campaign. The regiment and trooper William H. Goodwin (seated in front at far left) would spend the war guarding the border. *Courtesy of the Robert Goodwin Collection*

case of the Irish, the feelings were really more anti-British than pro-German, but the results were the same. Ultimately, it was the many German provocations—intentional or accidental—that finally forced the United States to end its neutrality and join Britain and France on the side of the Allies. President Woodrow Wilson and the US government had made their intentions of remaining neutral quite clear and expressed no desire to join in a European conflict that appeared to many Americans as a power struggle between royal families. In fact, the most important point of Wilson's 1916 reelection campaign had been "He kept us out of war." Even with maintaining neutrality, there were issues that continued to push the United States into the Allied camp. Wilson warned the German government that his country would sever diplomatic relations with Germany if they were to continue attacking neutral shipping and passenger vessels traveling across the Atlantic. On 4 May 1916, Germany agreed to his demands. In what became known as the "Sussex pledge, " they promised not to attack any more neutral ships.[1] That pledge soon proved worthless when Germany resumed their attacks. As a result, many US citizens now wanted the United States to enter the war. Yet, President Wilson still hesitated to commit the country to that course, realizing the cost in human lives such a commitment would require. However, the provocations continued. Making matters much worse, Germany was caught trying to recruit other countries to attack the United States; a telegram to this effect sent from Germany to Mexico was intercepted and deciphered by British intelligence in January 1917. German foreign minister Arthur Zimmerman sent a telegram to the German legation in Mexico, asking the ambassador to contact the Mexican president and request that they join Germany in a war against the United States as soon as it appeared that the US would declare war on Germany. The ambassador was also requested to ask the Mexican president to mediate between Germany and Japan—then at war with Germany—with an eye toward forming an alliance between them. In return, Germany would ensure that Mexico regained their lost territory in Texas, Arizona, and New Mexico. Although the British had intercepted the message in January, they needed to be patient to protect the capabilities of British intelligence from German discovery, so they delayed sharing the telegram with the US government. On 24 February 1917 the telegram

One of the few benefits of serving along the Mexican border was the abundance of open space to play baseball. In this rare photograph, Lt. Houghten of the 13th Cavalry Regiment takes his turn at bat. It is interesting to note that the lieutenant is still wearing his spurs as he waits for the pitch. *Courtesy of the Robert Goodwin Collection*

was presented to Woodrow Wilson. The incendiary details of the telegram were then provided to the American press on 1 March and were quickly published by them.[2]

The "Zimmerman telegram" immediately inflamed public opinion and gave Woodrow Wilson and the US Congress no other option but to declare war on Germany on 6 April 1917. Just two months earlier, the US War Department, at the direction of Secretary of War Newton Baker, had recalled the National Guard troops from the border and the Regular Army from within Mexico. The Army had been unable to capture Pancho Villa, but it had kept him on the run, and he never again attacked the United States. Now, with the political situation with Germany worsening every day, the Army was needed back in the Unites States to be ready in case war became necessary. Just as it had taken several weeks to send the National Guard to the border, it took nearly as long to bring them home. Some units returning to their home states were unpleasantly surprised to find that they were not going to be released from federal duty. Instead, these selected units were immediately deployed around key East Coast industrial sites, rail centers, bridges, and seaport complexes to guard against potential attacks or sabotage by the Germans.

When war was declared by the United States, it had already been recognized that a much-larger army than that which currently existed would be required to be sent to France. Although volunteers would be solicited to join the Regular Army and the National Guard, many more men would be necessary. It was obvious to most in the Army and the US government that a system of national conscription would be necessary. Under such a program, all men in the country would then serve as the manpower pool from which the draftees would be selected.

On 18 May 1917, just six weeks after declaring war, Congress passed the Selective Service Act of 1917, giving the government the authority to draft men from the twenty-one to thirty-one age group. Quickly, some 4, 684 local draft boards were established and

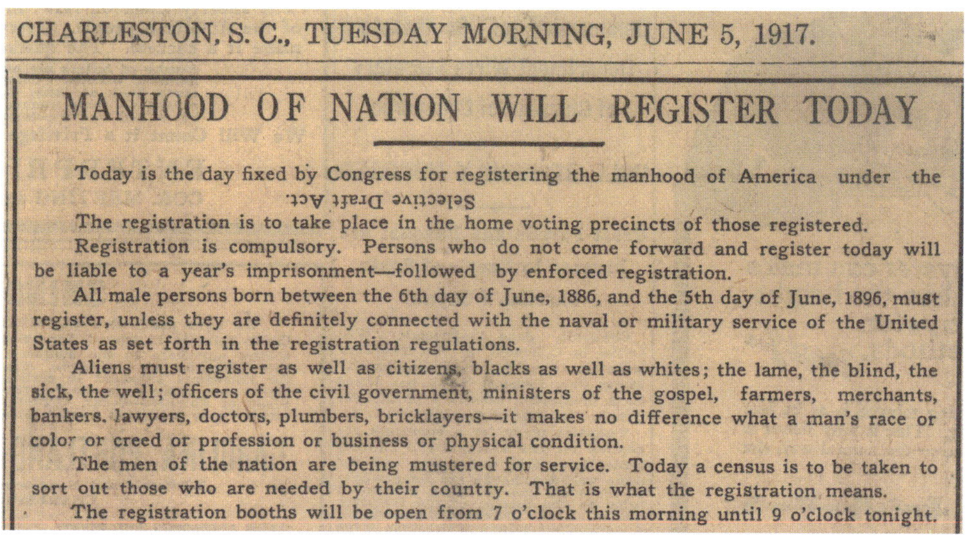

CHARLESTON, S. C., TUESDAY MORNING, JUNE 5, 1917.

MANHOOD OF NATION WILL REGISTER TODAY

Today is the day fixed by Congress for registering the manhood of America under the Selective Draft Act.

The registration is to take place in the home voting precincts of those registered.

Registration is compulsory. Persons who do not come forward and register today will be liable to a year's imprisonment—followed by enforced registration.

All male persons born between the 6th day of June, 1886, and the 5th day of June, 1896, must register, unless they are definitely connected with the naval or military service of the United States as set forth in the registration regulations.

Aliens must register as well as citizens, blacks as well as whites; the lame, the blind, the sick, the well; officers of the civil government, ministers of the gospel, farmers, merchants, bankers, lawyers, doctors, plumbers, bricklayers—it makes no difference what a man's race or color or creed or profession or business or physical condition.

The men of the nation are being mustered for service. Today a census is to be taken to sort out those who are needed by their country. That is what the registration means.

The registration booths will be open from 7 o'clock this morning until 9 o'clock tonight.

Clipped from a Charleston, South Carolina, newspaper from 5 June 1917, this announcement—hurriedly printed with three words upside down—makes it clear that all men between ages twenty-one and thirty-one, without exception, are required to register for the draft. Only after everyone had registered would consideration be given to exempting some men from serving in the military.

This 1918 recruiting poster depicts a pitcher either in a stylized Canadian or US Army uniform winding up to throw a grenade. The intended message is clear: good baseball players will make great soldiers. *Courtesy of Library of Congress*

supervised by the Office of the Provost Marshal General in Washington. These boards were set up under civilian control in all forty-eight states, the District of Columbia, and the territories of Hawaii, Alaska, and Puerto Rico. Each board was responsible for the registration, classification, and potential exemption for family care or current employment in war-related work of each age-eligible man in their local community. District boards each had jurisdiction over approximately thirty local boards. District boards could also hear appeals for exemption from serving in the military. Each local board handled an average registration of 5, 000 men. During the course of the war, there were three large-scale registrations: The first, on 5 June 1917, registered all men between ages twenty-one and thirty-one; the second, on 5 June 1918, registered all men who had turned twenty-one since the first registration (a supplemental registration was held on 24 August to register the men who had turned twenty-one subsequent to 5 June 1918); and the third, on 12 September 1918, registered all men between eighteen and forty-five.[3] The expansion of the age groups took place after hearings at the House Committee on Military Affairs, in which Secretary of War Newton D. Baker testified and said, "There are two ways of fighting this war. One is to make every possible effort and win it soon, and the other is to proceed in a somewhat more leisurely fashion and win it late."[4]

With the declaration of war in April 1917, the songwriters now included Uncle Sam in the fight. Of note here, besides the cheering Doughboys in the background, is the fact that Uncle Sam is a left-handed hitter like Ty Cobb and Babe Ruth. *Courtesy of Library of Congress*

Obviously the first option was the better one, and thus it was chosen. Even with the United States entering the war and the Selective Service Act in place, professional baseball teams played the entire 1917 season. The season had started off tumultuously with the possibility of a player strike. The strike had nothing to do with the war, or any national event, but for what was known in the baseball world as the "10-day clause." This clause worked on behalf of the club owners and ensured that teams would not have to pay players who were injured for more than ten days. While obviously unfair to players hurt during the course of a game or over the course of a career, it was hard for the professional baseball players advocating the strike to gain any traction. In part this was because the players' union was not recognized by the owners, and so there was no official cohesive and consolidated representation to stand up for the players against the "10-day clause." For the baseball fans, any hint of strike caused a negative reaction, and little public sympathy existed for the players. Fortunately, David L. "Dave" Fultz, a former American League player and practicing attorney, was serving as the president of the "Players Fraternity." Fultz had organized the Fraternity—a union-like organization—in 1912 and had the support

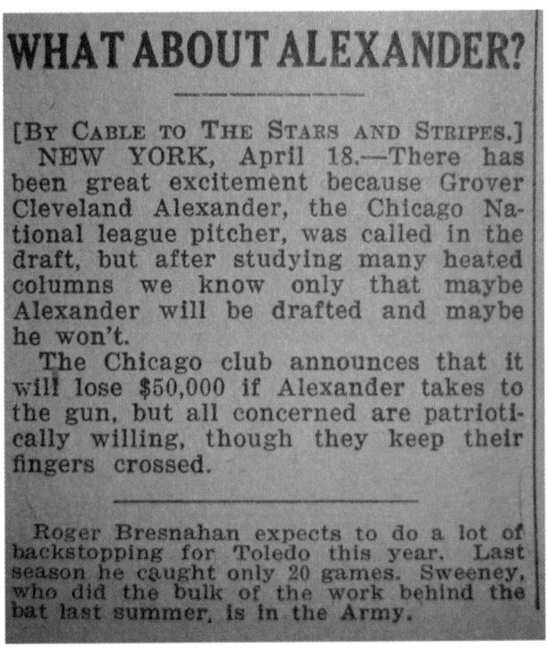

WHAT ABOUT ALEXANDER?

[BY CABLE TO THE STARS AND STRIPES.]

NEW YORK, April 18.—There has been great excitement because Grover Cleveland Alexander, the Chicago National league pitcher, was called in the draft, but after studying many heated columns we know only that maybe Alexander will be drafted and maybe he won't.

The Chicago club announces that it will lose $50,000 if Alexander takes to the gun, but all concerned are patriotically willing, though they keep their fingers crossed.

Roger Bresnahan expects to do a lot of backstopping for Toledo this year. Last season he caught only 20 games. Sweeney, who did the bulk of the work behind the bat last summer, is in the Army.

Another clipping from the Paris edition of the *Stars and Stripes* provided the draft status of famed major-league pitcher Grover Cleveland Alexander. Updates such as these were avidly followed by the Doughboys already in France, as they tracked who was joining them in military service and who was not. *Courtesy of the* Stars and Stripes

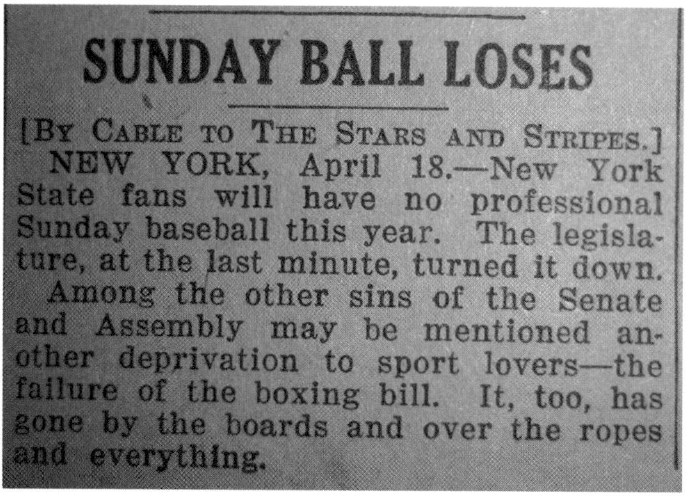
SUNDAY BALL LOSES

[BY CABLE TO THE STARS AND STRIPES.]

NEW YORK, April 18.—New York State fans will have no professional Sunday baseball this year. The legislature, at the last minute, turned it down.

Among the other sins of the Senate and Assembly may be mentioned another deprivation to sport lovers—the failure of the boxing bill. It, too, has gone by the boards and over the ropes and everything.

A quick update in the *Stars and Stripes*, letting the soldiers of the American Expeditionary Forces (AEF) know that there would be no professional baseball played in New York State for the foreseeable future and that boxing might also be banned in the state. *Courtesy of the* Stars and Stripes

of many current major leaguers. After some intense negotiations with the owners and little progress made, Fultz at first supported the idea of a player's strike. He came to realize that he did not have the support of all the players and that the time was not right to challenge the owners. After further negotiations with the team owners that slightly improved the players' working conditions, Fultz was able to convince them that a strike was not in their best interest.[5] And so the season continued.

The bad publicity arising from the potential "10-day clause" shutdown and the subsequent declaration of war against Germany, Turkey, Bulgaria, and the Austro-Hungarian Empire were just two of the factors that started the 1917 baseball season off on a sour note. Mother Nature also seemed against the 1917 season, since bad weather played a big role in delaying games at the start. Forty-eight games in the National League alone were postponed in the first month of the season.[6] Financial losses from these delays and postponements hit team bankrolls very hard. It was particularly devastating in the minor leagues, where several teams—always struggling to meet their team payrolls—folded before season's end.[7]

It did not help the owners or the players that many newspapers, as well as members of the general public, questioned why baseball was not doing more to support the war effort. Owners, conscious of the negative publicity, proved somewhat sensitive to the bad publicity and were willing to give in to public pressure. They encouraged their players to reach out to their local communities to boost morale and support the Army. Some players and coaches even learned military-style drills and then put on shows before games to demonstrate their willingness to support the country's military efforts. These drills were also advertised as preparing the ballplayers in case they were drafted or chose to volunteer.

In spite of the many problems and controversies, the season played on. Yet, questions continued to be raised about why these seemingly healthy baseball players were not joining in the fight. In a period when the greatest insult was to be called a "slacker, " the term was being heard more and more regarding professional athletes. By the end of 1917, the country was on a war footing. Large training camps were filling up with draftees and volunteers all preparing for their chance to fight for their country.

In France, Gen. John J. Pershing commanded the growing American Expeditionary Forces (AEF). It was expected that in 1918, the American force would take on a greater role in the war as the buildup continued. Industries were converting from prewar production to making weapons and equipment. Furniture factories began making stretchers for medical units, and the nation's clothing industry turned to making thousands of uniforms and overcoats. Families planted vegetables in their backyards and vowed to forgo meat on Mondays and wheat on Wednesdays. Opera goers and bird watchers donated their personal binoculars to the Army and Navy, which were desperately in need of such items. Now, with the American people increasingly energized to support the war effort, many were questioning whether the 1918 baseball season should be played at all.

Some team owners, such as Harry H. Frazee—owner of the Boston Red Sox—attempted to come up with solutions that both organized baseball and the draft boards could agree on for the 1918 season. Many of the teams began their spring training by visiting Army training camps and putting on exhibitions, still not knowing what the future held for them and for baseball.

The season started on schedule, without the weather issues of the previous year, but questions continued to be asked about the appropriateness of playing ball while American soldiers were fighting and dying in France. The biggest blow to baseball came in May 1918. It was Provost Marshal Gen. Enoch Crowder's edict that all men must be engaged in some "useful" occupation or else face the draft, regardless of their draft status or exemption classification. This was dubbed the "work or fight" edict, and it was primarily aimed at men who worked at such non-war-supporting jobs as pool room managers, bartenders, sales clerks, attendants, footmen, elevator operators, and the like. Organized baseball held its collective breath and waited to see whether the declaration applied to professional ballplayers. The final decision, promulgated by Secretary of War Newton Baker in early July 1918, was bad news for professional baseball. It lumped ballplayers into the work-or-fight category with all of the other "nonessential" job holders.[8]

The club owners were obviously as concerned as the players about the decision and looked desperately for a way to remain a viable sport, yet at the same time support the country's growing war efforts. On 19 July 1918, Frazee sent a letter to Chairman of the National Baseball Commission August "Garry" Herrmann about shortening the season:

Aug. Herrmann

Chairman National Commission,

Cincinnati, O.

If the President confirms Secretary Baker's order of today I urgently suggest that we close our seasons after playing one hundred games and the winners in each league play nine games to decide Worlds championship Please wire answer

Regards
H. H. Frazee[9]

In a photograph dated 16 April 1918, the New York Giants are led onto the field for opening-day ceremonies by a US Army band. With many people questioning why such athletic young men were not serving in the military, having a military-style entrance was a method used by the major leagues to mute some of the criticism. *Courtesy of Library of Congress*

Ultimately, it was decided the regular season would end on Labor Day, 2 September 1918. This was two months longer than the government had originally proposed, and it shortened the season by only two weeks, but it was an acceptable compromise to all concerned. It meant that a total of 140 games would be played by each team instead of the normal 154, and the World Series was scheduled to be played from 5 to 11 September 1918.

In spite of these agreements, there were still many adjustments to professional baseball that would be made as a result of the war. Provost Marshal Gen. Crowder's order meant that all men eligible for the draft who were working nonessential occupations must apply for work related to the war efforts or expect to be called into military service.[10] In spite of its activities in support of the war effort and to entertain the soldiers, professional baseball was now considered a nonessential business. Therefore, its players were not exempt from the draft. Now, in addition to playing baseball, the men on each club and the umpires had to be registered for the draft, then also apply for exemptions if desired. There were actually a number of ways a man of draft age could be considered

exempt: among them were physical disability (certainly a hard case to make for most professional athletes), being the sole source of income for a spouse or dependent family members (a potentially easier case for those ballplayers with wives and children), employment in a critical war service industry, or by being a member of the clergy, or a divinity school student.[11]

As it turned out, very few ballplayers were found under these conditions to be exempt from the draft; only thirty-six National League players out of the 206 available were exempted. Even fewer (20) were exempted in the American League. Active players were not the only ones who were found to be draft worthy; many coaches, scouts, front-office employees, stadium workers, and even retired players were also in the age groups subject to the draft.[12]

While the draft was taking players left and right, some were able to return to their teams for a few games because of short furloughs from their military training camps. Future Hall of Famer Sam Rice of the

The New York Yankees—armed with baseball bats instead of rifles—work on their marching skills under the steady cadence of a US Army sergeant. The two men in civilian clothes in the leading rank are Yankees' owners Tillinghast L'Hommedieu Huston and Jacob Ruppert; surprisingly, all the players and the two owners appear to be in step. *Courtesy of Library of Congress*

Washington Senators was able to return for a three-game series against Boston to great applause from the crowds. Eventually Rice managed to play a total of seven games in the 1918 season before he was obligated to return to his training camp and focus on Army duties.

By the second month of the season, the players had registered and were now being drafted. Some tried to appeal their selection by the draft board by going directly to Newton Baker in the hope that the secretary of war might intervene on their behalf. A very few succeeded and they were allowed to remain in the league. With the constant refrain from the Army that more and more troops were needed, Baker was not usually inclined to exempt a healthy man from the service. He also agreed with Gen. Crowder that baseball was not essential to the war efforts, but allowed exceptions to be made for certain players if recommended by their local draft board. Among these players was Ty Cobb, who had already announced that he planned to enlist at the end of the 1918 season instead of waiting to be drafted. Benjamin Michael

"Bennie" Kauff, a star outfielder of the New York Giants, was not as lucky; he was ordered to report to military training camp before July. And so he did, reporting to Camp Sherman, Ohio, on 25 June, and was assigned to the 158th Depot Brigade. His War Service Record (AGO Form 724) reflects a rather uneven military career. It appears that Kauff was promoted to corporal shortly after arrival at Camp Sherman but was demoted to private just two months later. After the war he returned to big-league baseball and was involved in a strange episode involving the theft of a car. Although eventually found innocent by a court of law, recently appointed Major League Commissioner Judge Kennesaw Mountain Landis banished him from baseball.

Others ballplayers and coaches, such as Boston Braves catcher John Henry, were also unsuccessful in their appeal for exemption and received their training-camp orders.[13] The Yankees had five of their players ordered to register for the draft by 13 June.[14] Eventually, an average of about fifteen players per team were drafted or had enlisted

Benjamin Michael "Bennie" Kauff strikes a typical outfielder's pose for his portrait. A star outfielder for the New York Giants, Kauff received his draft notice in June 1918 and reported to Camp Sherman, Ohio, for training in July. Kauff was hitting .315 when he reported to the Army; he never hit that high again in his professional career. *Courtesy of Library of Congress*

Bennie Kauff's wartime service record, showing that although he was living in New York City, he reported for induction in his hometown of Pomeroy, Ohio. Kauff served in the Army from July 1918 until his demobilization on 10 February 1919. *Courtesy of New York, Abstracts of World War I Military Service, via Ancestry.com*

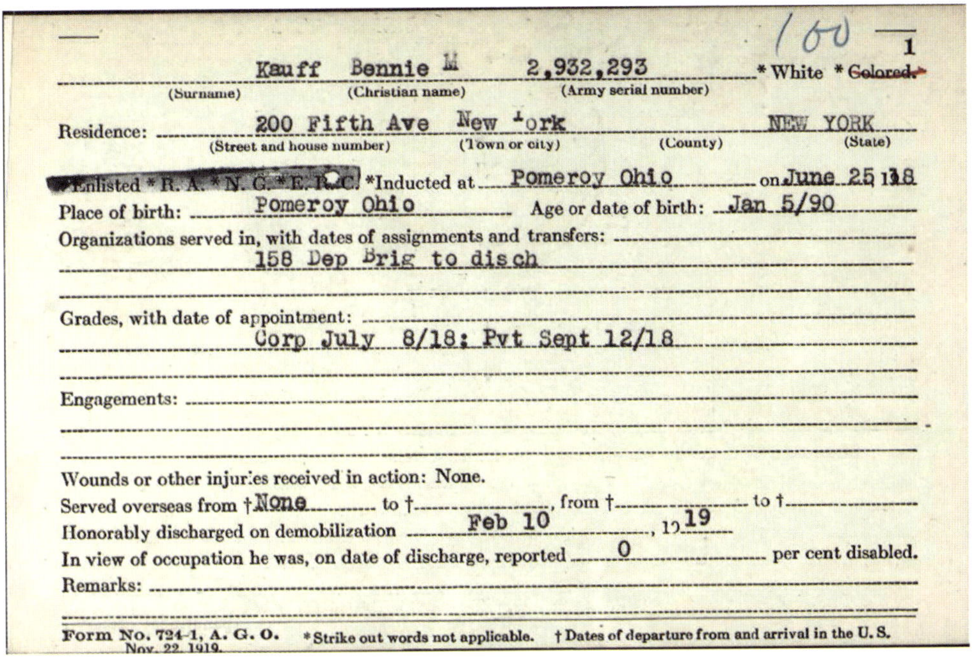
100 1

Kauff (Surname) Bennie M (Christian name) 2,932,293 (Army serial number) * White * ~~Colored.~~

Residence: 200 Fifth Ave (Street and house number) New York (Town or city) (County) NEW YORK (State)

~~*Enlisted * R. A. * N. G. * E. R. C.~~ *Inducted at Pomeroy Ohio on June 25 1918

Place of birth: Pomeroy Ohio Age or date of birth: Jan 5/90

Organizations served in, with dates of assignments and transfers: 158 Dep Brig to disch

Grades, with date of appointment: Corp July 8/18; Pvt Sept 12/18

Engagements:

Wounds or other injuries received in action: None.

Served overseas from †None to †, from † to †

Honorably discharged on demobilization Feb 10, 1919

In view of occupation he was, on date of discharge, reported 0 per cent disabled.

Remarks:

Form No. 724-1, A. G. O. Nov. 22, 1919. *Strike out words not applicable. † Dates of departure from and arrival in the U. S.

in the Army or Navy. Teams found it difficult to replace players who were drafted, but they did their best to keep the season going.[15]

Some ballplayers, having no desire to serve in the Army or Navy, chose to find war-related jobs in the many industrial complexes gearing up to produce war materials. Within many of these industries were baseball leagues that now allowed the professional players to "work" for the industries as well as play baseball on their teams. The Bethlehem Steel League was one of the larger industrial baseball leagues to which major- and minor-league players flocked. Other similar leagues across the country were created at "essential to war" facilities, such as the huge Delaware River Shipyards. Originally, most of the players in these leagues were local workers, a few retired players, and a few minor leaguers. As the requirement to "work or fight" was starting to be strictly enforced, more and more major leaguers and other professional athletes—including an up-and-coming heavyweight boxer named Jack Dempsey—started to take on "war-essential work." If fear of being drafted was not enough of a reason to join war service–related industries and their teams, the salaries in these industrial leagues were also quite lucrative. Depending on the relative fame of the player, a man might earn as much as $250 a game in addition to what he was being paid as a worker.[16] At times, some players signed up to play in multiple leagues, which was possible if the different leagues' teams were close enough together. Players were often interchanged to make a nine-man starting lineup.[17] Joe Jackson of the 1917 world champion White Sox was one of those who jumped from the major leagues to play both in the Bethlehem Steel League and the Delaware River Shipyard League. Ostensibly employed as a painter at the Harlan shipyard in Wilmington, Delaware, Jackson was joined by a number of other players, including well-known and future Hall of Fame pitcher Chief Bender.[18] On the West Coast it was the same story. Even eighteen-year-old minor-league ballplayers such as Willie Kamm were helped by their teams to find work in a war industry. Kamm signed up for work in an Oregon shipyard in 1918, so he could play baseball on the weekends in the Shipyard League.[19] After Jackson and some other well-known players, such as future Hall of Fame pitcher Eddie Plank, had left the major leagues for war work and the industrial leagues, American League president Ban Johnson—never shy about sharing his opinion—spoke out in the press. He commended the players who went to the steel industry to sincerely help the war effort, but condemned those who were there only to escape military service.[20] Many of the industrial baseball leagues proved to be short lived, and players returned to their former major-league teams as soon as the war was over.

In spite of the many personnel and public-perception problems, the 1918 season limped along until it was September, and time for the Boston Red Sox to play the Chicago Cubs in the World Series. Of note, beyond the game statistics and players involved, some sixty wounded soldiers recently returned from France were present at one of the games. The Red Sox won the series four games to two. With the last out, professional baseball in 1918 was over. Even World Series hero Babe Ruth, who was the winning pitcher in two of Boston's four victories, was now obligated to report to a war service job at Bethlehem Steel. Unfortunately, he first paid a quick visit to his family in Baltimore and was exposed to the Spanish flu, then was very sick for several days before he could report for duty at the steel plant.[21]

Many of the other ballplayers who were not already learning the nuances of the military or working in war-related fields were on their way to joining the military war effort in Army, Navy, and Marine Corps training camps. We must now turn our attention to those military training camps to begin to understand the story of where American baseball truly flourished in 1917 and 1918.

237 BASEBALL STARS MUST WORK OR FIGHT

Reprieve Until September 1 Granted by Secretary of War

[BY CABLE TO THE STARS AND STRIPES]

AMERICA, August 1.—While club owners asked for a reprieve until October 15, Secretary of War Baker couldn't see it that way, although he finally granted a reprieve until September 1 so far as the "work or fight" order went.

This "work or fight" decree affects 237 stars, which means, of course, that it will bring an end to any big league campaign on that date. The managers, however, believe that they can now finish the season by doubling up on games and that by selecting the best men from smaller organizations they can put a world's series across.

So there will be 31 more days of big league baseball before the stars of the game who are still playing will have either to work or fight in a final forced realization that the only real game left today is that of beating the Hun.

A short article from an August 1918 edition of the *Stars and Stripes* reporting that baseball players would have until 1 September either to find war-related work or prepare to be drafted into the military. This announcement effectively ended the 1918 baseball season as of that date, although the World Series was allowed to be played.

Songs lauding the skills of individual ballplayers were commonplace during the period and served as another indication of how important baseball was in the American culture during the period leading up to the war. *Courtesy of Library of Congress*

3rd Inning
Baseball in the Training Camps

The Punitive Expedition—chasing Pancho Villa through the Mexican desert, and the subsequent mobilization of the National Guard to protect the United States' southern border—had forced the Army to reassess its basic combat doctrine. It was clear to most senior US Army leaders that they needed to include motor vehicles, radios, and aircraft, among other things, in the mix required by a modern military force. The standard Army unit for combat had also changed from the regiment—with a few thousand soldiers—to a division with more than 28, 000 men. With so many men under the command of a two-star general, all aspects of training had to be strictly focused to ensure that each man understood his role in these newly formed divisions' combat mission. Likewise, the need to keep the men entertained with wholesome activities while off duty was also an important factor in maintaining a unit's morale and end strength. Even Secretary of War Newton Baker understood that a balance of military training and exercise had to be reached to make the soldiers a viable force. He had written that "plenty of hard work and clean fun make for vigor and manhood—the prime requisites of a soldier."[1]

The austerity of the Texas, Arizona, New Mexico, and Baja, California, borders had challenged officers trying to keep their soldiers engaged in the importance of the mission. Many of the men guarding the border crossings had grumbled that they wished Pancho Villa would come back and attack just to give them something to do. Failing that, the men spent their off-duty hours chasing rattlesnakes, cleaning their rifles, and drinking alcohol. One report stated:

> There was nowhere to go for any sort of decent diversion in their "off" time . . . there was no movie show, no library, no club room for lounging . . . in Laredo, and Brownsville, Texas, and in Douglas, Arizona. . . . And so, when they had any free time, many naturally gravitated to the saloons . . . and it was not an uncommon thing to see drunken men in uniform.[2]

Similar problems were noted by all commanders and eventually even reached the desk of Secretary of War Baker, who would later comment that "homesickness, liquor, prostitution, and cheap motion-picture shows seemed to be the greatest cause of military delinquency . . ."[3]

Cpl. Hunter Ashby Pendleton poses in front of his Camp McClellan tent in Alabama while wearing his Virginia National Guard baseball uniform. By the time this picture was taken, Pendleton had served on the Mexican border and was now part of the 111th Field Artillery Regiment. After the war, Pendleton would attend a field artillery officer-training course and be promoted to lieutenant. He also served in WWII as an officer in the Ordnance Corps. *Courtesy of Virginia Army National Guard*

When the US entered the war in April 1917, Baker was determined to better attend to the needs of the troops in training camps. He recognized the vast majority of soldiers in the Army would be draftees, with little experience of training or camp life, and therefore would require a greater degree of entertainment and diversion than the more experienced soldiers of the Regular Army or the National Guard. To that end he established the War Department Commission on Training Camp Activities. This commission was charged with linking various service organizations, such as the Young Men's Christian Association (YMCA), the Young Women's Christian Association (YWCA), the Salvation Army, the Jewish Welfare Board (JWB), the Knights of Columbus (K of C), the American Library

Taken in August 1918 at one of the stateside training camps, Doughboys are playing baseball while wearing their gas masks as part of their chemical-warfare training. Behind them, and wearing a bemused smile, is one of the ladies who volunteered for the service organizations, such as the YMCA and the Salvation Army. *Courtesy of National Archives*

Association (ALA), and the War Camp Community Service, into a cohesive support structure. Collectively, these organizations became known as the "Seven Sisters." They were tasked to support the moral, physical, and spiritual health of the thousands of soldiers who would soon be undergoing training in the States.[4] It was a huge mission, and the members of the commission saw it as their duty to "keep the men of the army and navy fit for fighting, first by keeping them physically well, and second by keeping them contented, interested."[5] Similarly, Gen. Pershing realized early in his command of the AEF in France that his soldiers were going to be exposed to things in Europe that their comparatively conservative American upbringing had not prepared them for. Pershing had seen much of the world during his Army career and knew that soldiers needed to be kept busy as much as possible to avoid misbehavior stemming from boredom. To fight this problem, during their off time they would need entertainment—preferably wholesome entertainment. Pershing was also well aware of the good

Songwriters and music-publishing houses also wanted to show their patriotism, and a number of Doughboy- and baseball-themed songs were published. One of them was the musical story of "Bobby the Bomber." *Courtesy of Library of Congress*

work that was being done in the training camps back in the States by the many service organizations. By 1918, there were 178 training camps for the Army and Navy in the United States, and the YMCA alone had almost 700 buildings and clubhouses at these sites. The YWCA maintained facilities at most camps to allow for female workers and visitors, and the other organizations also had dedicated huts and clubs at most locations.[6]

By 1918, the US Army was very diverse. Some of this diversity came from the regional makeup of the combat divisions, which were originally either recruited (Regular Army, National Guard) or drafted (National Army) from specific parts of the country. As a result, there were a great number of Hispanic soldiers in the Texas, Oklahoma, New Mexico, and Arizona National Guard units, while many Native American soldiers served in units from Minnesota, Wisconsin, and the western states. A number of Japanese, Korean, and Chinese Doughboys served in the units raised from New York City. Millions of immigrants from southern and eastern Europe had been arriving in the United States since 1880. As a result of this large immigrant population, and the Selective Service Act, 20 percent of the Army was born in a country other than the United States. Large numbers of Italians, Greeks, Irish, Polish, Russians, Armenians, Canadians, and Dutch served in the ranks of the US military. They were joined by men from India, Australia, South America, Central America, the Philippines, and the Caribbean. In short, except for African immigrants or African Americans, a majority of the units in the US Army became a mixing bowl of nationalities, races, and religions. This interesting phenomenon also spilled over into sporting events and most unit athletic teams.

Without a doubt, baseball was the most popular sport for the Doughboys while in their training camps. The 115th Infantry Regiment recorded that "athletics were encouraged by the military authorities and an effort was made to get every man interested and playing. This was done of a twofold purpose . . . to keep the men contented and happy and to develop them physically."[7] With so many of the soldiers arriving at their camps in autumn 1917, initial plans included establishing a number of football leagues. Unfortunately, the weather in the South during the winter of 1917–1918 was so cold and harsh that even playing a winter sport such as football proved to be nearly impossible. Indoor basketball leagues were formed but never received the same enthusiastic support as baseball. Therefore, whenever the weather cleared for even a short period, baseball games were played.

By early autumn 1917, before the bad weather set in at most camps, it became obvious that the Army needed to work harder to focus the Doughboys' attention in the proper direction. British and French instructors in trench warfare, machine gun operations, and hand-to-hand combat were dispatched to each of the training sites. While these experts taught the necessary combat skills to the Americans, the association of service organizations ministered to the soldiers' spiritual and athletic needs. In all the camps the Doughboys' hunger for outside entertainment was evident, none more so than at Camp McClellan, Alabama, where the 29th Division was training. The 1917 World Series between the New York Giants and the Chicago White Sox was followed carefully by some 10, 000 soldiers there who "saw" the action portrayed on a large electronic scoreboard and listened to the "play by play" commentary as it was read off a ticker-tape machine by a narrator.

The camp for Battery A, 111th Field Artillery (the Richmond Howitzers), at Camp McClellan, Alabama. The 111th spent over nine months in training at McClellan before deploying to France in June 1918. While training there, the soldiers enjoyed monitoring the events of the 1917 World Series through the use of a large electronic scoreboard and a narrator. *Courtesy of Virginia Army National Guard*

With better weather in the western part of the country, baseball enthusiasm remained high. At one training camp in the West, "there is a big field where sixteen base-ball diamonds have been laid out, and it is not uncommon for sixteen games to be going on there simultaneously."[8] It was even believed by some of the sports administrators that the skills gained on these fields would serve the Army well in France: "What bomb-throwers those pitchers will make! How resourceful those first basemen will be in battle."[9]

Whether throwing a baseball or fielding an infield position appreciably enhanced combat skills is open to debate. One thing is certain: to play baseball, the soldiers needed good weather; and that was a problem. Soon after many of the National Guard soldiers and initial draftees reached their training camps, the worst winter in many years covered most of the country. When a great deal of the "Sunny South" was covered in snow and lashed intermittently by blizzards, the Doughboys in the National Guard camps huddled by the stoves in their tents and dreamed of better weather. Drafted men living in wooden barracks in National Army

An August 1918 postcard depicting baseball being played at Camp Lee, Virginia. Writing to his girlfriend, Marie, in Damascus, Pennsylvania, the soldier complains he has not received any mail from her in five days, and he has begun to think she has a new fellow. He ends by imploring her to "rite soon." *Courtesy of Steven Moore*

An advertisement from the 2 August 1918 edition of the *Stars and Stripes* intended to let the Doughboys know that Alex Taylor & Company of New York strongly supports their efforts. Mr. Taylor's "glad hand" and wish that he was there in France with them probably gave a laugh to many of the soldiers who wished he were there instead of them.

camps—constructed primarily in the Midwest and the North—had better living conditions, but equally nasty weather. They too dreamed of springtime and better weather conditions to get in a game or two.

When good weather finally returned, they were ready. At Camp McClellan, Alabama, it seemed that any open space large enough to hold a game was used until darkness ended the action. Every type of unit, from large infantry regiments to machine gun battalions, and even the small transportation companies, fielded teams to play within their organization and then against outsiders. Large crowds turned out for all the games, and "every Wednesday and Saturday afternoon and all day Sunday the games were on with hot rivalry."[10] At Camp Sheridan—also in Alabama—it was estimated that 255 formal games and another 2, 047 impromptu pickup games were played in one month. At the same post there were fourteen separate baseball leagues. Because Sheridan was the training site for the 37th Division, which was composed primarily of the Ohio National Guard, the soldiers received a real morale boost from their home state's major-league baseball teams. In November 1917, the Cleveland Indians traveled south and played three games against teams from the 145th Infantry Regiment, the 112th Ammunition Train, and the divisional hospital units. The following year, the Cincinnati Reds attempted to prove their patriotism by moving their 1918 spring training site to Montgomery to stay close to their fellow Ohioans' training base.[11]

A damaged photograph but worthy of study; this is the baseball team from the 326th Field Artillery Battalion that trained at Camp Wadsworth, South Carolina. Originally comprising National Guardsmen from Connecticut and other New England states, the 326th was destined to be in federal service over two years, because they would also serve almost a year of occupation duty in Germany. The SAC logo on the standing soldier's shirt stands for Army Signal Corps.

A similar scenario was played out at Camp Wadsworth, in Spartanburg, South Carolina. New England and New York National Guardsmen, as well as many of the newly formed Pioneer Infantry regiments, were training at Wadsworth. With most of the 27th Division coming from New York State, and the largest part of several Pioneer Infantry regiments coming from New England, a matchup between the Boston Braves and the New York Yankees was guaranteed to draw a large crowd. In a low-scoring contest, Home Run Baker and the Braves beat the Yankees in a pitching duel. After the game, the Yankees players autographed a game ball to be auctioned off. The auction was won by an officer from the 53rd Pioneer Infantry Regiment, who picked up his prize of $17.50. Just two days later, on the same field, the Philadelphia Athletics defeated the Pittsburgh Pirates by a score of four to two.[12]

The front and back views of Germany Schaefer's baseball card included in packages of *Recruit Little Cigars*. Although noted for his comical approach to the game, what was often overlooked was Schaefer's hitting ability, and his versatility in being able to play all the infield and outfield positions. *Courtesy of Library of Congress*

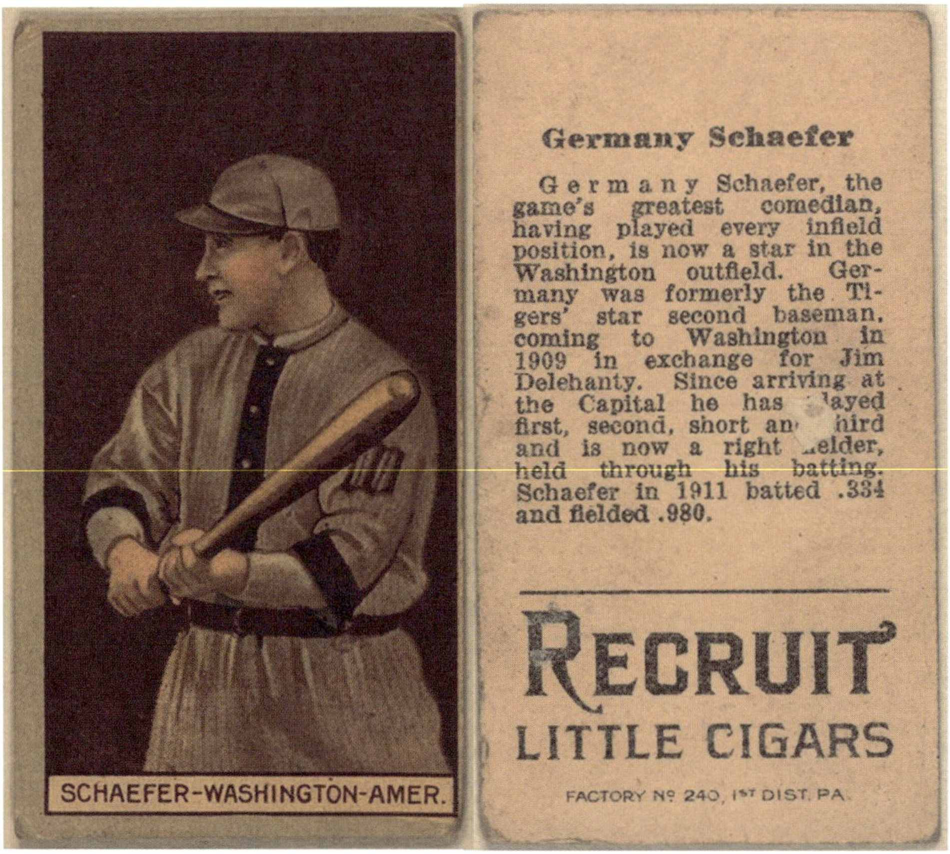

The National League New York Giants—losers of the 1917 World Series to the Chicago White Sox—spiced up their spring training. The team traveled down to the US Army Air Service's Rich Field in Waco, Texas, to play a team of aviators. The *Stars and Stripes* later reported that "The airmen arrived with enthusiasm, partly in airships. They then demonstrated that they do not play ball as well as they fly."[13] One of the major leaguers playing for the Giants that day was Herman A. "Germany" Schaefer, normally a middle infielder. Known as one of the major league's most famous jokesters, Schaefer had announced

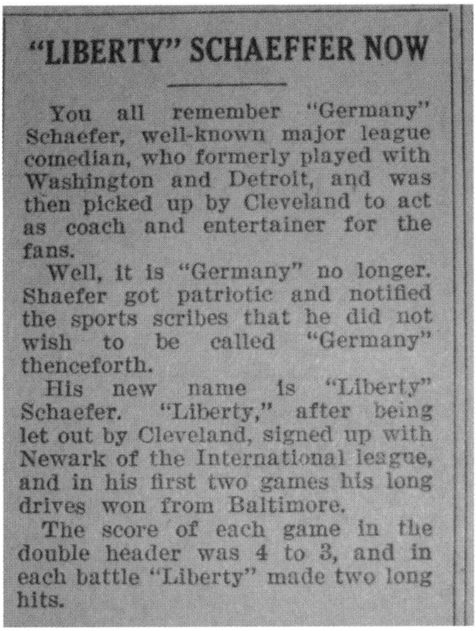

"LIBERTY" SCHAEFFER NOW

You all remember "Germany" Schaefer, well-known major league comedian, who formerly played with Washington and Detroit, and was then picked up by Cleveland to act as coach and entertainer for the fans.

Well, it is "Germany" no longer. Shaefer got patriotic and notified the sports scribes that he did not wish to be called "Germany" thenceforth.

His new name is "Liberty" Schaefer. "Liberty," after being let out by Cleveland, signed up with Newark of the International league, and in his first two games his long drives won from Baltimore.

The score of each game in the double header was 4 to 3, and in each battle "Liberty" made two long hits.

Always playing to the crowd, Herman "Germany" Schaefer was noted not only for his baseball skills, but also his stunts. Once he stole first base from second base, which led to a rule change. Fired up with patriotic spirit after the outbreak of the war, Schaefer first renounced his "Germany" nickname and played under his given name, Herman. Shortly thereafter, he "officially" announced that he was changing his name to "Liberty." *Courtesy of Library of Congress*

that he wanted to ditch his nickname and return to being called Herman. With the professional team staked to a large early lead, Schaefer took the mound and began pitching behind his back to the soldiers to allow them to score some runs. In the end it did not matter, and the Giants won easily. Schaefer had also announced earlier that he was changing his name to "Liberty" Schaefer as part of the war effort. Unfortunately, Schaefer would be one of the millions worldwide who died of flu or flu-related diseases in 1919.[14]

The infantry units at other training camps did not fare any better against the pros than the aviators had. The New York Yankees traveled to Macon, Georgia, to take on a team of National Guardsmen from the 124th Infantry Regiment training at Camp Wheeler. In front of a crowd of over 17, 000 enthusiastic soldiers, the Yankees jumped out to an eleven-to-nothing lead after the first inning and then coasted to a twelve-to-four victory.[15] At the same time, Babe Ruth was leading his Boston Red Sox teammates in taking three out of four games from the Brooklyn Dodgers in Little Rock, Arkansas, in front of a number of soldiers from nearby Camp Pike. It was reported that in each of Boston's victories, Ruth "played a big part walloping the ball wickedly."[16]

The Doughboys in training at Wadsworth were such baseball fanatics that a league with four conferences had to be formed just for nondivision organizations, such as the 51st, 52nd, 53rd, 54th, 55th,

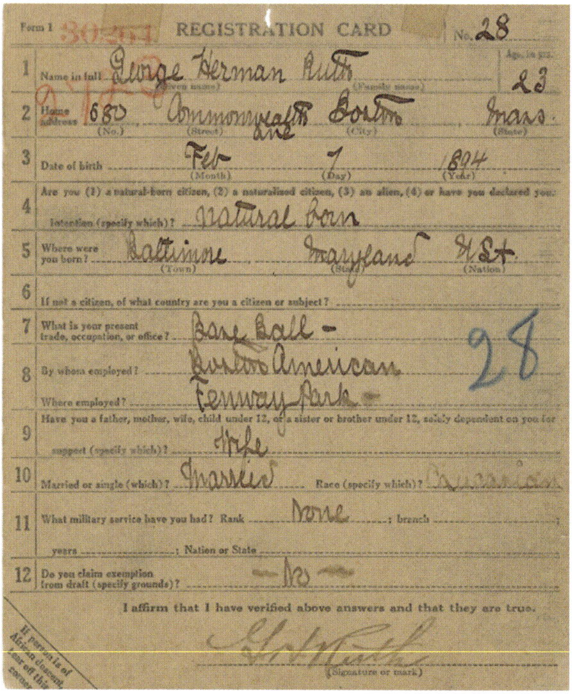

Form 1 30251 REGISTRATION CARD No. 28

1 Name in full George Herman Ruth (Given name) (Family name) Age, in yrs. 23

2 Home address 680 Commonwealth ave Boston Mass. (No.) (Street) (City) (State)

3 Date of birth Feb 7 1894 (Month) (Day) (Year)

4 Are you (1) a natural-born citizen, (2) a naturalized citizen, (3) an alien, (4) or have you declared your intention (specify which)? natural born

5 Where were you born? Baltimore Maryland U.S.A. (Town) (State) (Nation)

6 If not a citizen, of what country are you a citizen or subject?

7 What is your present trade, occupation, or office? Base Ball -

8 By whom employed? Boston American 28

Where employed? Fenway Park -

9 Have you a father, mother, wife, child under 12, or a sister or brother under 12, solely dependent on you for support (specify which)? Wife

10 Married or single (which)? Married Race (specify which)? Caucasian

11 What military service have you had? Rank None ; branch

years ; Nation or State

12 Do you claim exemption from draft (specify grounds)? — No —

I affirm that I have verified above answers and that they are true.

G H Ruth (Signature or mark)

If person is of African descent, tear off this corner.

Universal draft registration meant exactly that—by late 1918, if you were a man between ages eighteen and forty-five, you were required to register. Even if your name was George Herman "Babe" Ruth, and you listed your place of employment as Fenway Park, you were required to appear and register for the draft. Note that he listed his team's name as the "Boston Americans" instead of the Red Sox, which was a common practice in cities that had a team from both major leagues. *Courtesy of US World War I Draft Registration Cards, via Ancestry.com*

By far one of the largest and best-uniformed teams in the training camps was this group from the 90th Division. Consisting primarily of draftees from Texas and Oklahoma, the 90th trained at Camp Travis in San Antonio, Texas. During the Meuse-Argonne Offensive, the 90th compiled an admirable record for their fighting skills and their ability to drive the Germans out of their defensive positions.

56th, 57th, and 58th Pioneer Infantry Regiments and the 326th Field Signal Battalion. To accommodate all the other teams seeking playing fields, the camp commander posted a priority order for the eight official diamonds in the camp: "League ball teams will have preference on these diamonds. Regimental teams will have second choice and Company teams third choice."[17] It was good that the soldiers at Wadsworth were getting their fill of baseball. By May, the 27th Division would be on the move and heading to France, where they would spend the majority of their time in the war serving with the non-baseball-playing British army.

At the four large divisional training camps in Texas—Travis (San Antonio), Logan (Houston), MacArthur (Waco), and Bowie (Fort Worth)—the weather was somewhat better. However, the need at

This photograph of the 315th Cavalry Regiment's baseball team at Fort D. A. Russell in Wyoming is slightly mysterious for two reasons: the photograph is dated December 1918, and the soldiers are wearing 315th uniforms, but the unit was converted to the 71st and 72nd Field Artillery Regiments in August 1918; also, the coach on the far right appears to be an African American—an unusual occurrence in a strictly segregated Army. *Courtesy of National Archives*

each location to keep the soldiers busy while not training was still very important. A race riot and shoot-out in Houston in August 1917 was a powerful reminder to all concerned that problems between soldiers and civilians could quickly get out of control. The violence was the accidental result of the War Department's attempt to speed up the camp-building process. A battalion from a Regular Army African American unit (24th Infantry Regiment) was sent to Camp Logan to assist in camp construction. Almost immediately on arrival they had run-ins with local citizens. Being Regular Army soldiers, and rightfully proud of their long service in the US Army, the black soldiers refused to obey the segregation laws in nearby Houston. Very quickly, tempers flared on both sides, and a gunfight took place on 23 August 1917 in the streets of Houston. By the time it was finished there were several dead and wounded soldiers and civilians. Peace was not restored until other Regular Army units were brought into the city and the soldiers of the 24th were disarmed. In retribution for what was labeled a "mutiny, " a number of the 24th's soldiers were tried and executed, some only three days after their court martial.[18] Wishing to avoid similar problems, the camp staffs and the service organizations quickly turned to sports as a means to keep soldiers out of further trouble. The staff at Camp Travis—next to another Regular Army camp, Fort Sam Houston—established baseball, football, and basketball leagues to keep the soldiers of the 90th Division occupied.[19]

The War Department's Commission on Training Camp Activities issued their report in January 1918 and defined the areas of responsibility for each of the several service organizations. A "Recreative Activities" organization was established at all the large training camps. It was charged with encouraging the soldiers to participate in vigorous sports, noting that "stress is laid on hard competitive sports that develop the fighting instinct." Of particular favor was boxing, for its "intimate connection to bayonet fighting, " and baseball. Boxing in particular was seen as a way to combine sports with combat training. The War Department Commission on Training Camp Activities noted that

Anyone doubting the Doughboys' love of baseball need only examine this photograph taken in October 1917 at Camp Dix, New Jersey. A group of soldiers and civilians have braved the cold and rainy weather to watch a large bulletin board be updated with pitch-by-pitch results received over ticker tape, giving the details of the World Series game between the New York Giants and the Chicago White Sox. *Courtesy of National Archives*

> Boxing teaches the manly art of self-control as well as that of self-defense. It also makes better bayonet-fighters. Nearly every blow and position has its counterpart in bayonetting.[20]

The report also noted that the US government was providing only about 10 percent of the cost required to outfit the soldiers with baseball equipment. Obviously the service organizations were going to have to raise the rest from donations.[21] At Camp Grant, near Rockford, Illinois, the soldiers of the 86th Division did not wait for outsiders to provide gear and found ways to obtain their own. On 24 October 1917, they celebrated "Liberty Day" with a full slate of baseball games and boxing matches. Taking their divisional nickname "Black Hawk" from a local Indian legend, the soldiers of the 86th were destined to spend the war primarily training soldiers for service in other units. Over 115,000 men would pass through the division's ranks during the war, and when the "Black Hawk" Division finally reached France, once again they were "harvested" for soldiers to serve in other units. Nevertheless, under the

John Cleave "Rube" Benton was a well-regarded member of the New York Giants pitching staff before the war and most likely would have continued to post excellent numbers in 1918, if he had not been drafted after pitching in only three games. His later controversial involvement in the Black Sox scandal would lead to his banishment from baseball for a year. *Courtesy of Library of Congress*

physical-fitness guidance of Lawrence Whiting—a former college football player—they prepared as hard as any unit in the Army and played just as hard. That preparation showed on 4 July 1918 at Camp Grant. The 87th Division's boxers swept a seven-bout program against boxers in the Canadian Army. The Black Hawk baseball team did not do nearly as well, losing to the visiting team from Camp Dodge by a score of five to one.[22]

At an advance technical-training camp in Columbia, Georgia, a newly arrived soldier was invited to play in a company-level baseball game. Given the opportunity to pitch for his team, the soldier struck out twenty-five of the opposing batters during the game and hit a home run. When asked his name, the new Doughboy admitted he was John Cleave "Rube" Benton, until recently a member of the New York Giants' pitching staff. The previous year Benton had compiled a fifteen-win, nine-loss record for the Giants and had started the 1918 season with one win and two losses before he was selected by the draft.[23] Benton would later become embroiled in the "Black Sox" scandal as a tangential figure and was banned both by the American and National League presidents in 1922 as an "undesirable" character."[24] Commissioner of Baseball Judge Kennesaw Mountain Landis ultimately took Benton's side in the controversy. Landis allowed Benton to return to the major leagues in 1923, after a one-year absence. Although Benton ended his career with 154 victories,

Jack Barry, manager of the Boston Red Sox, poses at Fenway Park. In November 1917, along with four of the players on his team, Barry joined a US Navy Reserve unit in Massachusetts; by the end of December, eleven members of the team were either in Army or Navy uniforms. *Courtesy of Library of Congress*

the two years he lost—one to the Army and the other during his banishment—undoubtedly affected his career totals.

Of all the major-league teams, the Boston Red Sox were among the clubs hardest hit by the draft and selective-service rulings. In November 1917, five members of the team, including their manager, Jack Barry, reported for duty with a local Naval Reserve unit, while two others enlisted in the Navy. By the end of December, eleven members of the team, including Hal Janvrin, were in uniform and only two infielders remained on the roster. With these personnel losses, Boston was recognized as having lost more men to military service than any other big-league team. Nevertheless, in March 1918, what remained of the Red Sox, along with some new players, headed south to begin their spring training. Babe Ruth was still with the team and put on a hitting exhibition for soldiers from nearby Camp Pike before storm clouds and rain washed out the scheduled exhibition game against Brooklyn. The two teams met the next day in front of more than 6, 000 Doughboys. Ruth entertained the enthusiastic crowd by pitching for the first three innings and then moving to the outfield for the rest of the game. Remaining in Arkansas a while longer, the Red Sox were happy to get one of their pitchers back: Sam Jones had been classified as 2B by the draft board. The 2B category included those men who were married with a dependent spouse and children under age sixteen. The "2" meant that Jones was "Temporarily deferred but available for military Service" after all the men in category "1" had been drafted. The "B" after the "2" further explained that Jones had some injuries, but these were correctable with time and treatment. In Jones' case, these were probably the typical baseball injuries of bad knees, ankles, or shoulders but would not prevent him from serving as a soldier should he be called.

While their team was in spring training, the former members of the Red Sox serving in the Naval Reserve at Charlestown Naval Station in Boston were learning their Navy duties. One of these included the establishment of a unit baseball team. As time passed, the former Red Sox players enjoyed comparatively easy duty, since their job in the Navy was now essentially to play baseball. Their military service life remained easy until May 1918, when the Navy disbanded the unit. The news that the ballplayers might now have to serve as actual sailors was met with

Not to be outdone by the Army or Navy, the Marine Corps also fielded baseball teams wherever they were stationed. This cheerful group of ballplayers was at the Marine Corps training base at Parris Island, South Carolina. *Courtesy of USMC History Division*

sarcasm by the editors of the *Stars and Stripes*. The editors commented that the "Naval Reserve nine composed of many big league baseball stars, has disbanded because the cruel Navy prefers cannon ball pitching for them."[25]

Other major leaguers serving in Naval Reserve units fared better. US Navy Commissioner of Athletics Walter Camp declared in March 1918 that each naval station in the country would be encouraged to form a baseball team. As a result, a number of these bases quickly became destinations for baseball players from every league. In Charleston, South Carolina, former Boston Red Sox outfielder Jack Hoey built a team with several major- and minor-league players. At the Great Lakes Naval Training Station in Illinois, a team led by former White Sox outfielder Phil Chouinard had players from the Washington Senators, St. Louis Browns, Philadelphia Athletics, and the Pittsburgh Pirates. Other major leaguers playing for US Navy teams included such future Baseball Hall of Fame members as Herb Pennock, Harry Heilmann,

The US Navy was also well represented in the military's baseball world. This team of well-dressed sailors is from the Receiving Ship, Naval Station, in New Orleans in 1918. The embroidered patch on their uniforms is a highly stylized version of "USN." *Courtesy of National Archives*

Charles Dillon "Casey" Stengel, and Walter James "Rabbit" Maranville.[26] Stengel would later recall that life in the US Navy was fairly pleasant. At first "he was assigned to the commissary—but he also made good use of his major-league background by becoming a kind of physical-education director with emphasis on baseball."[27] Eventually Stengel was put in charge of the Brooklyn Navy Yard team, and, along with another professional ballplayer and Dodger teammate, Jimmy Hickman, they played many of the teams from visiting ships.

Even in the camps that were not fortunate enough to be visited by major-league teams, the drive to play ball at every chance was a common characteristic. The mania for fielding a baseball team was so prevalent among the soldiers that not only the larger units but even modestly sized units did so. The 11th Construction Company—a unit made up largely of bricklayers in the Aviation Section of the Signal Corps (later

This Marine baseball team, likely at Quantico in June 1918, is notable for showing two former major-league ballplayers: sitting in the front row (from left) is John B. "Dots" Miller, a second baseman from the St. Louis Cardinals; and Jay J. "Nig" Clarke, a catcher from the Cleveland Indians. Both men would play ball in France while serving in the Services of Supply. *Courtesy of National Archives*

A pair of Marines, most likely at Quantico, Virginia, stop playing long enough to have their picture taken. By 1918, the Marine Corps schools at Quantico were training Marines for service in France either with the 4th Brigade, which was part of the 2nd Division, or the 5th Brigade, which served in the Services of Supply.

assigned to the US Army Air Service)—fielded a "crack company base ball team" while stationed at the Aviation Mobilization Depot, Camp Sevier, South Carolina, in spring 1918. With an assigned strength of 160 men, the 11th managed to put together a team that went undefeated against teams from every part of the state, including "the base hospital and many regimental teams at Camp Sevier." The team was uniformed and equipped by means of a voluntary subscription from among the men in the company.[28]

By the end of 1917, the training camps were filled with soldiers, sailors, and Marines, but for many of the men, training time was over. The 361st Infantry Regiment, 91st Division, wrote in their history that there came a time when the troops knew they would soon be leaving for France. As a result, unit sporting events came to a close

> and passed into history. The inter-company baseball series was moving briskly, each team with its distinctive company uniform, when the orders to move to France closed the schedule and started the uniforms on their long journey to an A. E. F., S. O. S. salvage pile.[29]

The Army was growing in size and proficiency as soldiers sailed to Europe to build the force that Gen. Pershing would lead into combat. Among those soldiers were a number of current or former professional baseball players, as well as thousands of enthusiastic amateurs. It is to those members of the American Expeditionary Forces that we now turn our attention.

Most likely taken in 1917 or 1918, this is a very well-equipped US Navy Training School team. There is an NTS patch on each ballplayer's left arm, and someone has taken the time to write the position each sailor plays, but left no indication of their names. *Courtesy of Library of Congress*

Gen. Leonard Wood shakes hands with the manager of the New York Yankees, William "Wild Bill" Donovan, before the first game of the 1917 season at the Polo Grounds in New York City. On the far right are the two owners of the Yankees: Jacob Ruppert and Tillinghast L. Huston. Both owners had military experience: Ruppert had served in the New York National Guard, and Huston was a US Army captain in the Spanish-American War. The heavy coats reflect the fact that the start of the 1917 season was plagued with bad weather. *Courtesy of Library of Congress*

Introductions completed, Maj. Gen. Leonard Wood poses before throwing out the first pitch of the season at the Yankees game on 11 April 1917. Among Wood's many accomplishments were his service as personal physician to President Theodore Roosevelt, being a Medal of Honor recipient from the Indian Wars, his service as the US Army chief of staff from 1910 to 1914, and being a player/coach of the Georgia Tech football team. *Courtesy of Library of Congress*

In April 1918—and certainly unusual—two German POWs discuss the signals between pitcher and catcher as part of a baseball game at Fort MacPherson, Georgia. Some of these prisoners were interned when their ships were impounded in US ports after the US declaration of war. *Courtesy of National Archives*

4th Inning
Playing in France in a Continuous Rain Delay

The Doughboys' time in France can be generally divided into two parts: during the war and after the Armistice. The baseball season was endless. Teams that formed in the training camps continued to represent their units, and new teams appeared everywhere the soldiers went.

In any military operation, timing is truly everything that matters. The 29th Division, consisting of New Jersey, Virginia, and Maryland National Guardsmen, arrived in France in summer 1918, during the German army's Summer Offensive. As a result, instead of going to a training area as planned, the 29th was hurriedly dispatched to the Alsace region to replace the 32nd Division. In place of tactical training in a controlled environment, they would gain combat experience in a comparatively quiet sector of the front. Of course, regarding the western front, "quiet" was always a relative term. The Germans soon welcomed the National Guardsmen to the "quiet" zone with some trench raids and a number of artillery barrages. The 29th Division commander, Maj. Gen. Charles Morton, was determined to give something back to the Germans, and as a result, a schedule of machine gun barrages was set up to take place once a night in each of the division's regimental sectors. Of course, this activity soon elicited further German payback with their own artillery and machine gun fire. That "quiet sector" started to heat up quickly, and the soldiers of the 29th realized that they were now deeply into the war. Their love of the national pastime remained very strong, however. During this period Capt. John Cutchins, a Virginia National Guardsman serving on the 29th Division's headquarters staff, observed two teams of Doughboys playing baseball while wearing their gas mask carriers around their shoulders in case of attack due to their proximity to the front lines. Adding to the strangeness of the scene, Cutchins recounted that some French soldiers in a large observation balloon nearby appeared to be watching the game from their vantage point, as were several German aircraft that were flying overhead and scouting the area.[1]

It was a scene and attitude to be replayed over and over again. The Doughboys wanted to play baseball and petitioned anyone who would listen to send them the equipment they needed. The Knights of Columbus did one better than that. They sent a bona fide big leaguer—former

An interesting cartoon filled with layers of symbolism, showing a baseball analogy for the state of the Great War in 1917–1918. The French and British are stranded on second and third base; all that remains of Russia is an empty hat on the baseline, but the AEF is now coming to bat as the sun breaks through the clouds. The opposing team has Germany pitching, Austria catching, Bulgaria playing second base, and Turkey as the third baseman. The German pitcher is Kaiser Wilhelm (with a "W" on his jersey), and he is hoping that his "spitmarine" (submarines) will keep the Americans from driving in the winning runs.

This Signal Corps photograph was taken on 16 June 1918 in Varmaise, France, during a game between the 1st and 2nd Battalions of the 1st Engineer Regiment, 1st Division. By this date, many of the Doughboys of the 1st Division had already served almost a full year in France and would spend the next months in continual combat until the Armistice. *Courtesy of US Army*

all-star infielder John J. "Johnny" Evers—to France as their sporting-activity representative. According to the *New York Times*, Evers "paved the way for success for the game for the A.E.F. . . . He staged games with enemy airplanes swooping overhead, and was first to handle the enormous supply of athletic equipment which was given to the boys by the K of C."[2] Evers was joined in his efforts by William "Bill" Friel, another former big leaguer with extensive experience managing minor-league teams.[3]

It was not just the combat divisions that took every opportunity to play baseball; there were over 600, 000 American soldiers serving in the Services of Supply (SOS), and they too set up leagues to play at every opportunity. With almost two million American soldiers in France by late summer 1918, the need for baseball equipment soared. The need was so great that the president stepped in to provide equipment—not the president of the United States, but President of the American League Ban Johnson. Reaching out to the owners of the

This picture of a soldier throwing a grenade graced the front page of the 28 February 1918 edition of the *Stars and Stripes*. It was followed by some truly bad poetry describing how the Germans would suffer from the Doughboys' playing skills. Even by February 1918, the vast majority of American soldiers had yet to face the German army, so the truth behind those brave words had yet to be proven. *Courtesy of the* Stars and Stripes

FRANCE, FRIDAY, FEBRUARY 22, 1918.

WORLD'S SERIES OPENED—BATTER UP!

The outfield is a-creepin' in to catch the Kaiser's pop, and here's a southpaw twirler with a lot of vim and hop!

American League for help and contributions, Johnson was able to gather and ship "2000 balls, 500 bats, 50 first basemen's mitts, 50 catcher's gloves, 150 fielder's gloves, 100 chest protectors and 50 masks."[4] It was a nice gesture, but just a drop in the bucket compared to what was needed. The Services of Supply units clustered around the French town of Bourges even went so far as to dispatch one of their chaplains to England to purchase team uniforms that were not available locally. Base Hospital Number 8, mobilized in July 1917 and composed of the staff at the Post-Graduate Hospital in New York City, was in Savenay, in the Nantes section of France. It quickly became one of the largest US Army hospital complexes in France and handled over 35, 000 patients. Baseball was so popular that the hospital staff even devised a form of indoor baseball that could be played by their convalescent patients.[5]

As early as January 1918, the first official US Army leave order was published in the AEF and gave the news that "officers and men in good standing were to be given seven days leave in every four months . . ."[6] And while Paris was not one of the options given as a leave destination, thirty-nine other French cities and towns were soon available. Most were in the warmer areas of France and had direct rail connections, including Aix-les-Bains, Savoie, Biarritz, and the Riviera. Entertainment and guidance at these sites were provided by the YMCA as part of their mission. Contract hotels were set up, and soldiers were provided food and lodging at fixed rates within their budget. It was a great deal for the soldiers, and many applied for leave at the recreation centers. The German offensive in March 1918 caused the AEF to suspend the program, and it was not reinstated until May, with the proviso that only soldiers not actually involved in combat operations would be allowed to participate. In November, after the Armistice, the AEF lifted most of the restrictions and allowed for extended visits.

Also with the Armistice an edgy calm set in. Although extremely happy to have survived the fighting and, even better, to be on the winning side, many Doughboys realized that the Armistice had only quieted the guns, not ended the war. That end could come only after months of negotiations between the victorious Allies and the defeated Central Powers. As a result, most combat units continued to train for further combat, while some had to prepare to march into Germany to serve as an occupation force. The story of this occupation force, designated the US Third Army, must wait for a later chapter. For now, it is important to provide the story of the two US armies—the First Army and Second Army—that were still occupying the front lines at the time of the Armistice, and the very large logistical and administrative support force that was needed to keep them supplied with food, fuel, and ammunition, as well as to maintain all the equipment of a modern army.

In spite of the continued training requirements and basic logistical work required to sustain a two-million-soldier army, soldiers generally began to have more personal time for sports. Although many were working hard to get ready to send the AEF back home to the United States, there was time and official permission to pay a visit to some of the designated rest-and-recreation centers in France mentioned previously.

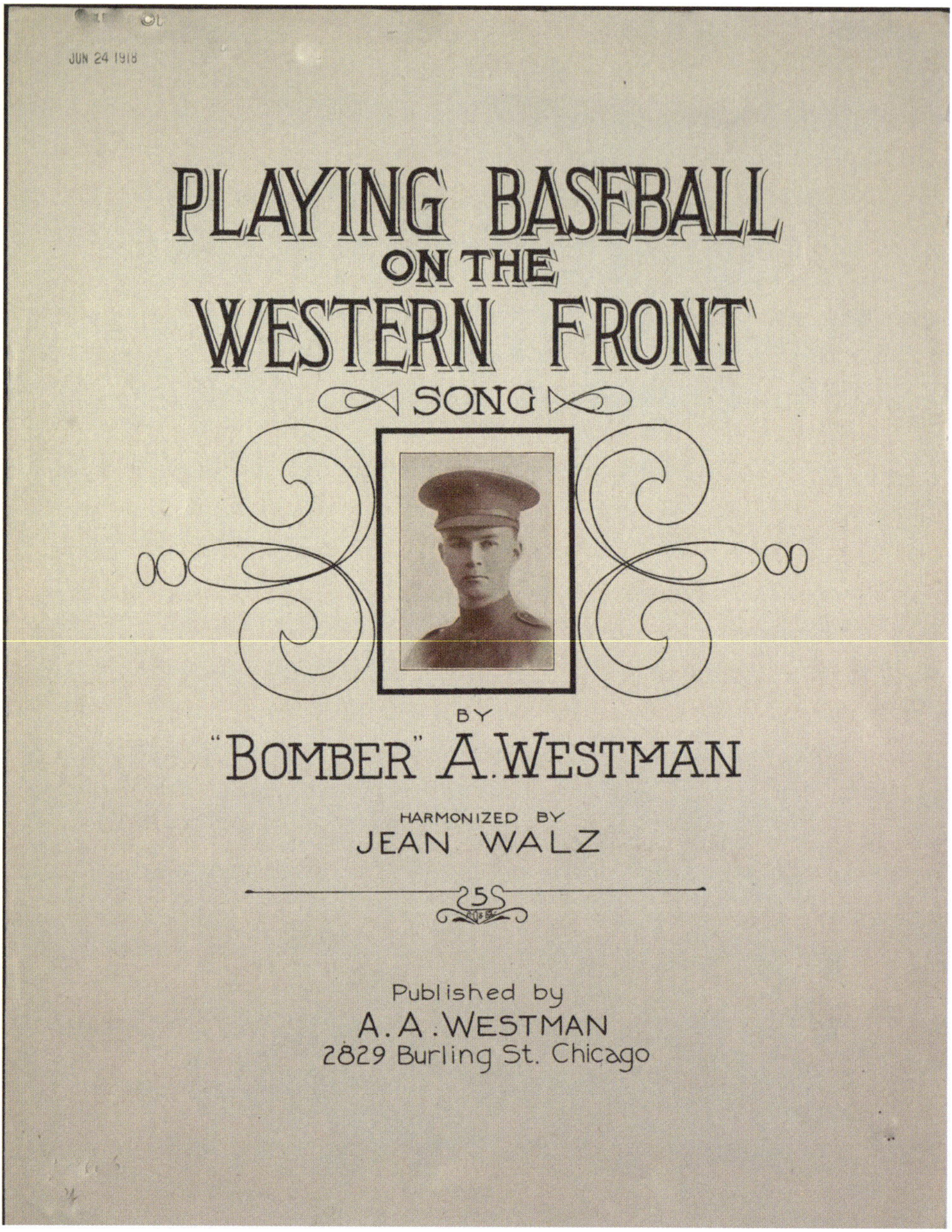

Songwriters again got in the spirit of things with such classics as "Playing Baseball on the Western Front," with lyrics that declared, "They don't use a diamond out in Flanders, when they play baseball out there. The pitcher doesn't wait, the batter to locate, he simply throws a hand grenade, the German is the plate." The song was sure to be a hit on the home front. What the American units serving in Flanders with the British army thought about the song is unknown. *Courtesy of Library of Congress*

With most of these being in the balmy southern part of the country, the soldiers were able to escape—at least for a short period of time—the dreary, wet weather of central and northern France. Some even wandered as far as Italy and Great Britain.

When the fighting ended, the service organizations also greatly increased their efforts to entertain the troops and occupy their leisure time again with wholesome activities. The Doughboys were quick to take advantage of the new facilities and diversions offered by various American welfare agencies: the Red Cross, the YMCA, Knights of Columbus, and the Jewish Welfare League. The YMCA alone established about twenty of their huts in each of the divisional training areas. The Doughboys who visited them were sometimes lucky enough to occasionally converse with one of the genuine American female canteen workers and for a few moments could pretend they were back home.

Not all the Doughboys were pleased by the liberal atmosphere they found in France. A Missouri National Guard field artillery captain

This group of Doughboys is using YMCA-provided equipment to get a game in. Of note are the three French soldiers in berets on the far right who are watching the game; they are most likely the French army instructors assigned to provide combat training for the US Army before the units went into the trenches. *Courtesy of National Archives*

Soldiers in the AEF were not the only baseball players in France; the Canadian Army also fielded a number of teams. In this remarkably clear photograph, Canadian soldiers are playing the game with local YMCA officer Capt. Robert Pearson serving as the umpire. *Courtesy of Canadian War Museum, George Metcalf Archival Collection: CWM 19920085-807*

named Harry Truman later wrote he had received leave to visit Paris and had visited the "Opera Comique to hear 'Carmen, ' and to the *Folies Bergeres*, a disgusting performance." Later, on a similar visit to Nice and Monaco, he was disappointed to find that while he could go inside the famous Monte Carlo casino, he was not allowed to gamble at the tables there because he was in uniform.[7]

Among the combat divisions assigned to the Second Army in late October 1918 was the 29th Division. While the 29th had performed well in the Alsace region—where Capt. Cutchins had observed the unusual frontline ball game mentioned earlier—and in the Meuse-Argonne Offensive as part of the US First Army, they had suffered a large number of casualties. As a result, they had been brought out of the front lines and moved into a reserve and refitting role to prepare them for the next offensive. With the Armistice that offensive was no longer necessary, and the guardsmen began to think about returning home. Their morale soared briefly when on 13 December, the 104th

An unusual sight: a group of English and American Red Cross workers put the finishing touches on a large order of baseball uniforms for the Doughboys stationed in Britain. *Courtesy of US Army*

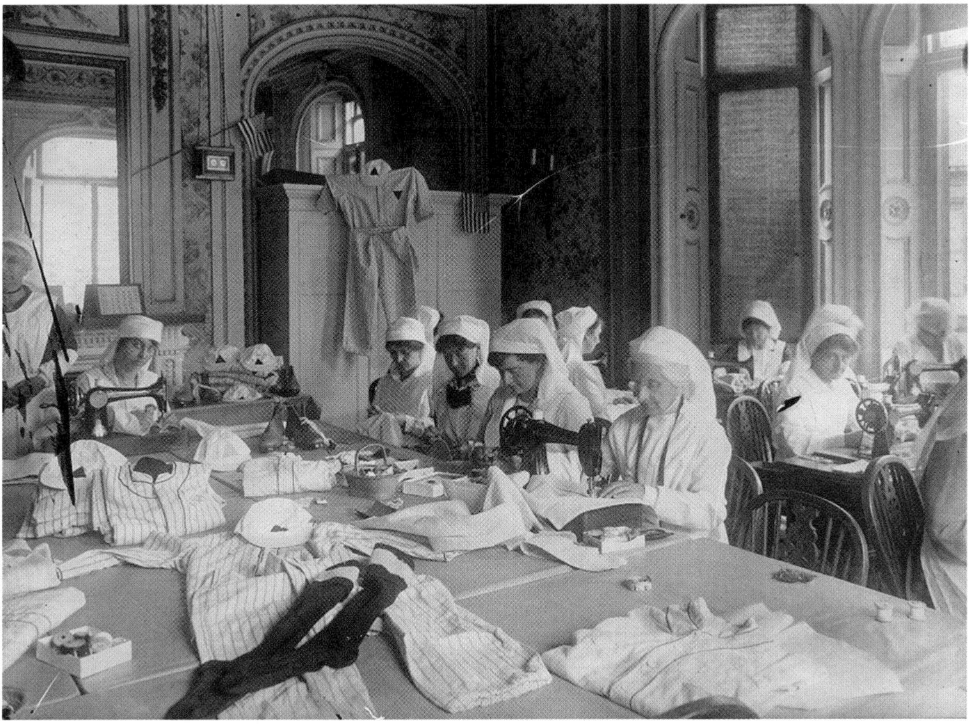

Trench Mortar Battery received orders to prepare for redeployment back to the States. They were sent to the port of St. Nazaire in February and boarded the USS *Mongolia*—a Navy-chartered troopship—and were back in New York City by early March. Unfortunately, this was the only unit of the 29th Division to receive such an early "port call." The rest of the division instead moved to the 11th Training Area near Bourbonne-les-Bains to practice their combat skills. It was becoming obvious that they would have to endure a European winter before it would be their turn to go home. Being good soldiers, the units of the 29th made their best attempt to ignore the rain, sleet, and snow while performing endless drills. The more astute among them did see the "irony in maneuvers against [a pretend] enemy, after having met successfully in battle an actual enemy."[8]

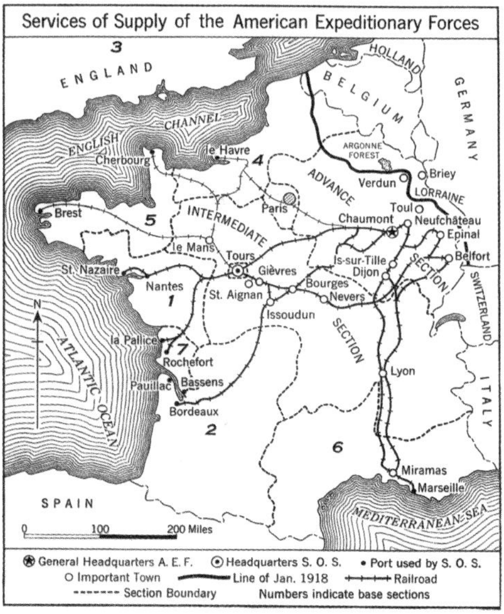

With over 600,000 men assigned to the Services of Supply, the American Army operated water ports, supply depots, hospitals, and maintenance facilities throughout France, as shown on this high-level map. Most of these base areas would field several baseball teams, as well as all the other sports teams. *Courtesy of US Army*

A National Guardsman from Pennsylvania in the 28th Division noted in the same spirit that the "[o]nly difference from war is, when we charged a hill before the Armistice, there was an enemy waitin' on the other side."[9] The African American 369th Infantry Regiment held the same opinion. Assigned to take courses in marksmanship, the men admitted that shooting at paper targets "had little appeal to men fresh from nine months of shooting at live targets."[10]

By early December, the American divisions that had been working with the British Army began moving slowly out of Belgium and northern France to rejoin their AEF brethren in the designated training areas clustered around Chaumont. The 91st Division took advantage of a former German army facility near the town of Meulebeke to delouse themselves. The division also managed to spend some time at an intermediate camp at Crombeke, near Ypres, in West Flanders. It was during this time that the speculative rumor spread through the ranks that the 91st was going to be converted into a cavalry division and sent to occupy some part of Russia. Thankfully for all concerned, this rumor proved false, and on 26 December they received word that the division was ordered to report to a transit and training area near Le Mans, France.

One divisional staff, reconciled to the fact that they would remain in France for the foreseeable future, began to work on setting up the three things they thought would keep their soldiers disciplined and content: "interesting work, comfortable quarters and healthful amusements."[11]

Taken in England at one of the many US Army Services of Supply hospital facilities in that country. As they would in France and later in Germany, the soldiers have taken a large open space and converted it to a diamond. *Courtesy of US Army*

With the typically inclement European winter weather, the Doughboys' favorite pastime of playing baseball was out of the question for a while. That said, most divisions quickly organized, trained, and fielded some very good football teams. Although football proved to be a good diversion for a period, most agreed it was only a placeholder while waiting for the constant cold, rainy drizzle to stop. Whenever there was even slightly better weather, baseball games broke out all over France in the training areas where American soldiers were working and living. In the area around the town of Bierne, the soldiers of the 77th Division believed they would be among the first units to return to

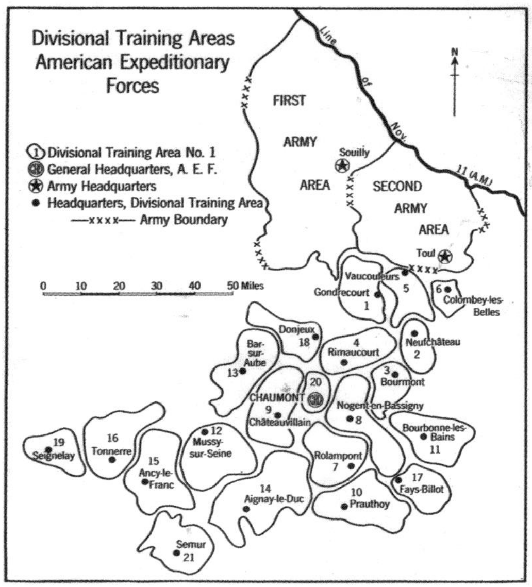

The large size of the AEF in France can be seen in this simple graphic showing the location of the two American armies and the associated training areas behind the lines. After 11 November 1918, each of these training areas contained thousands of Doughboys working on their equipment and preparing to return home. Sporting events—especially baseball—became one of the mainstays in keeping them busy. *Courtesy of US Army*

LE MANS IS VICTOR OVER CANADIANS IN DECIDING BALL GAME

(By Special Correspondent)

Paris, July 4.—By beating the Canadian team by the decisive score of 10 to 0 today, the Le Mans club, champions of the A. E. F. league, also became the military champions of the world. Canada's inability to solve the puzzling curves of Fuller, the American pitcher, is a part of the tale, as they only reached his offerings for one hit, a low fly over second base by Prichérick, the Canadian third baseman, in the seventh inning. On the other hand, the Canadians booted the ball around more or less, the nine hits of the American club

(Continued on Page 4.)

This clipping from a Doughboy's newspaper describes the victory by the AEF team from the Le Mans Base Depot over the Canadian Army's best team. Limiting the Canadians to only one hit, the Le Mans team was therefore declared and self-proclaimed the "Military Champions of the World."

America and were making preparations to move their equipment to the ports. In the meantime, they still managed to play a number of interdivisional ball games. As with most of the units waiting on orders to return to America, living and ball-playing conditions were dependent on local geography. The machine gun battalions of the 77th were living in "miserable billets; but were fortunate enough to have a good ball-field; and a good ball team [was evolving] to play in the division League." Company "G" of the 305th Infantry Regiment was billeted near the Chateau de la Barre. Turning the chateau's courtyard into a ball field, the soldiers enjoyed their games but complained that a lot of baseballs ended up in the chateau's moat.[12] The history of the 305th Infantry Regiment, written in 1919 by Capt. Fred Tiebout, even included a photograph of their brigade commander, Brig. Gen. Michael J. Lenihan, watching the 305th's team beat the team from the now-famous "Lost Battalion."

The 88th Division, comprising almost entirely National Army draftees, had arrived in France shortly before the Meuse-Argonne Offensive. The division was sent to the Alsace sector to relieve the National Guardsmen of the 29th Division so they could participate in the upcoming offensive. With the signing of the Armistice, the 88th moved to a divisional training area near Gondrecourt, about fifty miles from the former front lines. Almost immediately upon arrival the infantry and artillery units conducted vigorous combat training to maintain and further hone their skills should the peace talks break down. Eventually the command staff let up and allocated one hour a day to "organized athletics." This period was soon expanded to two hours a day. Taking advantage of the time, the soldiers quickly laid out football fields and baseball diamonds. The divisional football team proved very successful in competition against other AEF units, and the soldiers looked forward to spring to do the same in baseball.

Infantrymen Beat Marines

Company H of the — Infantry succeeded in downing the Marines of the — Company by a score of 7 to 5. Company H got off to a bad start, the soldiers of the sea hanging up four at the termination of the initial stanza, bot fusilades of hits by the infantrymen in the fourth and eighth innings, three runs coming over the platter in each frame, netted them the victory. The score:

Co. H ....10030003—7
Marines ....40001000—5

Two base hits—Schalk, Works. Struck out—by Halling 11, by Works 4, by Schinkel 7. Bases on balls—off Halling 7, off Works 2. Hit by pitched ball—Stratton by Works. Hits—off Works 3 in 4 innings (none out in fifth), off Schinkel 2.

Even something as innocent as baseball box scores were subject to the Army's censors. While the story of the game could be told, no unit designations were allowed. Similar censorship of combat stories would cause some animosity between the Army and the Marine Corps and last into WWII. The relatively small size of the Corps in comparison to the Army made every mention of Marines seem part of a publicity campaign to the detriment of the Army's equally hard-fighting units. *Courtesy of the* Stars and Stripes

By April, the 88th Division team had the makings of a good baseball club. They started off with a strong victory over the nearby Toul Replacement Depot team by a score of eighteen to one. They then went on a road trip to the First Army area north of their camp to play the 6th Division. They beat the 6th Division team twice, then moved on to do the same to the 36th Division team by a score of six to one. Next up was a team composed of soldiers attending AEF University at Beaune. Another one of the AEF's methods for keeping soldiers busy was to send as many as possible to French, British, or American army–established colleges and universities. Many of these soldiers had attended higher-level learning facilities before the war, and there were a number of former college ballplayers in the school at Beaune. It did not matter to the 88th Division's team, since they beat them five to one. This was followed by a trip to the 7th Division, where the 88th's team lost their first game on 5 May 1919, but they quickly rebounded against the same team the next day to win twelve to one.

Taken in spring 1919, this picture of the 317th Infantry Regiment's baseball team was sent home by Pvt. John C. Hosmer to his wife in Hartwell, Ohio. Hosmer (standing, center back row) was the team's third baseman and was wounded on 12 September 1918 near Ligny-en-Barrois. *Courtesy of Virginia War Memorial*

Their final game in France was against a strong Marine Corps team at the St. Nazaire port complex. They beat the Marines seven to two on 19 May 1919. After that, it was time to put away their gloves and bats; the 88th Division was finally going home.[13]

While the combat units trained and played ball to while away their time until the ships taking them home to the States were available, the thousands of soldiers in the Services of Supply knew their own time in France would be longer. Someone had to clean up and shut down training areas, ammo dumps, supply depots, and railroad yards, as well as run all the functions of the seaports until the Doughboys from the infantry, artillery, engineer, aviation, chemical-warfare, and tank corps had departed. Only then would it finally be their turn to go home. As a result, they plunged deeply into organized sports, and baseball, as usual, was the lead dog. Some of the biggest ordnance and repair depots in France were near the small town of Mehun, in central France.

Caught in midswing, this Doughboy and his comrades are using the wide-open spaces of the Tuileries Garden in Paris for a baseball diamond. Following the habit of playing baseball whenever time was available and there was enough room, these members of the AEF have managed to attract a crowd of Parisians to watch their game. *Courtesy of Library of Congress*

Thousands of American soldiers, French women, and Chinese laborers worked at these depots and factories to repair damaged weapons and equipment. They were also responsible for salvaging damaged or worn-out military clothing, footgear, and unit equipment items for reuse. Thousands more American soldiers and several thousand British ladies of the Woman's Auxiliary Army Corps (later renamed Queen Mary's Army Auxiliary Corps) worked at the nearby Central Records Office in Bourges to manage thousands of individual and unit files for the AEF. As would be expected, the soldiers took advantage of any slack time in the work schedule to play baseball. In February 1919, even before the winter snow had melted, some Ordnance Corps soldiers had already played their first game. Despite several inches of snow on the field, the soldiers said they "want[ed] to get back into shape, especially for the national pastime as soon as possible."[14] This enthusiasm was noted in one of the Doughboy newspapers:

> Within the confines of this camp . . . are hundreds of baseball stars; some have been in the big leagues, or perhaps in minor [league] circuits. There are others who merely played while at college. Why can't we get together and produce some real good teams at these posts? [It is] reported that there are more than nine men at the post in Bourges who have had big league experience. They play different positions and they alone could combine to and make a team . . .[15]

Whether there actually were nine current or former major leaguers in the Bourges area cannot be confirmed. By the end of the war, there were 247 big-league players serving in the US military, so it is entirely possible that at least nine were in the Bourges area.[16] Nevertheless, this "dream team" never materialized, and in its place, a great number of teams were formed in the area to represent their units. While not exactly consisting entirely of major leaguers, Bourges did manage to scrape together a pretty good team that included a former St. Louis second baseman named John B. "Dots" Miller and one of Cy Young's former catchers, Jay J. "Nig" Clarke. Clarke was a Canadian-born big leaguer who joined the Marine Corps in August 1917. After some stateside service at the Marine Corps Overseas Depot at Quantico, and playing on the same baseball team there, both he and Miller were assigned to Company L of the 11th Marine Regiment, 5th Marine Brigade, now assigned to the Services of Supply.[17]

Harold "Hal" Janvrin was another former big leaguer serving in the Services of Supply in the Bourges area. Janvrin had been a successful utility infielder with the Boston Red Sox for several years and played an important role in their 1915 and 1916 World Series victories. He had started the 1917 season with Boston and expected to return to them after the war. He was instead surprised to be notified while serving in France that he had been traded to the Washington Senators. Janvrin had been a solid .230 hitter in his six years with the Red Sox but struggled to regain that form when he later returned from the war. He was traded from Washington to the St. Louis Cardinals before the end of the season. He played for them for two years before spending his last two years with the Brooklyn Dodgers.

With hopes that the weather would cooperate, the Bourges Baseball League attempted to kick off its baseball season on 7 April 1919 with a full schedule of eight contests. These games were to showcase such unusual pairings as the Casualty Administration Division team against the Postal Express Service, and the Master Card Division (the organization that tracked all Doughboy individual movements and transfers in France) against the Administration Building staff team. One newspaper noted that despite the constantly rainy French weather, the "fields are in excellent shape as a result of a steam roller. . . . With backstops and benches erected,

Jay Justin Clarke was a Canadian-born ballplayer who played for five different major-league teams in his nine-year career. Clarke enlisted in the US Marine Corps in November 1917 and served in France in the 5th Brigade of Marines, assigned to the Services of Supply. After the war, he resumed his professional baseball career for a few years, then rejoined the Marine Corps in 1929. *Courtesy of Library of Congress*

Harold "Hal" Janvrin, a utility infielder for the Boston Red Sox, had the unusual experience of being traded to another team—the Washington Senators—while serving in the Services of Supply in France. Not surprisingly, Janvrin's baseball statistics suffered during his first few months with the Senators in the 1919 season, and he was soon traded to the St. Louis Cardinals. *Courtesy of Library of Congress*

the old drill field looks like a regular big league baseball diamond." Obviously spirits ran high as the Casualty team, led by a former University of Pittsburgh catcher, boasted that its team speed would make it a fast game, and predicted an easy victory. Their Postal Express opponents fired back that they were "just as keen for a chance at the bacon and will use every bit of strategy" to defeat the Casualty team.[18] Unfortunately the rain continued, and even a week later the opening games still had not been played. The headline in the local soldiers' newspaper sports page said merely in the Doughboy's fractured English/French: "With Rain, Pas Baseball." The rain continued, and the soldiers were "Pas" baseball" until early May.

Eventually the weather improved, and it was noted that there were some 55, 000 men playing on 3, 700 teams in France. A large tournament was held at Bordeaux from 25 May to 2 June to determine the very best teams to represent their organizations in a two-division league. Representing the Services of Supply were the highly regarded teams from the Le Mans area and the Nantes supply depot in Base Area Number 1.[19]

A sign of how seriously the Doughboys in France took baseball was seen in the 8 June 1919 edition of *The CRO*, the local US Army–produced newspaper. The headline said "BOURGES TEAM HAS LIGHT-FINGERED UMPIRE" and detailed how a bad call on balls and strikes by umpire "Percy Hackett, one of the cleverest arbiters in the AEF today, " cost the team from the St. Aignan Evacuation Camp a victory and also ended their

Baseball Season Delayed

Rain Prevents Real Baseball Opening

Two Exhibition Games to be Held Sunday on New Diamonds. Good Contests Are Expected

BIG START NEXT WEEK. PERHAPS!

Bad news traveled fast. The constantly inclement French weather delayed the opening of the 1919 Bourges Baseball League for over three weeks. With the heavy workload in the Services of Supply, most games were played on Sundays—the soldiers' day off. With such uncooperative weather, some doubted the season would ever start.

thirteen-game winning streak. It happened like this. With St. Aignan leading one to nothing in the bottom of the ninth, the first Bourges batter reached base with a single. The second batter, according to St. Aignan, was so overmatched by the pitcher that he stood no chance of hitting the ball. Here is where the "light-fingered" umpire enters the story. Umpire Hackett, apparently taking pity on the batter, called two obvious strikes as balls. According to the newspaper account, this gift "heartened the batter's failing spirits, " so he swung the bat and hit the next pitch, driving it for a single. This moved the runner on first all the way to third. At this point the excitement of the Bourges home crowd became too much to contain, and many poured onto the outfield. While the St. Aignan players waited for control to be restored, the runner at first walked over to second. The umpire refused to send him back to first, despite the protests of the St. Aignan team in the field. After order was restored, the next batter hit a deep fly to center field, and the runner on third scored the tying run.

Noted simply as "Our Nine of the 840th Aero Squadron." The 840th was formed in February 1918 and deployed to Latrecey Aerodrome, in northeastern France, as a repair squadron from May 1918 to March 1919. This photo, probably taken in 1918, shows that the soldiers played in their regular uniforms with only the addition of athletic shoes and baseball socks in place of leggings. *Courtesy of Charles G. Thomas*

One thing the Doughboys did not lack in France was self-confidence. In this cartoon from *The CRO*, the Doughboys' firm belief that the quality of baseball in the American Expeditionary Forces was the best in the world shows through clearly.

Certainly an unusual photo from *The CRO*, the Doughboy newspaper produced in the Bourges area for soldiers of the Services of Supply. In this rare action shot, the Bourges baseball team is playing a game against a pickup team in the rest-and-recreation center in Monaco.

The next hitter did exactly the same thing, and the runner on third, having moved there from second on the previous play, came in to score the winning run. The sportswriter, obviously a fan of the Bourges team, took advantage of the entire incident to admonish the St. Aignan team, saying that previously "Bourges has taken the worst end of decisions gamely and it seems too bad that our friends from St. Aignan . . . could not do like likewise. It is not the right spirit for champions."[20] Obviously, even back then, it was easier to talk about the "spirit of champions" when the breaks went to your team.

In any army, there is always good-natured, and sometimes not-so-good-natured, ribbing between units. Particularly strong are the jibes between the soldiers of "working" or "fighting" units and the soldiers assigned to comparatively safe, easy jobs in a headquarters. The writers of *The CRO* were certainly party to this belief and were not averse to belittling other opposing teams. In an article written to describe a victory by the hardworking Army Ordnance Corps players of the Mehun team, they pointed out that the next team coming to "shake bats" was from the Services of Supply Headquarters at Portiers, and "little trouble is expected from the lace curtain outfit."[21]

While baseball was the game of choice both in the stateside training camps and in France, the Doughboys did find time to play or watch other sports. In the following chapter, these "other" sports and their role in training or entertaining the Doughboys will be examined.

A group of African American Doughboys take advantage of one of the large parade grounds near the Services of Supply headquarters at Tours to play a game of baseball while still dressed in their work uniforms. It appears that a sizable crowd of other soldiers, French citizens, and children are beginning to gather. *Courtesy of Kautz Family YMCA archives, University of Minnesota Libraries*

A serious-looking soldier decides to pose with a baseball bat instead of his rifle. With many units unable to obtain proper baseball uniforms, it is possible that this unidentified Doughboy would also play ball in his work uniform. *Courtesy of Marvin-Alonzo Greer Collection*

Another African American soldier also chooses a baseball bat as a prop in his French-made portrait. Of note here is the fact that he is wearing an overseas hat instead of the campaign hat casually tossed on the ground behind him. Although many soldiers preferred the older-style campaign hat as a work hat, wearing an overseas hat was solid proof that the soldier was serving in France and not still in the States. *Courtesy of Marvin-Alonzo Greer Collection*

From 23 June 1918: the soldiers are playing on a diamond provided by the Red Cross. Most likely taken at one of the US Army hospitals in Britain during the war, a large crowd of soldiers and civilians have gathered to watch the contest. *Courtesy of Library of Congress*

Two wounded Canadian soldiers pose while attempting to play baseball at a hospital. The two nurses in the background appear to be wearing Canadian nurses' uniforms. *Courtesy of Library of Congress*

Under fairly dry conditions, the team from the 54th Field Artillery Brigade takes on an all-star team from the 29th Division. The 54th Brigade, composed of National Guard field artillerymen from Virginia, Maryland, and New Jersey, had the misfortune of being in a Brittany training camp when the Spanish flu struck that area, and the brigade suffered severely from that exposure. *Courtesy of US Army*

Another view of the game between the 29th and the 54th Field Artillery Brigade. The game was played on 3 April 1919, as the Guardsmen were preparing to return to the States. *Courtesy of US Army*

5th Inning
Those Other Sports . . .

While baseball was the obvious favorite sport for the Doughboys, both in France and back in the States, there was some room for other sports in their training schedules. The Doughboys were also enthusiastic fans of football and boxing; many units boasted excellent teams for both. As will be seen, there was also significant interest in soccer, basketball, volleyball, track and field, tennis, mountaineering, and even bicycle racing.

Football

With many of the National Army draftees and National Guard soldiers reporting to their training camps in fall 1917, football was by far the natural and favorite choice for outdoor sporting events. The National Army training camps for the most part were in the Midwest or in the northern part of the country, while the National Guard camps were almost all in the South. This was not an accident, but the result of analysis that showed there was only enough money to build the wooden buildings the National Army would need for living and training. Conversely, the National Guard units had tents as part of their basic unit equipment, so it was decided that the Guard would live and train in the South, where the winter weather was expected to be milder than what was normal in the North. It was a logical decision. However, Mother Nature proved to be as fickle and uncooperative as ever, and winter 1917–1918 in the southern United States proved to be among the coldest on record. National Guard soldiers huddled in their canvas tents and complained about the "Sunny South." As a result, most of the Guardsmen in training camps were more concerned about staying warm and healthy than about team sports. But for some men the cold weather was just right for playing football.

The National Football League as we know it today did not exist until after the First World War. College football was just entering its golden era when war was declared. Campuses across the country drew thousands of spectators to their football fields and stadiums on Saturdays. The entry of the United States into the war changed that. Some college football teams enlisted as a group, while others lost many of their star players to voluntary enlistments. Later they lost even more players to the draft. It appears that most of the college players who did join the US military gravitated toward officer training and therefore went to war as lieutenants and captains. As a result, most Army unit or training-camp football teams had a number of skilled former college players. Some college coaches and players who entered the service quickly became

Football was also played. Taken in March 1919, this photograph shows the strength and tenacity of the 33rd Division football team. It was their misfortune to run up against another even more powerful team when the 88th Division's team came to play them on 1 March 1919 in Junglinstein, Luxembourg. The 88th won the game handily by a score of thirteen to zero. *Courtesy of Serge Kugener Collection*

unit athletic officers and team coaches. There was also competition inside the larger units to get the top talent assigned to their camp and team. Even with the bad winter of 1917–1918, football teams were organized and games were played at most training camps. It was the same in France as Doughboys began to arrive in larger numbers, particularly in spring and early summer 1918.

Organizing and managing a unit football team required a lot more time, manpower, and equipment than pulling together a baseball team. As a result there never were as many football teams representing every level of unit organization as there were for baseball. There was a period when football took center stage for the Doughboys. After the signing of the Armistice and the movement into Germany of the US Third Army for occupation duty, those combat divisions remaining in France were moved to training areas to refresh their tactical skills, establish schools to teach vocational skills to the soldiers, and begin preparations for returning to the United States. While in these training areas, most divisions began to assemble football teams to play in an AEF-wide tournament that would clearly establish who had the best football team in the Army. With so many of the young officers having played in college

Showing the makeshift gear used by many of the Doughboy teams in Europe, these football players are practicing one of their plays. In contrast to today, most teams would have fewer than twenty players on a team, so the men were expected to play both offense and defense. *Courtesy of US Army*

before the war, each division boasted a number of elite college-level football players to fill out their teams.

One such team came from the 88th Division, which was stationed in the First Training Area, near Gondrecourt. For the National Army soldiers of the 88th, the location seemed a poor reward for their service. It was the "least desirable in the country: poor, stony, dirty, shambling villages and weather of the worst variety. The rain was almost constant, not in heavy downfalls, but in persistent, misty drizzles, and mud was everywhere."[1] Nevertheless, the soldiers of the 88th knuckled down and laid out both baseball diamonds and football gridirons. In spite of the constant rain, the football team began practicing near the division headquarters in the middle of January 1919. Playing on the team were two Native Americans of some sporting renown: Pvt. Tom Necklace had played on the Carlisle Indian football team with Jim Thorpe, and Sgt. Frederick Bender was the brother of famed major-league baseball pitcher Chief Bender.[2] One month after they began practicing, the 88th team took on the team from the 5th Division, a Regular Army unit serving in the occupation of Luxembourg. Not letting the lack of official football uniforms stop them, the 88th

> got aviation caps for their heads, Red Cross sweaters in place of jerseys, and padded their blue denim fatigue pants for use as football breeches. They went to [the nearby city of] Nancy and bought woolen stockings and for shoes they added cleats to their old Army kicks.[3]

Calling themselves the "Hunhuskers, " the 88th team was ready for action. Their game against the 5th Division's team ended in a 0-to-0 tie. Four days later the two teams played again, and this time the 5th Division won by a score of three to nothing. After a week's further practice, perhaps with an added focus on offense, the 88th's team beat the team from the US IX Corps by a score of thirty-three to zero. The Hunhuskers then traveled to Luxembourg and defeated the 33rd Division's team thirteen to zero. March 1919 found them in Germany to take on the team from the 89th Division near the city of Trier. It did not go well, and the 88th fell to the 89th by a score of thirteen to nine and were eliminated from further participation in the AEF tournament.

The football team from the 4th Division; their loss on 5 February 1919 by a score of fourteen to zero to the 89th Division's team set the stage for the 89th to travel to France for the AEF Football Championship round of games. There was a large turnout for the game in spite of the cold weather, and even the trees were filled with spectators. *Courtesy of National Archives*

Over in the 29th Division's training area, similar events were taking place. The 29th, composed primarily of Virginia, Maryland, and New Jersey National Guard troops, developed an internal divisional football league. From these teams, the best players were selected to represent the division against other teams from First Army units. Rising through the standings after competing against the other divisions, the 29th's consolidated team lost to the 36th Division in the First Army Championship game on a very muddy field by a score of three to zero.

At the same time, the football teams in the Third Army were practicing and playing along the banks of the Rhine River. Playing among themselves at first, and then against visiting teams from the AEF in France, two powerhouse teams began to emerge: the 89th Division team and the team from the 4th Division, a Regular Army unit stationed in the area

One of the football teams in the American Forces in Germany takes time from practice to pose. It appears there are fourteen players on the team and two coaches. *Courtesy of US Army*

The 26th Balloon Company's football team takes time for a photograph in France after the Armistice. The officer seated in the center is wearing wings on his uniform, indicating he was probably one of the aerial observers assigned to the unit, as well as a member of the team. *Courtesy of US Army*

FOOTBALL TEAM, TWENTY-SIXTH COMPANY, AMERICAN EXPEDITIONARY FORCES

around the city of Coblenz. The team from the 4th made quick work of the 42nd "Rainbow" Division's team, then knocked off the IV Corps team by a score of three to zero. Next up was the 2nd Division's team, the champion of the III Corps. In front of a large crowd, the 4th Division prevailed by a score of ten to seven. In the excitement of the victory, 4th Division commander Maj. Gen. Mark Hersey led his soldiers on a celebratory snake dance around the gridiron. The only thing now standing in their way to claiming the championship of the Third Army was the 89th's team. The 4th Division's history later noted that the game

> was attended by British generals from Cologne and French generals from Mainz who had come to see the final game of the football championship of the Army of Occupation. Hopes were high . . . [but] the 89th by a 14–0 score, won a splendid victory. It was a severe disappointment.[4]

In retrospect, the 4th Division's loss to the 89th Division should have come as no surprise to anyone in the AEF or in the Third Army. The 89th was coached by George "Potsy" Clark. Clark had built a solid reputation as a football star at the University of Illinois before the war and would later gain further fame as the coach of the National Football League's Detroit Lions. Among the members of the 89th's team, and quarterbacking the squad, was an aggressive and extremely athletic cavalry officer named Charles Gerhardt, the man who would command the 29th Division during the next war and lead them ashore on D-day at Omaha Beach.[5] Gerhardt was a former West Point football star and together with Clark made a powerful backfield combination for the 89th. Their experience showed as the season progressed.

By mid-March 1919, all the top teams in the AEF were assembled and began to play. Among the semifinal games was a tough battle between the 89th Division and the Services of Supply team from St. Nazaire. Nursing a seven-to-zero lead going into the second half, the 89th found itself in trouble when the SOS team drove to their one-foot line. The 89th took a deep breath and dug in their cleats. They stopped the SOS team on four successive plays. That goal-line stand seemed to deflate the SOS, and shortly thereafter player/coach Potsy Clark ran for a touchdown to make the score thirteen to zero, effectively ending the game.

By the time the dust, blood, and mud had settled from all the preliminary games, there remained four top-notch football teams in the

The 89th Division's AEF Football Championship team poses near their work area in the American occupation zone in Germany. The officer kneeling behind the center is Capt. Charles Hunter Gerhardt. By June 1944, Gerhardt would be a major general commanding the 29th Infantry Division and lead them onto Omaha Beach on D-day.

The view from the end zone. Another football game played in Luxembourg on 27 February 1919 pitted the 28th Division against the 5th Division. The 5th Division recovered a 28th Division fumble to swing the tide of the game in their favor. *Courtesy of Serge Kugener Collection*

AEF: one representing each of the three US Armies in Europe, and another for the Services of Supply. The playoffs featured the 36th Division representing the US First Army in the first game against the 7th Division from the US Second Army; in the second game, the US Third Army champs, the 89th Division, were pitted against an SOS team from the Intermediate Section. The 36th faced the 7th Division in front of 25, 000 spectators, including Gen. Pershing and his guests, King Albert and Queen Elizabeth of Belgium. Rain started to pour before the game and continued throughout, making the field muddy and the ball slippery. Film footage remains of the game and reinforces the written accounts. The field was so muddy and wet that the players are indistinguishable from one team to another. Only the referees' unmuddied white trousers help tell them apart from the players. The film also shows how packed the stands were, with thousands of soldiers rooting on their teams.

Soldiers were not the only ones to enjoy a good football game. The sailors at the Great Lakes Naval Training Station in northern Illinois are braving the cold weather to root on their football team. By the end of the war, the Great Lakes Station had trained over 125,000 sailors. *Photo by E. Ross Benedict, courtesy of Tod L. Benedict*

The game remained a scoreless tie until late in the fourth quarter, when one of the 7th Division's players fumbled the ball on his own twenty yard line. After a short drive the 36th punched the ball into the end zone from there, and the game ended shortly thereafter. Queen Elizabeth was so impressed by the game that she insisted on bringing her camera down to the field after the game to take pictures of the players.[6]

Facing the Intermediate Section's football team—known for their powerful running game—the 89th found themselves down three to nothing early in the game. It appeared likely that the score might remain that way until an Intermediate Section kick returner could not get out of the way of a bouncing punt; he was accidentally touched by the ball on the five yard line. The 89th recovered the ball and quickly took advantage of their good luck. Gerhardt threw a touchdown pass to Potsy Clark, who was playing in the halfback position. That opened the floodgates, and the 89th scored ten more points in quick succession to close out their opponents. With the conclusion of these games, everyone in the AEF knew it was time for a showdown between the 36th and the 89th.

The AEF championship game was played on 29 March 1919 in Paris, in front of 15, 000 fans. Included among the crowd were Pershing, Lt. Gen. Hunter Liggett, and the commanders of the 36th and 89th Divisions. Following what appeared to be a pattern, the 89th spotted the 36th Division team a six-point lead but appeared to get stronger as the game progressed. By the end of the game, Potsy Clark had taken over completely and scored all fourteen points for the victorious 89th

Division, the final touchdown coming on his tremendous sixty-five-yard run through the tired 36th Division defense. Clark was undoubtedly the best football player in the AEF, and in this game, in addition to scoring both touchdowns, he also kicked each extra point.

Never passing up a chance to speak to his soldiers, Gen. Pershing made his way onto the field after the game to congratulate both teams and said:

> You have carried out the letter and the spirit of the plan adopted to promote clean sports in the American Expeditionary Forces, You have gone at this athletic program and this game today with the same dash and spirit you showed on the [battle] fronts, and that is the spirit that makes America and Americans great.[7]

Although this championship game ended Doughboy football in France, the Army of Occupation in Germany maintained a football league until 1922, when there simply were not enough soldiers left in the force to make a game of it.

A sideline picture of one of the teams playing in the 11 May 1921 game between the Medical Department of the American Forces in Germany (AFG) and a consolidated team from the Cavalry and Machine Gun Detachments. Of note here are the yard markers, the turret in the center background from one of the local Rhine River bridges in the Coblenz area, and the soldier, seated among the spectators, who is reading a newspaper instead of watching the game.

Boxing

As a form of exercise designed to instill the martial spirit into men who previously had been store clerks, college students, and farmers, boxing was the early answer. Even before some units had been issued rifles and uniforms, local boxers were brought to training camps to teach footwork, fighting skills, and, most importantly, self-confidence. As training progressed, the soldiers' enthusiasm for the sport generated a need for unit teams. With the arrival at the camps of YMCA, Salvation Army, and Knights of Columbus volunteers, boxing took on an even-greater role in entertaining the troops. Along with providing places of worship, libraries, and clubhouses, these organizations were charged with providing sporting equipment and encouraging the men to stay active. That some of these facilities were integrated was noted by one writer, who wrote while watching two African American soldiers taking their turn in a boxing ring during an "Amateur Night" that there was

> the most interesting audience from a racial standpoint that I have ever seen—a sprinkling of Jews, a few Slavic types, negroes, some Scandinavians, and a pronounced Gaelic element—raw material being fused in the crucible of democracy.[8]

This is certainly an interesting observation coming from an army that maintained a rigid segregation between some of the races. Almost as interesting was the arrival in June 1918 of a hundred prisoners of war from the German navy at Camp Grant, Illinois. The white-uniformed sailors had come primarily from ships that had been interred since the beginning of the war. Initially, the Germans were concentrated at Fort MacPherson, Georgia, where some had even begun to pick up the rudimentary elements of baseball as a means to pass the time while in the stockade. But now they were not at Camp Grant to show off their baseball skills: they were to be an additional labor force. They "were put to work at once building the giant boxing arena . . . constructed in a natural amphitheater beside the Rock River [with a] seating capacity of more than 10, 000." The new arena got its first big test on 4 July, when the 86th

Some of the more popular events at many Knights of Columbus Huts were the boxing matches held to instill a more "warlike" spirit in the soldiers.

Coming from the New Jersey National Guard–based 112th Field Artillery Regiment of the 29th Division was middleweight boxer C. J. "Ritz" Walters (*right*). His trainer, Teddy Raymond, is seated at his side and also served in the 112th, a heavy-artillery unit equipped with 155 mm artillery pieces. *Courtesy of USAMHI*

Division's boxing team hosted a Canadian Army team in a seven-bout card. The US boxers won all seven fights: the first six by technical knockout, and the last when the Canadian was unable to answer the bell.[9]

After the Armistice was signed, the soldiers maintained their high level of interest in their unit boxing team but also began to closely follow the professional boxers who were making headlines. The Paris edition of the *Stars And Stripes* and the *AMAROC News* covered every nuance and detail of the famed Jack Dempsey–Jess Willard fight in July 1919. Jess Willard, considered a giant at six feet six inches tall, had been the heavyweight champion for more than four years. His opponent, Jack Dempsey, was younger and some five inches shorter but had been suspected of dodging the draft by working in a shipyard. Among the Doughboys, opinion was split as to who would emerge victorious on 4 July 1919 in Toledo, Ohio. As early as May, the boxing writer for *The CRO* had no doubts:

> If Dempsey is the man that he is touted as . . . there seems to be nothing that can prevent him from taking the crown. Willard's record as a fighter is not the best in the world . . . he has done little but lounge around and live the life of the proverbial Riley."[10]

At the same time, the sportswriter for the *AMAROC News* had doubts about Dempsey's ability to withstand the power of Willard. He wrote:

Barney Myers had a wonderful night, copping a decision over Dougherty of Clamecy in two rounds. The visitor assimilated a terrible licking, being knocked down several times in each round. The good nature of his opponent was the only thing that saved him from going out for the count.

Barney Meyers

One of the favorite US Army boxers in the Bourges area was Barney Meyers. Although wounded in the Meuse-Argonne Offensive, Meyers recovered well enough to have a successful boxing career in the Services of Supply.

> But the little dope bird also tells us that the champion will outweigh Dempsey at least 50 pounds or more, and that is an advantage that is mighty hard for any fighter, be he ever so clever and speedy, to overcome.[11]

As the time for the fight got closer, it appeared that it might be a nonevent. An anti-boxing-movement group in Ohio—scene of the scheduled fight—had influenced the Ohio state legislature to petition the governor, James M. Cox, to halt the fight. While the discussion in Ohio went back and forth, a number of Ohio Doughboys stationed on the Rhine decided to make their feelings known. Never shy about expressing their opinions and thoughts, the American soldiers sent their own petition to Governor Cox, demanding that the fight be allowed, while others sent antifight petitions. Groups of soldiers and sailors at other locations also sent petitions with thousands of signatures. Whether these ultimately influenced Governor Cox's decision is unknown, but nevertheless, the fight was on.

Perhaps the Buckeye soldiers should have saved their efforts. With an estimated 80, 000 spectators, the fight lasted just eight minutes.

One of the many boxing matches held by the Armies of Occupation in Germany; this well-attended bout is taking place in July 1921. In the center it is possible to see American commander Maj. Gen. Henry T. Allen arriving and being saluted by a British officer. The two boxers for the match, their backs to the camera, are seated at center, wearing white undershirts.

Dempsey knocked Willard to the canvas in the first round, the first time that champ had been knocked off his feet. It would not be the last. The challenger knocked him down several more times before the bell sounded to end the first round. Willard managed to last another two rounds, but essentially the fight was over after the first round, and Dempsey was the new champ. A Doughboy newspaper reported: "Jack Dempsey Sends Big Willard to Slumberland in Third Round."[12]

In the 91st Division—a National Army unit composed originally of draftees from the Pacific Northwest—interest in boxing had started during their training at Camp Lewis, Washington. After 11 November 1918, one of the chaplains who had originally trained the unit's boxers restarted the pugilistic program of what he called his "Sunday School Class" while the unit was recovering and resting from their frontline exertions. The history of the 361st Infantry Regiment reported that after the Armistice:

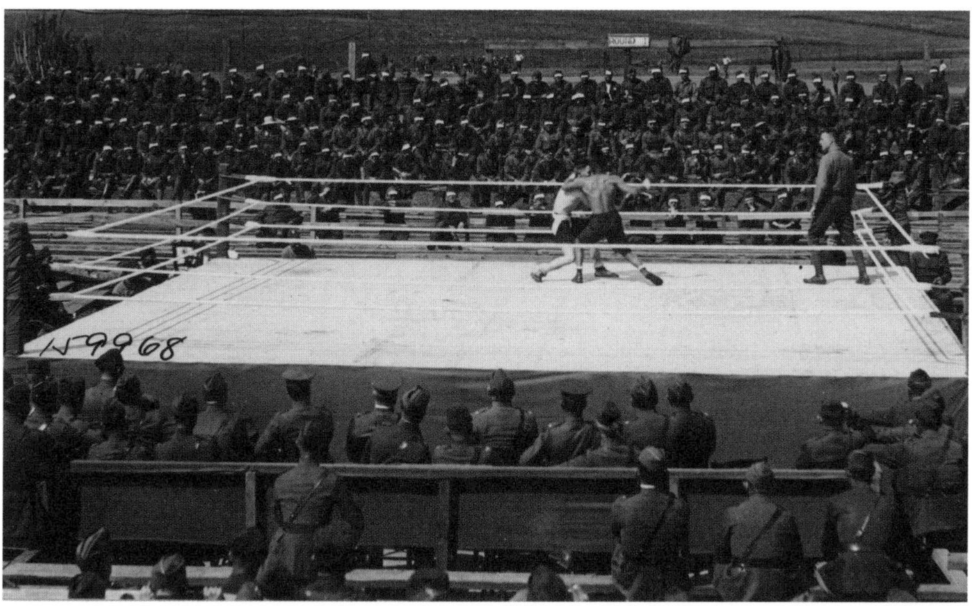

In this 7 June 1919 Army Signal Corps photograph, Kid Farrell, a 5th Division boxer, is taking on an opponent from the US Third Army. The fight, staged in Esch, Luxembourg, took place outside in bright sunlight, so the soldiers facing the camera have made paper "brims" for their overseas hats to shield their eyes. *Courtesy of Serge Kugener Collection*

> the old favorite diversion of boxing was again indulged in with the result that the divisional team included among its members Sergeant Woodhouse of Company "A, " Sergeant Simonich of Company "A, " Corporal Pedersen of Company "A, " Private O'Brien of Company "E" and Private Robertson of Company "G." These included all of the 361st Infantry boxing representatives who had won divisional championships in Camp Lewis, except Corporal Wells and Private Ferdon, both of Company "A, " both of whom had been wounded in action and had not returned to the regiment. . . . No one of these men was ever beaten and each inter-divisional contest in which they took part was won by this division.[13]

By late fall 1919, most of the AEF was gone from France, and the Third Army, although still in the Rhineland, was shrinking in size from 260, 000 soldiers to only 20, 000. Boxing remained as popular as ever among the soldiers on the Rhine, and there were many boxing matches against Allied soldiers from the French, British, and Belgian armies. The new commander of the American occupation force, now officially renamed the American Forces in Germany (AFG), was Maj. Gen. Henry T. Allen. Allen, a well-known explorer of the Alaskan frontier before the war, was a firm believer in all forms of sporting activities and took care to put in appearances at all of his soldiers' events. Under his guidance, the AFG soon became known as an elite unit both for their physical fitness and their soldier skills. The degree to which boxing contributed to this overall fitness can be gleaned from the YMCA's records, which recorded that in the time since the American forces in Germany had been established there had been

Another indication of the popularity of boxing among the soldiers: this small pamphlet on boxing techniques was published and sold by the *AMAROC News* in the American occupation zone. Note that it is modestly dedicated "to the fiercest fighter and the fairest sportsman in all the world—the American Doughboy." AMAROC is the contraction of "American Army of Occupation."

Two images of Clive Mason: before the war as a cowboy in California, then as a military intelligence soldier in Germany in 1921. Mason, a Native American, served as an investigative agent in the Military Intelligence office in Coblenz. During his off-duty time he fought as a light-heavyweight boxer under the name "Chief" Mason. Mason later put his many talents to work as a private detective in Los Angeles, then as a rancher.

"two thousand one hundred thirty-seven bouts . . . lasting nine thousand seventy-five rounds. There had been eighty-six international boxing contests held locally, of which the Americans won fifty-five, lost twenty-six and tied six."[14] The Doughboys occupying the Rhineland were certainly aided in their sporting accomplishments by access to a number of indoor and outdoor swimming pools, as well as a skating rink, golf course, and thirty-six tennis courts in the Coblenz area. It is small wonder than one observer noted that "The AFG [is] the Army University of Athletics."[15]

A final note of the effect of boxing on the Doughboys, and vice versa, comes from the pen of Maj. Gen. Johnson Hagood. Returning to the United States after commanding a field artillery brigade in the occupation of Germany, Gen. Hagood had the opportunity to talk to Jack Dempsey and thank him for putting on a boxing exhibition for a group of US Army officers. Dempsey waved off the thanks and told Hagood that "The Army and YMCA saved the boxing game to America. Before the war we were being hedged in more and more by state laws, until we were just about through. But when the chaplains and the YMCA people saw what boxing did for the soldiers in France, they put us back on the map."[16]

Basketball, Volleyball, and Soccer

Although baseball, football, and boxing were the most-popular sports among the Doughboys, many men played basketball, volleyball, or soccer. Some units in the northern US training camps even fielded hockey teams. Once again, service organizations such as the YMCA and the Salvation Army provided what uniforms and equipment they could to outfit the soldiers. A Camp Lee periodical reported that the 1918 volleyball season at the large training base in Virginia had to be delayed until November because of the Spanish flu.[17] The camp, near the city of Petersburg, was one of the training sites hit hardest by the epidemic, and, to lessen the chance of passing the disease, all large gatherings of soldiers were prohibited. Likewise, the Camp Lee basketball team had to wait for the disease to slacken, then opened its season with a vengeance.

Taken at the Great Lakes Naval Training Station in 1918 or early 1919, this photograph shows a serious-looking naval basketball team. Of note here are the heavy kneepads some of the sailors wear and the roundel with wings patch on their shirts, indicating perhaps they are from a naval aviation unit. *Photo by E. Ross Benedict, courtesy of Tod L. Benedict*

One of the better-known basketball teams in the central Virginia area at the end of the war was this group of soldiers from Camp Lee. Drawn mainly from the staff of the camp hospital, they pose in front of one of the hospital buildings. By October 1918, there were over 57,000 soldiers at Camp Lee, many sick with the Spanish flu; as a result, the basketball season was delayed two months. *Courtesy of US Army, Fort Lee*

Members of an AFG basketball team pose for a portrait in front of a door labeled "Poodle Dog Café." While they are equipped with sport shoes, it appears that cutoff uniform trousers and Army-issue undershirts compose the rest of the team's uniforms.

Traveling down the Virginia peninsula to Camp Eustis, and then the naval base at Norfolk, they quickly established a reputation as a solid team. In a high-scoring affair that went into overtime, they defeated another highly regarded team from their own camp, the Camp Lee Post Office team, by a score of twenty-nine to twenty-five.

Among the many foreign-born soldiers serving at Camp Lee in 1918 were several from England. Getting together, they organized a camp soccer team and began play against other Army teams, then civilian teams from the local area. One of their biggest rivalries was with a civilian team from the nearby Richmond Athletic Club. Traveling the twenty miles to and from Camp Lee to downtown Richmond for games, the Doughboys even brought the camp band along to help entertain the crowds.

It was the same at all the training camps. Camp Sheridan, Alabama—training site for the Ohio National Guard, which would form the 37th Division—reported that there were 160 basketball teams in the YMCA leagues on post.[18] Started primarily as a means to keep the troops in shape and out of trouble, many of these sports continued as a means to keep the soldiers busy until they could be demobilized after the war was over.

Basketball leagues were set up throughout France, and there was a very active league in Paris itself, where seven teams from various US Army organizations stationed in the city played on a regular basis. Not awaiting demobilization, the soldiers of the AFG played to keep in shape and because they enjoyed it. By the end of 1919, there were four basketball leagues in the American zone, and each unit in the AFG fielded teams down to the company level. The 1920 season was a busy one with many games. At the end of the season, the top players were selected to form an AFG team. They traveled south to the French occupation zone headquarters in Mainz and defeated the French army teams there.

A combination of college and amateur basketball players made up the roster of the team representing the Overseas Depot, Quantico, in 1918. The two Marines standing in the back row appear to be corporals and are most likely the training and coaching staff for the team. *Courtesy of Library of Congress*

After a soccer match held in Grevenmacher, Luxembourg, in January 1919 between a team of Doughboys and the local citizens, the participants pose together for a group photograph. As usual for the period, any kind of sports activity has drawn a large crowd of local children. *Courtesy of Serge Kugener Collection*

The Other "Other" Sports

Included among the many other athletic activities that were popular with the Doughboys were track and field events, polo, tennis, and even bicycle racing. Mountain climbing and mountaineering were encouraged at one of the rest-and-recreation centers opened to the Doughboys in southern France. Unfortunately, because of this new interest, Camp Hospital Number 45, opened July 1918 at Aix-les-Bains, became a busy facility, and the majority of the patients whom the staff treated were for injuries incurred from bicycle accidents or mountain climbing while on their "rest and recreation" leave.

Track-and-field events were less hazardous and certainly capable of drawing large crowds. In late June 1919, the Inter-Allied Track and

A typical medal provided by the YMCA and awarded to a track meet participant at one of the many competitions hosted by the US Third Army in the American occupation zone. This particular medal was awarded for a second-place finish in the 400-meter relay.

Field meet in the Bois de Vincennes, near Paris, drew thousands of participants and spectators. Built by American Army engineers on the site of an old training ground for the French army, the athletic complex was soon known as "Pershing Stadium." It was designed to hold 22, 000 seated and 18, 000 standing spectators, and the inside of the track was large enough to allow rugby games to be played. More than 1, 000 athletes from eighteen countries participated and competed in nineteen different sports. After the closing ceremony, the stadium was presented as a gift to the people of France. The facility was closed in 1960, and the site is now an open-air recreation park but is still known as *Le Stade* Pershing.

In Germany, the Third Army / AFG maintained a strong track-and-field program, and the American teams hosted many meets in Coblenz; they also traveled to the other Allied occupation zones. Polo was also popular among the officers and cavalrymen of the AFG. Two officers playing for the American Army polo team in Germany would go on to become very well-known generals in the Second World War: Terry Allen and Johnathan Wainwright. At times, even the commander of the AFG would ride for one of the AFG teams in competition. During 1920 and 1921, the AFG polo team would travel as far as Spain to play at a high level of international competition. In 1920, a polo team from the AFG represented the United States in the Olympics held in Antwerp, Belgium. Led by Col. Nelson Margetts, the US team won the bronze medal.[19]

The soldiers of the Third Army were also fortunate because one of the first actions taken by the Army on arrival in Coblenz was to commandeer the huge *Festhalle* in the center of town and turn it over to the YMCA to operate. The *Festhalle* had been the center of Coblenz's social life before the arrival of the Americans and could

Among the many events in this August 1921 Inter-Allied track-and-field meet in the American zone was the obstacle course. It was specifically designed to showcase useful soldier skills, such as running, climbing, and jumping. The black soldier in the center, approaching the barrier, is most likely from one of the French colonial regiments serving in the French occupation zone.

seat some 1, 850 people in its main hall. There were also "numerous rooms used for reading, writing, pool, billiards, and other games; a small assembly room seating about two hundred; a large restaurant; a garden with tennis and croquet grounds . . . and facilities for movies lectures and religious programs."[20]

With the departure of the AEF from France, the only US Army units of any size remaining in Europe were in the AFG. To fully understand their story, as well as the continuing saga of the Doughboys and the national pastime, it is now necessary to travel to the large American occupation zone in the heart of the German Rhineland.

Doughboys were never shy about trying any sport, and this cartoon pokes fun at a soldier who is going to play tennis. Left unsaid is the real question: Does he really want to play tennis, or simply get some time alone with one of the many attractive British Women's Army Auxiliary Corps ladies who worked for the US Army in the Bourges area?

Having survived the war and the Spanish flu, these Doughboys from a machine gun battalion have decided to take on mountaineering as a sport while on rest-and-recreation leave. So many soldiers would be hurt attempting this sport that one hospital in southern France was dedicated to treating accidents from mountain climbing and bike riding.

6th Inning

Playing Away Games in the German Rhineland

Among the least-known stories of the American military in the Great War is the occupation of the German Rhineland after the Armistice. One of the provisions of the Armistice required the occupation of the German land west of the Rhine River by the British, French, Belgian, and US armies. As a result of this mandate, some 260, 000 American soldiers and Marines marched from France through Belgium and Luxembourg in November and December 1918, into the area around the German cities of Treves (Trier) and Coblenz (Koblenz). An important component of the US Army occupation mission was the seizure and control of the Rhine River bridges within its sector, including a pontoon bridge and a railroad bridge at Coblenz and the railroad bridges at Engers and Remagen. To the north, the British army and Commonwealth troops controlled bridges in the Cologne and Bonn area. The French army was responsible for the crossings in the area around Wiesbaden and Mainz. The German army had used these bridges while moving into position to invade Belgium and France in 1914. The Allies were determined to prevent a similar use should peace talks fail.

After arriving at their assigned sectors in Germany, the Doughboys of the US Third Army were expected to govern the local German population and receive the war reparations material the German government was required to provide to the victors. Obviously neither of these missions was extremely time consuming, so unit commanders needed something to keep their troops busy. Arriving as they had in December, baseball was not an option, but football was; soon every unit was fielding teams. With many of the officers in the Third Army having been college athletes, the quality of play was very respectable.

Taken against the background of one of the old German fortifications in the Coblenz area, the members of Company F, 8th Infantry Regiment's track-and-field team pose. Undoubtedly, the large corporal standing on the left is the "hammer throw" participant.

Also considered an important sport for instilling soldier skills, polo was popular in the American occupation zone, particularly among the members of the US Cavalry detachment. Several polo players pause for a smoke before returning to the game.

A period map of Germany showing the American occupation zone in pink, the British zone in light blue, and the French zone in yellow. The green band represents the "Neutral Zone" established by the Armistice to separate the occupation zones from unoccupied Germany. The semicircular area in pink on the east side of the Rhine River was guarded and administered by the 1st, 2nd, and 32nd Divisions. "Carnival Island," site of many baseball and football games, is in the Rhine River near Third Army Headquarters in Coblenz (Koblenz).

As seen previously, after many games the 89th Division's football team represented the Third Army and won the AEF championship game in front of a large crowd in Paris in 1919.

As soon as the weather in the Rhineland began to improve, soldiers turned their efforts to their favorite sport, and leagues sprung up throughout the American sector. The earliest Third Army newspaper was called *Die Wacht Am Rhein: A Journal of Truth*. It was printed before the *AMAROC News*, which began circulation in April 1919, became the most popular and commonly available newspaper for American soldiers in the occupation zone. In the 1 April 1919 edition of *Die Wacht am Rhein*, the editor noted that

> with the passing of the football season in the Army of Occupation and the fulfillment of the promise of warm spring days a question of a few weeks only, our thoughts naturally turn to the pastimes that have regaled us at this season in past years . . . if we are to believe the statements of the auxiliary organizations [YMCA, Salvation Army, Knights of Columbus, etc.] of the Third Army we will experience no difficulty in securing the necessary paraphernalia. . . . It is already a common sight to see a half dozen O.D. clad warriors playing catch or batting up flies in the vacant lots around town.[1]

The editor further urged each unit to take on the challenge of fielding a team and making a schedule of games. Noting that "everyone seems content to wait until someone else takes the necessary first step, " he even called on his own unit to begin preparing for what he called the "Coblenz Baseball Classic of 1919." Little did he know how powerful a response this call to action would get, and that soon there would be more teams and leagues in the Third Army than could be counted. Among them appeared a powerhouse team from a field artillery unit in the 89th Division. Representing the 342nd Field Artillery Regiment was a lineup packed with former major and minor leaguers and college players. The team roster included Grover Cleveland Alexander from the Chicago Cubs;

The 1919 champions of the Third Army: Motor Transport Corps Repair Unit 310. Although small in size in comparison to many of the units they would face on the field, the 310th was fortunate to have a number of men with professional and semipro experience on their team. Of note here is the uniformity of the players' hats and jerseys; the Third Army patches on the hats and the "310th" numbers on the shirts were most likely created by local German tailors.

Lloyd Waite, a catcher from the St. Louis Cardinals; Winfield Charles "Win" Noyes, a pitcher from the Philadelphia Athletics; Otis Lambeth, a pitcher from the Cleveland Indians; Clarence Mitchell, a multifaceted player from the Brooklyn Dodgers; Charles William "Chuck" Ward, an infielder also from the Brooklyn team; Eddie Croix, from a St. Louis farm system team; and several players from Harvard and the University of Illinois. Quickly compiling an unbeaten record in the Third Army, the team looked to be dominant.[2] Fortunately for the rest of the teams in the Third Army and the AEF, the team was broken up when several members, including Alexander, were sent back to the United States for demobilization.

For most German citizens, the Doughboys were quite congenial occupiers, especially in comparison to the French army just to the south. One German wrote that while he would like to have no foreign troops in Germany, "he prefers Americans . . . because they are much more considerate and spend more money."[3] There were two aspects of American culture, as demonstrated by the soldiers now living in their

The 42nd Division fielded many baseball teams, and included in its ranks was a very well-known Major League baseball player, Hank Gowdy, in the 166th Infantry Regiment. This photograph of the division's engineer regiment's baseball team was most likely taken in Germany in spring 1919, before the 42nd returned to the United States. *Courtesy of Charles G. Thomas*

towns and cities, that were extremely puzzling to the locals. First was the growing temperance movement back in the United States, which was constantly being discussed by their American soldier tenants. The Moselle Valley, running west to east from Luxembourg almost to the Rhine, was world renowned and celebrated as the center of Germany's wine industry. The citizens of the region were accustomed to drinking wine on every occasion and with most meals. The area around Coblenz was also notable for a number of very large and well-known breweries. German beer, even in those days, ranked among the world's best. Growing up in this culture, with easy access to alcoholic drink, the average German citizen could not fathom why any civilized country would decide to enact a prohibition against drinking alcohol. The Germans were of course unaware of the strong feeling against alcoholic beverages that had come into prominence in the United States since the commencement of the war.[4] The second most puzzling aspect was the American soldier's obsession with baseball.

Several Doughboys from the 5th Field Artillery Regiment, 1st Division, pose with their new German friends while attempting to explain to them the intricacies of the great American pastime. Although obviously enthusiastic about learning the game, the German children seem equally interested in what the soldiers will share from their lunch.

This Doughboy cartoon shows that nothing much has changed in the American attitude toward schools and classrooms. With the war over, the Army attempted to provide training for soldiers in every possible civilian job skill—including bookkeeping—to prepare them for their lives after the Army. In spite of these good intentions, Eddie's buddies want him to go play baseball with them.

Try as they might, the Germans could not understand the Doughboys' fixation with the sport. It seemed to the local citizens that wherever the soldiers could find a patch of open ground, it immediately became part of a baseball diamond. This "play everywhere you can find some room" attitude had some interesting repercussions and also led to some unusual ground rules.

Eventually, a semblance of order took over athletic activity in the Third Army. Teams from the larger units were formed into four leagues: the Coblenz League consisted of teams from military police units, the 54th Pioneer Infantry Regiment, some evacuation hospitals, and Air Service units; the Lutzel League, with the 56th Pioneer Infantry Regiment, the 41st, 638th, and 141st Aero Squadrons, and several logistics units; the Rhine League, with the 1st and 3rd Pioneer Infantry, the 322nd Field Signal Battalion, Evacuation Hospital No. 22, and the Motor Transport Corps' Repair Unit 310; and the Moselle League, with the 51st Pioneer Infantry Regiment, the 138th Aero Squadron, two evacuation hospitals, and several other logistics support units. While this appears to be a fairly formal and fixed format, in reality the teams changed constantly, as some units were sent back to the States and other new units came from the United States or France to join the Third Army. Nevertheless, a structure had been laid down and the games began in earnest.[5]

In the area around Cochem castle, the units belonging to the US IV Corps also established four baseball leagues. Every US Army Corps had a large number of combat support and logistics units, so there were a number of different-sized units in these leagues. Field hospitals, remount

With fifteen players and four coaches, this tough-looking team from the 6th Engineer Regiment of the 3rd "Marne" Division was larger than most teams in the Third Army. Of equal interest here is the fact that the coach standing on the far left is still armed with his .45 pistol.

squadrons, truck companies, pioneer infantry regiments, corps-level field artillery units, military police companies, and even a telegraph battalion fielded teams. It was recognized that there had to be a way to balance out the different unit sizes. To solve the problem of balancing the league, the *Fourth Corps Flare* published the guideline:

> Within each league the winning team will be picked by a number of methods owing to the different number of teams and the variety of organizations. In the 1st league the highest percentage will decide, in the 2nd and 3d a round robin series is to be played among the winners of each of the three groups, in leagues 3 and 4 a series of three games are to be played between the winners of the two groups in each.[6]

It was a complicated arrangement, but the soldiers took baseball seriously. They expected each unit to get a fair shake, and this structure

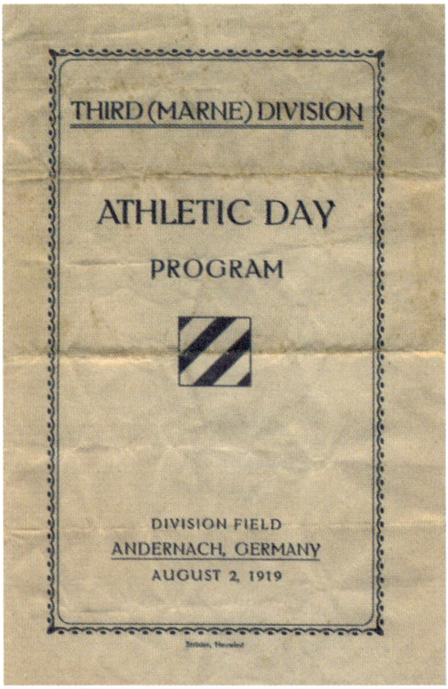

The front cover of a program printed in Germany with all the scheduled events for the 3rd Division's "Athletic Day," which took place near the town of Andernach, on the west side of the Rhine River. Included in the events was a baseball game between the 3rd Division's team and a team of "All-Stars."

appeared to be a reasonable solution. The newspaper concluded the league format information with a short reminder that the Third Army had won the AEF football championship, and all concerned expected that the baseball teams would do just as well. They closed with this: "Even if we all can not be stars, we can help make stars and improve those who are already such."[7]

The soldiers took the games as earnestly as their comrades back in France or still in stateside training camps. In flowing and dramatic terms, the 18th Field Artillery Regiment's newspaper reported on 9 May 1919 about a crushing defeat their team suffered at the hands of the team from the 7th Infantry Regiment, 3rd Division:

> In the first place the 18th could not get acquainted with the offerings dished up by York [the 7th Infantry Regiment's starting pitcher] nor did they do much better when Troley [the relief pitcher] was the opposing hurler. Alibi number one—their batting eyes were not in evidence. Foozles [errors], oodles of them, by the infielders, gardeners [outfielders] . . . made it a holiday for the 7th. Alibi number two—they couldn't field. . . . Thus ended a poorly played game. The game was the best umpired of any played in Polch this season.[8]

For a field artillery unit to lose to an infantry outfit was bad enough, but to have the infield commit so many foozles made it so much worse. At least the umps did a good job.

Unfortunately, reality crept back into the Allied armies' occupation zones, and for a period in late May to the middle part of June 1919, baseball had to take a back seat in importance. German hesitance to sign the surrender documents at Versailles had forced the Allied occupation armies to place their units back on a war footing. If necessary, the Allies planned to attack from their occupation sectors, through the neutral zone, and into unoccupied Germany, thus forcing the Germans to sign the Treaty of Versailles. One of the US Army units designated to support the attack was the 417th Motor Supply Train, with its complement of 360 trucks. As tensions rose, the 417th moved across the Rhine and took up positions in the 1st Division's area to transport the infantry, artillery, and machine gun units when the order was given to attack. The 417th noted that during their stay in the 1st Division's sector they "hauled members of the 1st, 2nd, and 3rd Divisions to and from various ball games which were being held in the area."[9] Finally, on 23 June 1919, the Germans signed the treaty, much to the relief of many on both sides who had little desire to be in a shooting war again. It had been a close thing; the Germans agreed to sign with less than eight hours

This team from the 302nd Remount Squadron defeated the baseball team from the 301st Remount Squadron by a close score of four to three. As a reward, their captain treated them to ice cream and cake. The photograph was taken on 15 April 1919 in Coblenz. *Courtesy of Walter Erickson Collection*

More Doughboy humor; these cartoons appeared in *The Indian*—the 2nd Division's news magazine—and point out some of the unique features of how baseball is played in the German Rhineland. Melsbach Field was about six miles east of the Rhine River, in the 2nd Division's sector.

remaining before Allied forces were to attack. With the signing, the soldiers of the Third Army could return their attention to two important things: baseball season in the Rhineland, and waiting for the day they would return to America.

In the published history of Motor Transport Corps Repair Unit 310, which fielded a team in the Rhine League, the unit historian devoted more pages to the story of his unit's Third Army championship baseball team than he did to any other topic. Each game they played was described in some detail, including complaints about playing surfaces at some of the ball fields. One of the more interesting games was against the team belonging to the 322nd Field Signal Battalion. Played on the 322nd's home field in their barracks area, the victory by the 310th came as a result of a sharply hit ball to left field that rolled into an open cellar window and was ruled a home run. Another victory in their march to the championship came at the expense of the Third Army's Headquarters Troop team. Incensed at what they perceived to be a bad call by the umpire at home plate, the Headquarters team walked off the field and was declared to have lost the game by forfeit. Victories over the teams from Evacuation Hospital Number 49, Evacuation Hospital Number 27, and the 139th Military Police Company followed as the 310th

One of the stars of the 310th's team was Lt. F. D. Patterson, who converted from outfielder to pitcher halfway through the season and became part of the mound rotation. He also batted .315 for the season. Patterson had played college ball for Northwestern in his native Chicago before joining the Army.

Having played baseball for Knox College in Illinois before the war, L. G. "Red" Stillman starred for the 310th's basketball team before becoming the baseball team's catcher. Here Stillman shows the form that made him a top catcher in the league.

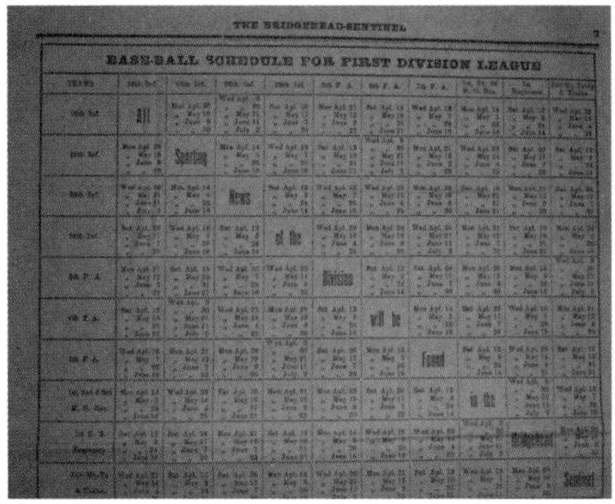
THE BRIDGEHEAD-SENTINEL

BASE-BALL SCHEDULE FOR FIRST DIVISION LEAGUE

Not willing to be outdone by any of the other divisions in the Army of Occupation, the Doughboys of the 1st Division had their league schedule printed in the 12 April 1919 edition of their divisional newspaper, the *Bridgehead Sentinel*. With a full slate of games from April to early July 1919, the soldiers of the 1st Division probably should have extended their season, since it would be late September before they would return to America.

continued its winning ways. The championship of the Third Army was to be decided in a three-game series against the powerful team from the 3rd Battalion, 39th Infantry Regiment, 4th Division, in late July 1919. Playing on a field in the town of Coblenz-Lutzel in front of a crowd of more than 3, 000 soldiers and local citizens, the 4th Division team won the first game by a score of four to three. The second game was a pitchers' duel and ended with the 310th winning two to one. The following day, the two teams met for the winner-take-all final game. With the score tied at four to four in the twelfth inning, the 310th managed to push across the winning run and brought the pennant home.[10] Or so they thought.

Almost immediately after the 310th had been proclaimed the champions, a protest arose from Evacuation Hospital Number 49. The heart of the protest lay in a decidedly gray area concerning two games that had been washed out early in the season by typical rainy German Rhineland weather. The hospital team's supporters also claimed that the 310th had fielded a "ringer" named Farr from the 320th Aero Squadron to play shortstop. With claims and counterclaims on both sides accusing the other of selective memory or imperfect knowledge of the rules surrounding the forfeiture of games, there appeared to be only one way to settle this argument: on the field. But before that could happen, a Quartermaster Corps team from the Bendorf Supply Depot came forward and also challenged the 310th's claim. In response, and adding fuel to the flames, the 310th announced that they would be willing to play the team from Evacuation Hospital Number 49 if there would be a side bet of 10, 000 *deutsche mark*—a large but not unman-

310th M. T. C. HAS CHAMPIONSHIP
OF COBLENZ AREA BY DEFEATING
39th INFANTRY IN CLOSE AFFAIR

DECIDING GAME GOES TWELVE INNINGS WITH FINAL COUNT FIVE TO FOUR. TWO PREVIOUS TUSSLES WERE WON BY ONE TALLY. PLENTY OF BLOWS ARE GARNERED IN BATTLE BY SLUGGERS

The column headline from the 21 July 1919 *AMAROC News* declaring the 310th Repair Unit, Motor Transport Corps, as the winner of the Third Army Championship after a tough game with the 4th Division's 39th Infantry Regiment team. Although some units would dispute the 310th's title as Third Army champs, the athletic officer for the Third Army would uphold their claim.

ageable sum, given the state of the German economy and monetary inflation, even by Doughboy standards. It was at this point that the senior athletic officer for the Third Army conducted a quick investigation and determined that the games forfeited by the Evacuation Hospital's team had been rightly awarded to the 310th, and that because the 320th Aero Squadron—an aviation supply and maintenance unit—had been attached to the 310th during the period, their use of a shortstop from that squadron was perfectly within the rules. The 310th was therefore crowned the champion of the US Third Army. He also ruled that the 310th was free to play any further games they would like, but the official championship had been awarded. There is no record of a follow-on game with the Evacuation Hospital Number 49 team, but it is known that the 310th traveled to Bendorf on 31 July 1919 and beat the Quartermaster Depot team easily by a score of eleven to six.[11] A short while later, the 310th announced they were seeking matchups against other teams in the occupation zone. By this time, most of the large

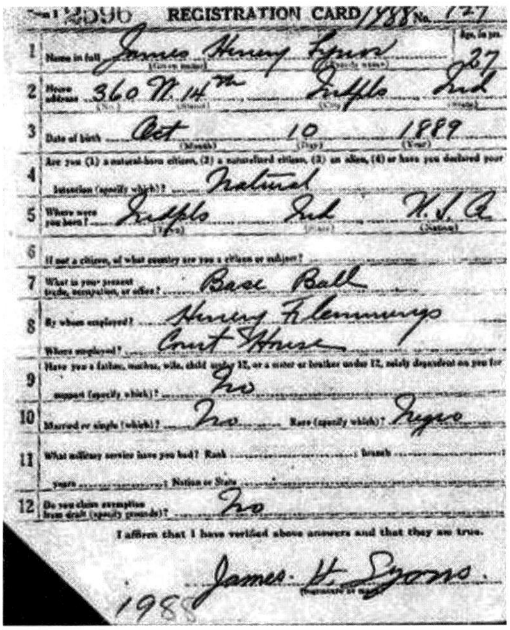

REGISTRATION CARD 1988 No. 127

1 Name in full: James Henry Lyons — Age, in yrs.: 27
2 Home address: 360 N. 14th, Buffalo, Ind
3 Date of birth: Oct 10 1889
4 Are you (1) a natural-born citizen, (2) a naturalized citizen, (3) an alien, (4) or have you declared your intention (specify which)? Natural
5 Where were you born? Buffalo, Ind, U.S.A.
6 If not a citizen, of what country are you a citizen or subject?
7 What is your present trade, occupation, or office? Base Ball
8 By whom employed? Henry Flemmings — Where employed? Court House
9 Have you a father, mother, wife, child under 12, or a sister or brother under 12, solely dependent on you for support (specify which)? No
10 Married or single (which)? No — Race (specify which)? Negro
11 What military service have you had? Rank — branch — years — Nation or State
12 Do you claim exemption from draft (specify grounds)? No

I affirm that I have verified above answers and that they are true.

James H. Lyons

1988

The draft registration card for James Henry "Jimmie" Lyons, the former Negro League ballplayer who led the efforts of the Services of Supply team against the Indians of the 2nd Division. Note that Lyons's registration card lists his occupation as baseball player and that the bottom left corner of the card has been clipped off to indicate he is "colored." *Courtesy of US World War I Draft Registration Cards, via Ancestry.com*

A truly unique photograph; a look at a soldier in action who would later become a major leaguer. Paul B. "Birdie" Speraw playing for the 310th Repair Unit, Motor Transport Corps, against the Military Police team crosses the plate under the careful watch of the umpire. The MP's catcher has dropped his mask and moved up the third-base line to catch the inbound throw. In 1920, Speraw would play for the St. Louis Browns against the Boston Red Sox.

combat units were in the process of preparing to return to the States for demobilization, and the soldiers of the 310th MTC Repair Unit would soon follow suit, so no record exists of this challenge being accepted.

The Doughboys' desire to play baseball reached areas not even in the American zone. Another seldom-recognized postwar mission was conducted by the US soldiers assigned to run prisoner-of-war (POW) camps in unoccupied Germany. These camps were filled with Russian prisoners who had been captured on the eastern front and were awaiting rail transportation back to Russia. On 4 June 1919, *AMAROC News* reported that the US Army detachments assigned to operate these camps had established athletic programs to keep the POWs busy. As a result, over 200, 000 Russian prisoners were being taught the intricacies of baseball and basketball. In another instance, one of the many small detachments of Doughboys tasked with supporting the rail movement of Haller's Polish army from France, through Germany, and into Poland was stationed in the French zone near the town of Bad Ems. Consisting of one officer and four enlisted men, the detachment petitioned the Third Army for some baseball equipment. Their request was met by the athletic officer assigned to Coblenz, who dispatched the desired equipment to the men. The only remaining question in the Third Army headquarters was "Who were the men going to play?"[12]

There was no question about team matchups in the American zone; there were teams representing each division and corps in the Third Army. These teams played at the AEF level against other divisions and major organizations still in France, as well as against each other in the American zone. Although the 1st Division's newspaper the *Bridgehead Sentinel* bemoaned the fact that there were no "big-name" major league players on any of its divisional teams, it acknowledged that there were a number of skilled former college players in the ranks. One writer even suggested that major-league scouts would do well to come to Germany, watch a few of the games, and think about signing some of the players to big-league contracts.

Among the most successful teams in the Third Army was the team made up of the 2nd Division's soldiers and Marines. The 2nd Division team took as their team name the "Indians" in homage to the Indian-head symbol on their divisional shoulder patch. After winning games at Heddesdorf against the 4th Division by a score of six to four, they then defeated the III Corps team by a score of eleven to five. Next, the 2nd Division Indians took on the team from the Third Army at the Carnival Island baseball diamond, on an island in the Rhine River very close to the city of Coblenz. They beat them soundly, and the 2nd Division's newspaper later reported that although it was "a trifle one-sided, it was a good game."[13] The 2nd Division team continued its winning ways when it beat the 1st Division team on their home field in Montabaur. In the audience that day was the most famous soldier in the Army, Gen. Pershing.[14]

Considered by many to be Pershing's favorite division because of their "old Army" roots and longevity of service in the war, the 1st Division shortly thereafter hosted a visiting team from the 5th Division. The "Red Diamonds" of the 5th were occupying a portion of the Duchy of Luxembourg, and the travel by their team to Germany may be the very first instance of teams crossing international borders to play baseball. Regardless, it was a good thing that Pershing was not around to watch his Big Red One team in action this time, since they lost four games in a row to the visitors. In another surprising upset, the 3rd Division team swept a 4 July doubleheader at Andernach from the Marines of the 5th Brigade, who were visiting from France.[15]

In early July 1919, there was an unusual event for the occupation zone: a three-game series of integrated baseball games. The games pitted the all-white team of the 2nd Division—the Indians—against an African American all-star team from the Army Services of Supply camp at Nantes, France. Played at Heddesdorf, in the 2nd Division sector, over 15, 000 soldiers and Marines showed up for the first game on 3 July. In that opening game, the visitors from Nantes defeated the Indians by a score of three to two. The Third Army newspaper, the *AMAROC News*, laid the defeat squarely on the Indians' "failure to keep wide awake on the bases and lack of a timely swat." Despite loading the bases in the seventh and eighth innings, the Indians were unable to drive in any more runs, and the black soldiers proved victorious.[16] The paper also noted that an African American soldier, Pvt. Lyons, had been the hitting star for Nantes that day with a home run, two runs batted in, and two stolen bases.

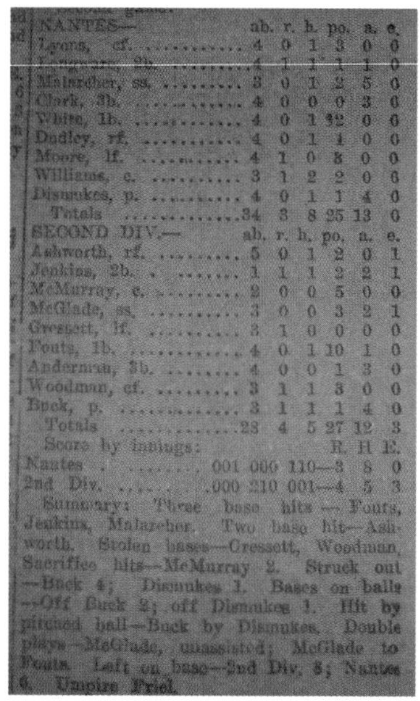

NANTES—	ab.	r.	h.	po.	a.	e.
Lyons, cf.	4	0	1	3	0	0
[illegible], 2b.	4	1	1	1	1	0
Malarcher, ss.	3	0	1	2	5	0
Clark, 3b.	4	0	0	0	3	0
White, 1b.	4	0	1	12	0	0
Dudley, rf.	4	0	1	1	0	0
Moore, lf.	4	1	0	3	0	0
Williams, c.	3	1	2	2	0	0
Dismukes, p.	4	0	1	1	4	0
Totals	34	3	8	25	13	0

SECOND DIV.—	ab.	r.	h.	po.	a.	e.
Ashworth, rf.	5	0	1	2	0	1
Jenkins, 2b.	1	1	1	2	2	1
McMurray, c.	2	0	0	5	0	0
McGlade, ss.	3	0	0	3	2	1
Gressett, lf.	3	1	0	0	0	0
Fouts, 1b.	4	0	1	10	1	0
Anderman, 3b.	4	0	0	1	3	0
Woodman, cf.	3	1	1	3	0	0
Buck, p.	3	1	1	1	4	0
Totals	23	4	5	27	12	3

Score by innings:		R.	H.	E.
Nantes	001 000 110—	3	8	0
2nd Div.	000 210 001—	4	5	3

Summary: Three base hits — Fouts, Jenkins, Malarcher. Two base hit—Ashworth. Stolen bases—Gressett, Woodman. Sacrifice hits—McMurray 2. Struck out—Buck 4; Dismukes 1. Bases on balls—Off Buck 2; off Dismukes 1. Hit by pitched ball—Buck by Dismukes. Double plays—McGlade, unassisted; McGlade to Fouts. Left on base—2nd Div. 8; Nantes 6. Umpire Friel.

The box score for the third and deciding game of the series between the African American All-Star team from the Services of Supply and the white team from the 2nd Division. Played in Germany in July 1919, the games drew some 20,000 spectators from local Army and Marine Corps units.

The next day the two teams met again, this time for a doubleheader. For this twin bill the attendance was even greater, estimated at 20, 000, making it probably the most heavily attended sporting event in the history of the American occupation. In the first game of the day, Lyons—the hitting star from the previous day—moved from his normal position in center field to the pitching mound. He gave a solid pitching performance until he was lifted for a relief pitcher in the sixth inning.

Pvt. 1st Class George M. Colburn from Council Bluffs, Iowa, poses in his 13th Field Artillery Regiment baseball uniform, holding his "spikes," in 1919. Colburn served in the Medical Detachment assigned to the 13th and was billeted in the 4th Division's occupation sector in the area around Ahrweiler, Germany.

As good as Lyons's pitching was, the 2nd Division's pitching proved to be even better in this game. The only slip by the Indian pitcher occurred when he allowed a leadoff triple by Lyons to start the game in the first inning. Fortunately for the Indians, Lyons was quickly erased at home plate, attempting to score on an infield grounder. After that, the Indians' pitcher settled down and the Services of Supply soldiers never mounted any further threats in the game, ultimately losing by a score of three to zero. When Lyons returned to his regular center-field spot after relinquishing the mound to a reliever, he was cheered by the crowd, acknowledging his performance in the games. The crowd continued to cheer Lyons even after he robbed the Indians of a run with a dramatic two-out, run-stopping catch in the outfield.

The second game of the day was a different matter. The Indians sent a private named Buck out to pitch the third and deciding game of the series. With Lyons back to patrolling the outfield, the Nantes team sent their previous day's winning pitcher, Dismukes, out to take the mound. As the game progressed it became a back-and-forth battle, with each team managing to put three runs on the board. The game was still tied three to three in the bottom of the ninth inning when the Indians managed to get a man on base. Coming through in the clutch, Ashworth, the Indians' right fielder, smashed a double to drive in the game-winning run and sweep the day's doubleheader.[17]

During the three-game series, Lyons went four for eleven with a home run and a triple. Given his hitting, pitching, and outfield skills, it is probable that the soldier in question was James Henry "Jimmie" Lyons, a noted ballplayer in the Negro Leagues from 1910 to 1925, with a break for his military service in the 809th Pioneer Infantry Regiment. Lyons was later recognized, along with his Chicago American Giants teammates Christobal Torriente and "Jelly" Gardner, as a member of one of the best defensive outfield trios in history.[18] Perhaps almost as impressive as a baseball series between white and black soldiers in the American occupation zone during the Army's highly segregated period was the large number of spectators at the games and the number of innings each man played during these three tough games in just a two-day period.

Not all games were played between the large corps or divisional organizations. Inside each organization there were numerous teams down to the regimental, battalion, and even company level. In addition to its Indians team, the 2nd Division had so many baseball teams that it was decided to mimic the major leagues and establish

Another indication of the enthusiasm of the Doughboys for baseball is seen in this crowd watching a ball game in Germany in 1919. On the basis of the 2nd Division patches visible on some of the shoulders, it is probable that this was taken in their sector on the east side of the Rhine River. *Courtesy of Library of Congress*

a National League and an American League. While the National League consisted of eight teams from the 9th and 23rd Infantry Regiments, the Marine Regiments, the 2nd Engineer Regiment, and two field artillery regiments, the 2nd Division's American League fielded ten teams from the divisional support units, such as the military police and the machine gun battalions. It was the same situation in the 3rd Division, as the "Rock of the Marne" soldiers filled their sector on the west side of the Rhine with ball fields and competition. In a shocking upset, the team from the 3rd Ammunition Train defeated the heavily favored 4th Infantry Regiment team in front of more than 3, 000 spectators to gain the 3rd Division championship.[19]

Supporting all this sporting activity were some professional baseball players of note now working for the Knights of Columbus baseball program in Germany, including Tommy "Buttermilk Tommy" Dowd, who coached the 4th Division team, and former Philadelphia Athletics star catcher Peter Noonan. Noonan soon became even more newsworthy when it turned out he had the good fortune to inherit a million dollars from a deceased relative while he was still serving overseas with the baseball program. The greatest sign of the importance of the baseball program to soldiers in the occupation zone was seen when an umpire, Tommy O'Mara, was flown 150 miles from Colombey-les-Belles, in France, to Trier to umpire a Doughboy baseball game. This could perhaps be the first known occurrence of the use of air travel as part of a baseball game.[20]

With the departure of the combat divisions and some of their support units, someone had to stay and maintain the occupation while the newly designated occupation unit, the 8th Infantry Regiment, was brought to Germany. Later, two undersized infantry regiments—the 5th and the 50th—which had been scheduled to be part of an Allied peacekeeping mission in Upper Silesia, were sent instead to the American zone. There they joined the 8th Infantry Regiment as the main body of the occupation force on the Rhine. Waiting for these units to take over the occupation mission were some of the very last original Third Army units to leave the American zone and go home. This temporary role fell to the versatile pioneer infantry regiments. Because of this, they kept their athletic programs going right up until it was time to catch the train taking them to the port. The 1st Pioneer Infantry Regiment recorded that

> amusements were not entirely lacking. Soldier shows and travelling companies made frequent visits and ballgames as well as athletic carnivals were frequent in which our teams and boxers took a most successful part. It must be understood that these amusements were only incidental to the immense mass of work performed, but helped to pass the long, long time till our bugles should sound the assembly for our homeward march.[21]

In addition to the newly arrived 8th Infantry Regiment, the burden of policing a large part of the American zone fell to military police (MP) units that had been hurriedly transferred to Germany from the American forces still remaining in France. Almost immediately after arrival, the MPs organized what became known as the MP League. Soon they too were playing games throughout the American portion of the Rhineland. In particular, they used the ball field built by earlier Army units on Carnival Island. The island's proximity to the American headquarters building and other American facilities in the city made it a convenient location. The MPs could be counted on to be playing in league play there almost every afternoon.[22]

Yet, for all the baseball being played in the organized leagues, one immutable fact remained: the Third Army was changing. First, in July 1919, its name was changed to the American Forces in Germany (AFG). Maj. Gen. Henry T. Allen—who would lead the occupation force for the rest of its existence—took command about the same time. The composition of the force also changed dramatically; by November 1919, all the units that had made the march to Germany were gone. The original 260, 000 Doughboys were now reduced to some 20, 000, and this number would continue to shrink. Yet, some of the original soldiers remained, and the newly arriving men and women were just as baseball crazy as their predecessors. As one observer wrote:

> The season of 1920 was a very interesting one. There were all varieties of base ball offered, from the big league stuff, down to the famous girl's game between the Army Nurses and the YMCA ladies. Interest was keen throughout the season and there was no let up in this interest. The commencement of football [season] was all that drove the men off the base ball diamonds.[23]

Even at reduced strength, the AFG kicked off the 1920 baseball season in fine shape, with several leagues in action. In the Coblenz area, there were twelve teams and a two-month season running from mid-April to Decoration Day—the name then in use for Memorial Day. As usual, the writers of the *AMAROC News* were deeply involved and supportive of the games:

> Baseball is now hitting on all cylinders among the Yanks in the Rhineland. It's a bum outfit indeed that hasn't got some kind of a ball club on the field. Old King Baseball always was popular among Americans and never more so than this year. It is a game that calls for red blood and keen brains. It makes poor soldiers good soldiers and good fighters better fighters.[24]

After the season's games were finished, the 3rd Battalion of the 8th Infantry Regiment was the clear champion, followed by the AFG Cavalry Detachment in second and the Provisional Guard Detachment from the US military prison in third. At the bottom of the league were the teams from the Quartermaster Corps, the 1st Engineers, and a winless team composed of Army field clerks.

Almost as soon as the championship game was completed, play began again for a second season that ran until the championship game was played on Bastille Day (14 July 1920), which was celebrated throughout the Allied occupation zones to honor their French comrades. In this second season, once again the infantrymen of the 8th Regiment took the championship after a hard-fought contest against the US military prison guard team.

While the Coblenz League was playing, three other leagues began their seasons: the Mayen League, with seven teams from organizations

Representing one of the least-known periods of the US Army, this finely embroidered banner pays tribute to the Army's occupation of Germany in 1920–21. During this same period, baseball fever remained as high as ever, even though the number of teams decreased due to the downsizing of the US force. The "A inside an O" in the four corners copies the US Third Army / American Forces in Germany shoulder patch signifying "Army of Occupation." *Private collection*

working and billeted near that town, and two separate leagues formed in the Andernach area, comprising soldiers from units stationed along the west side of the Rhine River and near that town. If that were not enough, there was also a league called the "Coblenz League of Second Teams, " formed from units that were not big enough to compete against the larger units. For a while it appeared that every soldier in the AFG was playing on one team or another, and this perception was borne out when the nurses of the Army Nurses Corps took on the female workers assigned to the YMCA on 6 August 1920. Advertised throughout the American zone, the game drew almost 8, 000 spectators to the Carnival Island baseball diamond. What they saw was an entertaining if not particularly exciting game, as the nurses beat the YMCA ladies easily by a score of twenty to twelve. The seven-inning game took only two hours and seventeen minutes to play and was considered a great success for all. The victorious nurses were credited with fifteen hits, including two home runs and two triples, while the YMCA team could manage only eight singles.[25]

A short time later, a team of sailors off the cruiser USS *Pittsburgh* traveled to the Rhineland to play baseball against the Army teams stationed there. The *Pittsburgh* had a checkered past; it had been renamed from the USS *Pennsylvania*, suffered some fifty-eight deaths among the crew from Spanish flu, and had run aground in the Baltic. Nevertheless, the crew was determined to make a strong showing while visiting the American occupation zone. Playing in turn the

The hard-hitting nurses of the Army Nurses Corps pose for a team picture. Their 6 August 1920 victory over the ladies of the YMCA's team was seen by some 8,000 spectators. *Private collection*

ARMY NURSE BASE BALL TEAM, A. F. IN G.

1, Brady; 2, McKay; 3, Murphy; 4, Mellos; 5, Sergeant Thompson; 6, Haddleton, Y. M. C. A.; 7, Keagris; 8, Colarty; 9, Williams; 10, McDermott; 11, Cavanaugh; 12, Rudolph; 13, Burke; 14, Burkhardt; 15, Alexander; 16, Gamble.

Machine Gun Battalion, the 5th Infantry Regiment, and the Quartermaster Detachment, the sailors lost the first two games but managed to win the third.[26] At the end of August 1920, all baseball came to a halt and the seasons were declared over. The large AFG maneuvers started and all soldiers were expected to participate. Although they were good ballplayers, the men of the AFG proved to be even better soldiers, and their annual military exercises and maneuvers were a showpiece of individual and unit combat skills. Starting at the individual soldier level and working up through squad, platoon, company, and higher tactical-unit levels, the training program culminated with an exercise in the autumn that lasted for over two weeks and in which the entire AFG participated. Conditions for realistic training were optimal mainly due to the administrative authority maintained by the AFG over the zone. The local German countryside was conducive to large-scale maneuvers, with a variety

A photograph taken during that seven-inning contest shows the YMCA team at bat while Nurse Mellis is pitching. Mellis proved to be the difference in the game by limiting the YMCA team to eight singles. *Private collection*

ARMY NURSES VS. Y. M. C. A. GIRLS, A. F. IN G., AUGUST 6, 1920

Mellis (A. M. C.) pitching; Glover (Y. M. C. A.) batting; Sanford (Y. M. C. A.) taking a lead off second base.

of forested areas, open fields, and hilly terrain. When a specific area was needed for training, it was necessary only to notify local German authorities. Because the exercises and maneuvers were held in the autumn after any crops had been harvested, there was little damage to the chosen areas. In cases where there actually was damage, the local property owners received monetary compensation from the German government as part of the defeated country's requirement to pay for the occupation. With almost unlimited stocks of small arms and artillery ammunition left by the departure of the much-larger Third Army, the AFG was able to use live fire as part of the maneuvers on a scale undreamed of before or since. From late August to the middle of September 1920, the troops were engaged in brigade-level maneuvers in part of the old 4th Division sector in the country southwest of Mayen and near the current site of the famous Nürburg Ring racetrack. Every member of the AFG, except a very few soldiers excused to stand guard duty at key sites, participated in the tactical exercises. Even the 108 musicians of the AFG's headquarters band placed their instruments in storage and became part of a provisional machine gun battalion. The actual exercises were preceded by forced marches that incorporated tactical battle drills along the route, leading to a battlefield almost eighteen miles long. At the culmination of the maneuver, the two US infantry brigades came together to form an "AFG" division. They then practiced relief of a division on a front line, attacking prepared positions and exploiting a breakthrough. The opportunity to see the American Army in action, with an unlimited supply of live ammunition and unconstrained usage of field artillery in the training area, brought observers from most of the European armies. The commander of the Swiss Army even made the journey to the American zone to see the show.[27]

Over the next two years, enthusiasm for baseball remained high, but the number of players and teams steadily dwindled as the AFG continued to shrink in size. The 1921 baseball season opened with the Quartermaster team shutting out the previous year's champion team from the 8th Infantry Regiment. The pitcher for the Quartermasters, a Texan named Martin, no-hit the infantrymen and allowed them only one base runner, and that came from a walk. The constant drawdown and transferring of soldiers and units back to the United States in 1921 had significant effects on all aspects of the AFG, including their sporting events.

The AFG was a constant hotbed of athletics and sporting competitions. In addition to baseball, football, and boxing, the American soldiers competed against each other and soldiers from the other Allied armies in many sporting events. This swimming trophy was awarded to a British soldier for first place in the 400-meter freestyle event in July 1921. *Courtesy of Alison Hutton*

The American occupation of Germany lasted until February 1923. Although the forces there were reduced to only 1,000 soldiers at the end, they continued to play baseball up to the last minute. The names of the players on this team from the 6th Field Artillery Regiment provide a good measure of the diverse ethnic background of the soldiers in the AFG.

ARTILLERY BASE BALL TEAM, A. F. IN G.

1, Roberts; 2, Alberts; 3, Cherneski; 4, Brunnele; 5, Petrush; 6, Bolcer; 7, Garcia; 8, Brannigan; 9, Vrana; 10, Blallock.

In 1920, there were over 16, 000 soldiers assigned to the AFG. By December 1921, the number was reduced to half that size. President Wilson's successor, Warren G. Harding, had opposed America's entry into the League of Nations, and under his guidance Congress passed the Knox-Porter Resolution, bringing an official end to hostilities between all of the Central Powers (Germany, Austro-Hungarian Empire, Turkey, and Bulgaria) and the United States. It was signed into law by Harding on 21 July 1921. Logically, with the United States and Germany now officially no longer at war, much of the rationale for maintaining an American force on the Rhine was disappearing. In America, the rush to disarm and downsize the Army was in full force for economic reasons, and in some corners it was suggested that the sole purpose for the continued existence of the AFG was for politicians to have an excuse to visit Europe on the taxpayer's dollar. Yet, strangely enough, the AFG continued to survive because it suited the purposes both of the conservatives and the liberals in Congress. Conservatives believed that to ensure the victory gained at such a high cost in the Great War, Germany must be suppressed. Therefore, the French deserved America's continued support and the presence of the AFG in the Rhineland. At the same time, liberal factions in Congress believed that maintaining an American presence on the Rhine was the only way to keep the French army and French government from further oppressing the suffering German people and crushing their fledgling democracy, known as the Weimar Republic. And so the AFG and baseball stayed on the Rhine, in ever-decreasing numbers.

By February 1922, orders from the US War Department had reduced the AFG to 3, 200 officers and enlisted men. By the end of the year, this number had been cut by two-thirds. In January 1923, the AFG received orders from the War Department to cease operations and turn over the American zone to the French army. In a solemn ceremony, the remaining

Of the many strange habits the Doughboys brought to Germany, none seemed as inexplicable to the local citizens as the game of baseball. Although many believed the game was putting down solid roots in the German Rhineland, most soldiers recognized the futility of trying to explain the complexities of the game to the Germans. This cartoon pokes fun at both sides of that cultural divide.

1, 000 American soldiers lowered for the last time the large United States flag that had flown over the fortress of Ehrenbreitstein since December 1918. They then marched through the streets of Coblenz to the train station to start their journey home.

With them, baseball marched out of Germany. In 1920, one enthusiastic observer of the AFG wrote:

> The great national game of the Americans has been established in the Rhineland and has left its marks, and when the Yanks pull out, there is no doubt in anyone's mind who is interested in the pastime, but that it will take hold among the German populace.[28]

He could not have been more wrong. With the American soldiers gone and replaced by less amiable French soldiers, the Germans had no inclination to play baseball. It would take another US Army occupation of Germany in 1945, after the end of the Second World War, before baseball would again be played in the Rhineland.

7th Inning
Players, Coaches, Judges, and Umps

Several hundred major-league or former major-league ballplayers ended up in uniform during the war. Although many of them remained in the States, others did perform frontline service. In that way, they took the same chances as other American soldiers, sailors, and Marines. Likewise, many hundreds of Negro League, minor-league, and semiprofessional-league ballplayers served in the military. Some professional and former professional baseball players died while in military service. The men had varied professional baseball experiences. Most men served their stint in the low minors before being able to break into the big leagues, and many made several trips between the majors and the minors. Truly this was the era of "living out of a suitcase" for minor-league ballplayers. Their longevity in the majors also varied, from Newt Halliday's "cup of coffee" with the Pittsburgh Pirates, during which he made a single appearance, to Eddie Grant's very successful career.

What follows are select short biographies of the greats, near greats, and not so greats who went to serve their country on a bigger stage than any baseball diamond. Some paid the ultimate price for this service, while others survived the war and came home to attempt to pick up where they left off. As a group, they are an interesting collection of ballplayers, managers, commissioners, and writers. We start this lineup card in the "A"s with Hall of Famer Grover Cleveland Alexander and end in the "W"s with the multitalented Pearl "Specks" Webster. No doubt, as a baseball team they would have been unbeatable.

Grover Cleveland Alexander (26 February 1887–4 November 1950)

Alexander was born in Elba, Nebraska, and grew up working in the cornfields near the town of St. Paul. Although his father wanted him to go to law school, "Old Pete, " as he became known, went in a different direction. He worked as a lineman for a telephone company so he could play baseball on the weekends. In 1911, he made his debut with the Philadelphia Phillies, and his twenty-eight victories set the record for most wins by a rookie pitcher in a single season. For his career he averaged twenty-seven wins a season.

In spite of his success, Alexander remained "a country boy pure and fresh, and all [the other opposing ballplayers] thought he was tops, even though we knew he was going to stand us on our heads."[1] He played for the Phillies until 1918, when he was traded to the Chicago Cubs because the management of the Philadelphia team feared he would be drafted. The Phillies were right: Alexander was drafted and sent to Camp Funston for training during spring 1918, after winning two out of the three games he pitched in the big leagues that season.[2] He served as a sergeant in the 342nd Field Artillery, 89th Division, and by July 1918 he was in France. When his battery was caught in a German artillery counterbarrage, nearby shell concussions left him deaf in one ear, and in the parlance of the period, somewhat "shell shocked." A teammate later recalled an episode in a postwar spring-training game when some "kids up in the grandstands started shooting off fireworks" near the bench where Alexander was sitting, and some of the players "gave a little start with each burst. But Alex never budged. He just sat there stiff as a board, teeth clenched, fists doubled over so tight his knuckles were white, staring off into space as if hypnotized."[3]

When Alexander returned from the war, he was nearly as dominating a pitcher as before, both with the Cubs until 1926, and then with the St. Louis Cardinals from 1926 to 1929. In his twenty-year career he amassed 373 wins, tying him for third all-time with another Hall of Famer and fellow Doughboy, Christy Mathewson.[4] His life outside baseball was not nearly as successful. He still suffered from hearing loss in one ear and experienced epileptic seizures. He also struggled with alcohol throughout most of his career, and his war experiences undoubtedly contributed to many of his later problems.[5] He was inducted into the Baseball Hall of Fame in 1938. Ironically, while named for one US president, Alexander was played by US president Ronald Reagan in the 1952 movie *The Winning Team* about his life. When he died in November 1950, he was buried with full military honors in St. Paul, Nebraska, near the cornfields of his youth.[6]

One of the more famous ballplayers to serve in the AEF was Grover Cleveland Alexander, a pitcher for the Chicago Cubs. Shown here before the war while at bat for the Philadelphia Phillies, Alexander served as a field artilleryman in the 89th Division in the Meuse-Argonne, and later in the occupation of Germany. *Courtesy of Library of Congress*

Calvin Bryant
(13 November 1891–11 November 1918)

Bryant was born in Blue County, in the Choctaw Nation (now Oklahoma). His father was a local sheriff and a representative to the Choctaw legislature. As a youth, Calvin excelled in football and baseball. In 1911, he played baseball as an infielder in the Class D Texas-Oklahoma League. His team, the Altus Chiefs, folded after Bryant played in only one game; an indication of the fragility of the low minor leagues of a century ago. After joining another team in the same league, Bryant finished the season batting .240. He played two more seasons in the same league, finishing his baseball career having played every position except catcher. For the next three years Bryant played semipro ball with a variety of teams.

On 19 October 1917, Bryant entered the Army and served in the 358th Infantry Regiment, 90th Division. Promoted to corporal, he played football for the regimental team in 1917 and 1918. Overseas, the 358th was engaged in combat during the St. Mihiel and Meuse-Argonne Offensives. On 8 November, Bryant, now a sergeant, was gassed and sent to a hospital; he soon returned and participated in the final assault of the war. Sgt. Calvin Bryant was killed in action shortly after 10:00 a.m. on 11 November 1918, less than an hour before the Armistice went into effect.[7]

Alexander Thomson "Tom" Burr
(1 November 1893–12 October 1918)

Alexander Burr was born in Chicago, Illinois. Although primarily a pitcher, he made one appearance as a center fielder with the New York Yankees in 1914 before being sent to the minors. In August 1917, Burr applied to travel to France to join the American Field Service, driving ambulances for the French army. It is unknown whether he made the trip, but he was soon commissioned and became a pilot in the 31st Aero

Squadron, US Army Air Service. In October 1918, while undergoing gunnery training in Cazaux, France, Lt. Burr's airplane collided with another airplane and crashed into Cazaux Lake. His body was recovered twelve days later.[8]

Harry E. Chapman (26 October 1885–21 October 1918)

Chapman was born in Severance, Kansas. He played semipro ball for many years before breaking into the Class D minors in 1910. Chapman made his major-league debut with the Chicago Cubs on the final day of the 1911 season. The next year Chapman did a short stint with the Cincinnati Reds before being sent back down to the minors. In 1914, Chapman joined the new Federal League; the league folded the following year and Chapman ended up on the American League's St. Louis Browns. For the 1917 season Chapman was back in the minors. After that season he entered the Army, a bit older than the average recruit or draftee. Chapman died from influenza-induced bronchopneumonia in October 1918.[9]

LaVerne "Larry" Chappell (19 February 1890–8 November 1918)

Chappell was born in McClusky, Illinois. In 1911, he broke into the Class B minor leagues. The left-handed-hitting outfielder was called up by the Chicago White Sox in 1913; he batted .231 in sixty games for the Sox that year. Due to an injury he suffered the next spring, Chappell played in only twenty-one games during the 1914 campaign. After making only one appearance for the Sox in 1915, Chappell was released to the Class AA minors. In 1916, Chappell was back up to the big leagues, and he made appearances with the Cleveland Indians and the Boston Braves before being released to the Class AA leagues late in the season. Chappell started the 1917 season with Boston again, but he made only four appearances with them before being sent down to the minors. In 1918, Chappell played for the Class AA Pacific Coast League; he did well in that very competitive league, leading the league with a .325 batting average. In July, he entered the Army. While serving in the US Army Medical Corps at Letterman General Hospital in San Francisco, Chappell became seriously ill in October 1918, and on 8 November he succumbed to influenza.[10]

LaVerne "Larry" Chappell shown in his Chicago White Sox uniform; he played for the White Sox, the Cleveland Indians, and the Boston Braves, as well as a number of minor-league teams before the war. *Courtesy of Library of Congress*

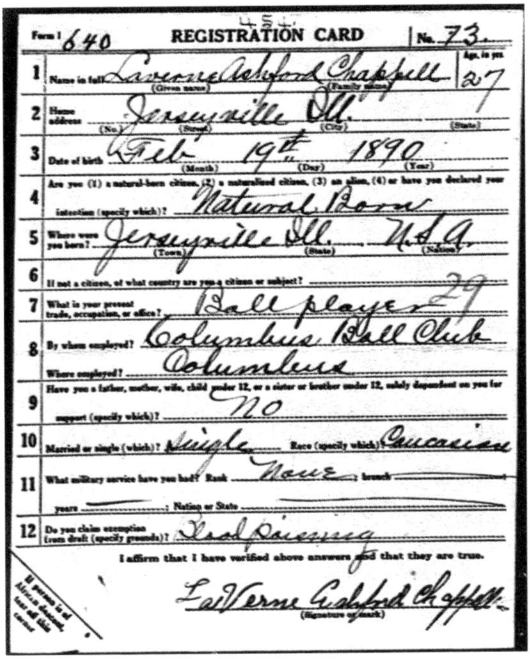

Form 1 640 REGISTRATION CARD No. 73.

1 Name in full Laverne Ashford Chappell (Given name) (Family name) Age, in yrs. 27

2 Home address Jerseyville Ill. (No.) (Street) (City) (State)

3 Date of birth Feb 19th 1890 (Month) (Day) (Year)

4 Are you (1) a natural-born citizen, (2) a naturalized citizen, (3) an alien, (4) or have you declared your intention (specify which)? Natural Born

5 Where were you born? Jerseyville Ill. U.S.A. (Town) (State) (Nation)

6 If not a citizen, of what country are you a citizen or subject?

7 What is your present trade, occupation, or office? Ball player

8 By whom employed? Columbus Ball Club
Where employed? Columbus

9 Have you a father, mother, wife, child under 12, or a sister or brother under 12, solely dependent on you for support (specify which)? No

10 Married or single (which)? Single Race (specify which)? Caucasian

11 What military service have you had? Rank None; branch; years; Nation or State

12 Do you claim exemption from draft (specify grounds)? Blood Passing

I affirm that I have verified above answers and that they are true.

LaVerne Ashford Chappell (Signature or mark)

The draft registration card for Larry Chappell showing his occupation as "ballplayer" and his current employment as the "Columbus Ball Club." Note also that Chappell was claiming exemption for "Blood Passing." His exemption was denied and he was inducted into the Army Medical Service. He died of complications from the Spanish flu in October 1918. *Courtesy of US World War I Draft Registration Cards, via Ancestry.com*

Tyrus Raymond "Ty" Cobb (18 December 1886–17 July 1961)

Ty Cobb was born in Narrows, Georgia, and is considered to be one the greatest baseball players to have ever played the game. He played twenty-two seasons in the major leagues. Twenty-one of those seasons were with the Detroit Tigers, and he served as the team's player/manager from 1921 to 1926. He joined the Philadelphia Athletics for his last season. When Cobb retired from the game he owned forty-three major-league records. He won nine consecutive batting titles from 1907 to 1915, and three more after that. Cobb had 4, 189 career hits with a career batting average of .366.[11]

In 1918, he requested duty with the newly established Chemical Warfare Service (CWS). Although some believed he was better suited for the infantry, he insisted on joining the CWS, explaining, "Christy Mathewson and Branch Rickey are in Chemical—they are guys I like and are friends."[12] In October 1918, he was sent to Chaumont, France, with Branch Rickey to join Christy Mathewson, who had already been in France for several weeks.[13]

Cobb became an instructor after he was given accelerated training in chemical and gas warfare. During a training exercise at Hanlon Field, near Chaumont, Ty Cobb, Christy Mathewson, and other participants missed the signal to put on their gas masks. As a result they inhaled what Cobb called the "sweet death" in the air. Eight of the soldiers died and many others were severely sickened. After a few weeks of suffering the aftereffects of the accidental exposure, Cobb felt that "Divine Providence" had touched him because the fluids draining from his lungs and body finally stopped. Cobb spent sixty-seven days in France before returning home.[14]

On returning to America, Cobb announced his retirement from baseball, but a few weeks later changed his mind and returned. He played eight more seasons. He was inducted into the Baseball Hall of Fame in the first class, along with his good friend and fellow Doughboy, Christy Mathewson, as well as Walter Johnson, Babe Ruth, and Honus Wagner.

William Paul "Bill" Coughlin (12 July 1878–7 May 1943)

Coughlin was born in Scranton, Pennsylvania. He played nine seasons in major-league baseball for the Detroit Tigers and the Washington Senators. Known as "Scranton Bill" and "Rowdy Bill, " he had a career batting average of .252 with 159 stolen bases. He was purchased from Washington by Detroit in 1904 and soon became a team leader for the Tigers. Coughlin was team captain for the American League pennant-winning Tigers in 1907 and 1908. Unfortunately, the Tigers lost both World Series to the Chicago Cubs. In 1918, at the request of the Knights of Columbus, Coughlin organized a team of Doughboys in southern France and quickly turned them into a championship club.[15] In 1919, Coughlin went to Coblenz in the American occupation zone, again at the request of the Knights of Columbus, to oversee the extremely popular baseball program for the Doughboys in the US Third Army. He also coached the Army of Occupation's championship-winning baseball team. When he returned to the United States, Coughlin became the head baseball coach for Lafayette College in Easton, Pennsylvania, until he died in 1943.

Nicles (Nick) DiGiacomo (5 April 1896–31 August 1918)

DiGiacomo was born in Monteodorisio, Italy, and came to the US with his family in 1912, settling in Baltimore, Maryland. In 1917, DiGiacomo, a laborer, played for the Hanover Raiders in the Class D Blue Ridge League. The third baseman played in thirty games, batting .260. Early in the season DiGiacomo transferred to the Frederick Hustlers in the same league; in July, he and other Hustlers players decided to quit baseball and enlist in the Army. On 19 July 1917, DiGiacomo enlisted in Company E, 5th Maryland Infantry Regiment, Maryland National Guard. Interestingly, he was naturalized as a US citizen that same day. When the National Guard was federalized, DiGiacomo found himself in Company E, 115th Infantry Regiment, 29th Division. On 13 March 1918 he was transferred to Company G, 163rd Infantry Regiment, 41st Division. The 41st was initially composed of men from the National Guard units of several western states; it, in common with all other divisions, soon received transfers from other divisions and other regions. DiGiacomo left the United States with his unit on 6 April 1918.

On arrival in France the 41st Division became a depot division, and it began to send replacements to other units that had suffered losses in combat. On 1 May 1918, DiGiacomo was sent as a replacement to Company M, 128th Infantry Regiment, 32nd Division; on 23 August, he was transferred to Company B of the same regiment. Just eight days later DiGiacomo was killed in action. During his short stint overseas, DiGiacomo had seen heavy combat with an excellent unit, having participated in the Aisne-Marne and Oise-Aisne Offensives and having fought in the Fismes Sector. His record as shown in *Maryland Military Men, 1917–1918* indicates he earned Serbian Order of St. Sava, but no other information is known.[16]

Considered by many to be one of the smartest baseball players in the major leagues, Johnny Evers was part of the famous Chicago Cubs double-play combination "Tinker to Evers to Chance." When his poor health did not allow him to serve in the military, Evers became a volunteer representative of the Knights of Columbus and went to France to teach baseball and supervise the Doughboy leagues. *Courtesy of Library of Congress*

John Joseph "Johnny" Evers (21 July 1881–28 March 1947)

Johnny Evers was born in Troy, New York, and was a major-league second basemen who made his debut with the Cubs in 1902. He played with them until 1913, when he was traded to the Boston Braves.[17] Evers was part of the 1914 "Miracle Braves" with Hank Gowdy and was considered to be one of the best second basemen in the game. He was given the nickname the "Trojan" because he was from Troy, New York. He played a total of seventeen major-league seasons.

Evers was barred from enlistment in the US military because of an old arm injury, but he still wanted to serve his country.[18] Using his celebrity status and membership in the Knights of Columbus Council

176 in Troy, New York, Evers petitioned them to send him to France as an athletic director. The Knights agreed, and soon Evers was in France, teaching French troops how to play baseball and traveling around to different camps and hospitals to organize Doughboy baseball teams. Using his Knights of Columbus connection, he was able to provide equipment and whatever other supplies were needed. Evers served overseas from July to December 1918.[19] After he returned to the United States, he continued his baseball career as a scout and as manager of the Chicago Cubs in 1921 and White Sox in 1924. Evers had one last chance to play in a major-league game in 1929, when he and another Doughboy baseball player, Hank Gowdy, convinced the manager of the Boston Braves to put them in as ninth-inning replacements.[20] Evers was inducted into the Baseball Hall of Fame in 1946 and died one year later.

David Lewis "Dave" Fultz (29 May 1875–29 October 29, 1959)

David Fultz was born in Staunton, Virginia, and attended Brown University in Providence, Rhode Island, where he was the captain of the baseball and the football teams. He graduated in 1898 with a law degree and was signed by the Philadelphia Phillies. Noted for clever base stealing and good hitting, Fultz jumped to the American League in 1901, when he signed with the Philadelphia Athletics. During his seven-year major-league career he compiled a .271 batting average, but he retired in 1905 after an injury.[21]

Having played some professional football in 1900 in the precursor to the National Football League, Fultz took on the job of coaching the University of Missouri football team in 1898 and 1899 during his time off from baseball. He later also coached the football teams for Lafayette College, Brown University (his alma mater), and New York University. He later also coached the baseball team of the US Military Academy at West Point. In 1906, he turned his efforts to building a successful law business, but in 1912 he returned his attention to baseball and was the driving force behind the creation of the "Players Fraternity, " a union-like organization formed to improve work conditions for professional baseball players. Fultz originally advocated a strike before the 1917 season against the "10-day clause, " a major-league tenet that allowed owners to withhold injured players' salaries after ten days. After defections by several players from the "Fraternity" during negotiations with the owners, Fultz realized there was little hope of winning. He settled for some small concessions from the owners and advised the remainder of the players against striking. When war was declared a short while later in April 1917, Fultz was forty-two years old but was determined to serve in the US military. Although many sources list him as a US Navy officer attending flight training, his New York State War Service Record shows that he was directly commissioned from "Civilian Life" into the US Army Sanitation Corps as a first lieutenant from July 1918 until January 1919. After the war Fultz also served as president of the International League.[22]

Harry Melville Glenn (9 June 1890–12 October 1918)

Glenn was born in Shelburn, Indiana. The left-handed-hitting catcher made his professional debut with the Class D league in 1910; he played in the minors until 1915, when he was called up by the St. Louis Cardinals. Glenn played six games behind the plate that season before being sent back down to the minor leagues. In June 1918, while still in the minors, Glenn was drafted into the Army. He was in the Army Air Service, training to be a mechanic at the Signal Corps Aviation Mechanics School in St. Paul, Minnesota, when he died of influenza in October 1918.[23]

Henry Morgan "Hank" Gowdy (24 August 1889–1 August 1966)

Hank Gowdy was born in Columbus, Ohio, and started his major-league career in 1910 with the New York Giants. He was traded to the Boston Braves at the end of the 1911 season after barely hitting above .200. In 1914, the Braves were twenty games out of first place in July before they came back to win the pennant, then went on to win the World Series, thus earning the moniker "Miracle Boston Braves." Gowdy gained fame by being named the World Series Most Valuable Player (MVP). Gowdy set the batting-average record for a catcher in the World Series, hitting .545 at the plate.[24] Gowdy was never able to repeat the success of his 1914 season, but he managed to play for seventeen years in the majors. On 1 June 1917—just two months after the United States declared war on Germany—Gowdy became the first active major-league baseball player to enlist. He joined the Ohio National Guard and became a member of the 166th Infantry Regiment in the famous 42nd "Rainbow" Division, one of the first US Army divisions to be shipped to the western front. Gowdy was commissioned a captain and arrived in France in November 1917. The 166th Infantry Regiment participated in the Champagne-Marne, Aisne-Marne, St. Mihiel, Meuse-Argonne, Lorraine, and Champagne Campaigns.[25] Gowdy was considered one of the best soldiers and a natural leader in his regiment. According to his commanding officer, Col. B. W. Hough, "He carried the flag . . . and he was one of them who heaved gas bombs at the enemy . . . he was fantastic!"[26] After the Armistice, Gowdy would make the long march into Germany with his unit as part of the American occupation force.

When Gowdy returned to the United States, he resumed his baseball career and played for the Boston Braves, New York Giants, and Washington Senators until his retirement as a player in 1930. He then coached for three different teams: the Boston Braves, New York Giants, and Cincinnati Reds. In 1942, he once again put his baseball career on hold and attempted to enlist in the military to serve in World War II but was rejected. One year later, at age fifty-three and refusing to accept "no" for an answer to his requests, Capt. Hank Gowdy was accepted into the Army and promoted to major.[27]

At Fort Benning, Georgia—known as the "Home of the Infantry"—the baseball diamond was named "Hank Gowdy Field" in his honor in 1925. It is close to another sporting field appropriately named "Doughboy Stadium."[28] A baseball diamond named "Gowdy Field" in Hank's hometown of Columbus, Ohio, was dedicated in 1952, but within two years it was converted into a landfill.

Edward Leslie "Eddie" Grant (21 May 1883–5 October 1918)

Grant was born in Franklin, Massachusetts, and played baseball and basketball while a student at Harvard. After his graduation in 1905, Grant played semipro baseball before being called up by the Cleveland Indians. In his debut on 4 August 1905, Grant played second base and stroked three hits in a losing effort. In his next game he went 0 for 4 with four strikeouts and was promptly released by Cleveland. After a brief stint with the Class A minor league, Grant was back to the big leagues the next year with the Phillies. In the ensuing years Grant played for the Cincinnati Reds and the New York Giants. Grant retired in 1915 with a career .249 batting average and later opened a law office in Boston.

That same year Grant attended a civilian training camp at Plattsburg Barracks in New York State to be better prepared if or when war should come. After the United States entered the war, Grant enlisted in the Army on 15 August 1917. He was commissioned a captain in Company H, 307th Infantry Regiment, 77th Division, at Camp Upton, New York. The 77th was initially made up of draftees from the New York City area; many of the men were recent immigrants who could speak little or no English. Grant trained his company for many months before heading overseas with his unit in April 1918. The 77th was engaged toward the end of the Aisne-Marne Campaign along the Vesle River. During the Meuse-Argonne Offensive, the 307th Infantry

Regiment fought in the tangled hell of the Argonne Forest. On 5 October, Grant was killed in action while he was leading his men in combat. He was the first former major-league player to be killed in action during the war.[29]

Newton Schurz "Newt" Halliday (18 June 1896–6 April 1918)

Halliday was born in Chicago, Illinois. The first baseman played in one major-league game, and he struck out in his only at bat with the Pittsburgh Pirates in the second game of a doubleheader in 1916. Halliday enlisted in the Navy on 1 September 1917 at Great Lakes Naval Training Station, about forty miles north of Chicago. In early 1918, Halliday came down with tuberculosis, and he succumbed to "Tuberculosis; pneumonia, acute" in April 1918, at Great Lakes.[30]

Ted Kimbro (8 September 1895–29 September 1918)

Kimbro was born in St. Louis, Missouri. After attending school in Oklahoma City, the eighteen-year-old shortstop and third baseman began playing for the West Baden (Indiana) Sprudels, an independent Negro team. From 1914 to 1917, Kimbro played on the Sprudels, Louisville White Sox, St. Louis Giants, and the New York Lincoln Giants. In 1917 Kimbro, living in New York City, registered for the draft, but he claimed exemption due to a rupture-related injury. During the 1918 season Kimbro played for the New York Lincoln Giants, Philadelphia Hilldale Club, and Grand Central Red Caps before being drafted into the Army on 18 July 1918. Kimbro was assigned to the 52nd Company, 13th Training Battalion, 153rd Depot Brigade at Camp Dix, New Jersey. He and his teammate, Pearl "Specks" Webster, played on a team at Camp Dix, as well as making appearances for the Lincoln

Giants and the Hilldale Club. Kimbro fell ill with influenza early in the 1918 flu season. As with so many influenza victims, Kimbro developed bronchial pneumonia as a complication, and he died at Camp Dix in September 1918.[31]

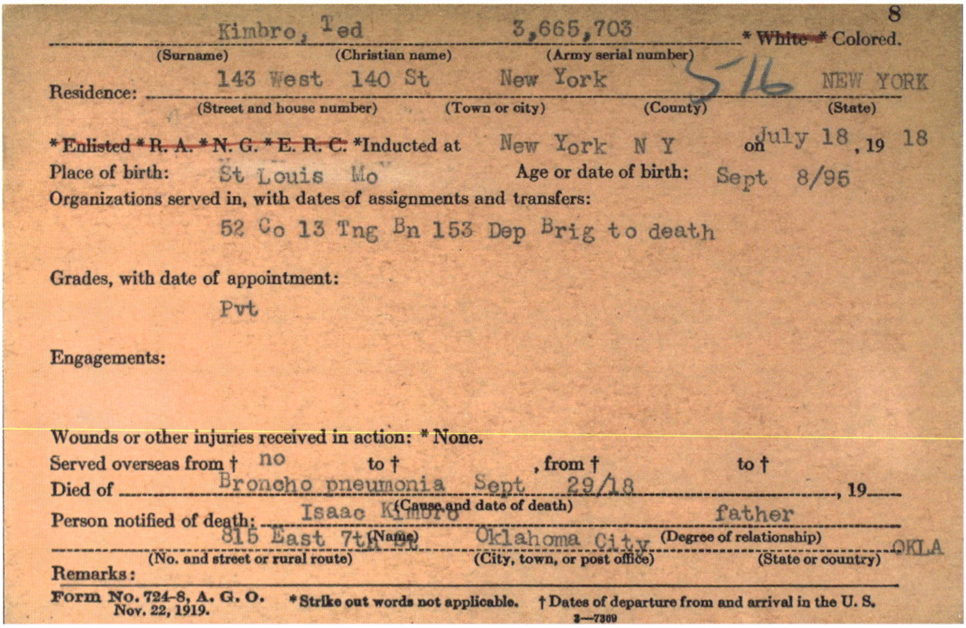

8

Kimbro, Ted — 3,665,703 — * ~~White~~ * Colored.
(Surname) (Christian name) (Army serial number)

Residence: 143 West 140 St — New York — 5/16 — NEW YORK
(Street and house number) (Town or city) (County) (State)

* ~~Enlisted * R. A. * N. G. * E. R. C.~~ * Inducted at New York N Y on July 18, 19 18

Place of birth: St Louis Mo — Age or date of birth: Sept 8/95

Organizations served in, with dates of assignments and transfers:
52 Co 13 Tng Bn 153 Dep Brig to death

Grades, with date of appointment:
Pvt

Engagements:

Wounds or other injuries received in action: * None.

Served overseas from † no to † , from † to †

Died of Broncho pneumonia Sept 29/18, 19
(Cause and date of death)

Person notified of death: Isaac Kimbro — father
(Name) (Degree of relationship)

815 East 7th St — Oklahoma City — OKLA
(No. and street or rural route) (City, town, or post office) (State or country)

Remarks:

Form No. 724-8, A. G. O. Nov. 22, 1919. — * Strike out words not applicable. — † Dates of departure from and arrival in the U. S.
3—7369

AGO Form 724 was the official form for recording an American's war service in the First World War. Here is the card for Ted Kimbro, a former Negro League infielder. Ted Kimbro's card is orange instead of the more common white, reflecting the fact that Kimbro died in service. Another victim of the Spanish flu epidemic that swept the country in late 1918, Kimbro died at Camp Dix, New Jersey. *Courtesy of New York, Abstracts of World War I Military Service, via Ancestry.com*

Kennesaw Mountain Landis (20 November 1866–25 November 1944)

Landis was born in Millville, Ohio, and was named after the battle where his father, Abraham Landis, a Union soldier, was wounded. Landis never completed high school but would go on to pursue a law degree from Union Law School, now known as Northwestern University.[32]

In 1891, having accomplished that goal, he opened a law practice in Chicago. Appointed federal judge of northern Illinois by President Teddy Roosevelt in 1905, Landis often interpreted the law in his own way, and not many wanted to have him as the judge at their hearing or trial. In 1915, the course of his career would take a turn in a different direction. A case came before his court about a dispute between the American and National Leagues of Baseball versus the relatively small Federal League of Baseball. The Federal League accused the other leagues of monopolizing the game of baseball, but the case was resolved before he could render a decision, when the Federal League was disbanded.

Landis proved to be a strong supporter of the United States' entry into World War I, and his stiffest judicial punishments were handed out to any who opposed the country's involvement. Landis had a vested interest in supporting the war, since his son, Reed G. Landis, was serving in the US Army Air Service and would become one of the AEF's top-scoring fighter pilots with twelve aerial victories.

In August 1918, Judge Landis gave a patriotic speech, then granted naturalized citizenship to 800 foreign-born soldiers assigned to the 86th Division at Camp Grant, Illinois. The judge made a point of shaking each new citizen's hand after the ceremony. This "naturalizing" procedure was repeated many times and at most training sites to prepare the units for departure to France.[33]

After the war, baseball would return to Landis's attention. In September 1920, eight Chicago White Sox players, including the famous "Shoeless" Joe Jackson, were indicted for fixing the 1919 World Series. The eight ballplayers were eventually acquitted of the charges in a court of law, but all eight were banned from the game of baseball for life by newly elected commissioner of baseball Judge Landis. Landis had been elected to the position by the team owners in November 1920, on the strength of his reputation for integrity and willingness to tackle tough issues, and the first task they gave him was to restore baseball's reputation. It has been written that Landis was

> no great intellect, [but had] an adamant sense of his own rectitude, and he brought into his courtroom the old rural and frontier values, adorning these

> rugged simplicities with thundering rhetoric as well . . . an unabridged cussword vocabulary. . . . Hardened by the granite patriotism of his origins, the judge was murder on anyone he deemed to be following an aberrant course.[34]

Baseball had needed a purging of its old ways, and Judge Landis was the man to apply the wire brush; he later suspended eighteen more players from baseball for life for a variety of other transgressions. Even Babe Ruth felt the wrath of Landis when he was suspended for forty games in the 1922 season because Ruth had angrily left the Yankee clubhouse without permission following the 1921 World Series.[35] As stern as Landis was, and as harsh as some of his decisions were, they did serve to clear away any hint of corruption in baseball. He served as commissioner from 21 January 1921 to his death in 1944. Landis was voted into the Baseball Hall of Fame a month after he died in 1944.

Christopher "Christy" Mathewson (12 August 1880–7 October 1925)

Mathewson was born in Factoryville, Pennsylvania. He played football and baseball at Bucknell University. After his freshman year, he signed with a minor-league club in Portland that eventually went bankrupt—certainly an inauspicious start for what would turn into a Hall of Fame career. In 1900, Mathewson played his first season with the New York Giants and pitched six games without a win.[36] Despite this rough start to his career, Mathewson went on to play sixteen years for the Giants and would become one of the all-time great pitchers in the National League. He ended his baseball career with 373 wins, which would leave him tied with his contemporary Grover Cleveland Alexander. His thirty-seven victories set the record for most wins in a season by a National League pitcher, and he won thirty games in three consecutive years. Ty Cobb called him "the greatest National League pitcher of them all."[37] After his playing career was over, Mathewson took on the job of managing the Cincinnati Reds. In 1917, he led the Reds to their first winning season since 1909.[38] In 1918, his managerial season was cut short because of the war and his decision to join the US military. He was thirty-eight when he entered the Army and was appointed a captain in the Chemical Warfare Service. With Ty Cobb and Branch Rickey, he served as a chemical-warfare instructor in France. While there, a training exercise went awry at the Allied Expeditionary Forces Gas School, and Mathewson, Cobb, and many others were accidentally exposed to mustard gas.[39] After the war, Mathewson returned to the United States and coached for the New York Giants. He was named the president of the Boston Braves in 1923. On 7 October 1925, Mathewson, his health still badly affected by his exposure to mustard gas, died at age forty-five. At the time it was said that Mathewson "had proved you could play professional baseball and remain a gentleman."[40] He was a member of the first class inducted into the Baseball Hall of Fame in 1936.

Herbert Jeffris Pennock (10 February 1894–30 January 1948)

Herb Pennock was born in Kennett Square, Pennsylvania, and came from a family with long ties to that state. Originally a weak-hitting first baseman, Pennock was converted to a pitcher by his prep school coach, and his true talent became obvious. He was signed to a professional contract by Philadelphia Athletics owner Connie Mack. Pennock made his first major-league start in 1912 and was traded to the Boston Red Sox in 1915. He missed all of the 1918 season while serving in the US Navy. His War Service Form 724 shows him serving at the US Navy base established in Gibraltar, but his postwar Pennsylvania War Service claim indicates service at a US Navy facility in Great Britain. This latter assignment would support the claim that he pitched in the famous "Army versus Navy" ball game witnessed by George VI, the king of England.[41]

After the war Pennock pitched for Boston until he was traded to the New York Yankees for the 1923 season. With that powerful team behind him, Pennock quickly established himself as one of the premier left-handed pitchers in the game. He retired as a player after the 1934 season but served as a coach or manager for other teams until his death in 1948. He was inducted into the Hall of Fame in 1948.[42]

Henry Grantland Rice
(1 November 1880–13 July 1954)

Grantland Rice was born in Murfreesboro, Tennessee, and became known as the "dean of sportswriters." Henry "Granny" Rice graduated from Vanderbilt University in 1901 and attempted a baseball career, but he made it only to a semipro team.[43] Within a year he gave up playing baseball and started writing about it as the sports editor of the *Nashville Daily News*. He then moved his writing talents to the *Atlanta Journal* in 1902, where he wrote the entire sports page and helped launch the career of an up-and-coming outfielder from Georgia named Ty Cobb.[44]

A man of many talents, Rice would also write poetry, in addition to covering the many sporting events he wrote about. He enjoyed adding rhymes and short phrases within long stories for the readers' entertainment. Some of his phrases and sayings are still in use today, such as "It's not whether you won or lost but how you played the game."[45] After Atlanta, Rice went to work first for the *Cleveland News* and then for the *Nashville Tennessean* until 1910, when he moved to New York to write for the *New York Evening Mail*. In 1913, he moved to the *New York Tribune*.[46]

When the US entered the war, Rice was already thirty-seven years old, but he still wanted to serve. He enlisted as a private in the 115th Field Artillery Regiment.[47] Almost immediately his education and maturity were recognized, and he was recommended for officer training, then commissioned a second lieutenant. When his unit was sent to the front lines, Rice was held back and instead assigned to write for the *Stars and Stripes*. After four months, he finally shook free of that job and managed to go to the front during the Meuse-Argonne Offensive. Following the Armistice, he participated in the "March to the Rhine" as a member of the US Third Army. While in Germany, he was a frequent contributor to the unit newspapers published there. One of his poems, a sarcastic takeoff on the famous "Bingen on the Rhine" poem, was titled "Coblenz on the Rhine." Among the many verses were the following:

A soldier of America lay starving in Coblenz.
His government had made him live four months on thirty cents.
A comrade stood beside him while his last Franc ebbed away
And bent with pity glances to hear what he might say.

Tell my brothers and companions when they crowd around to get
An earful of this bloody war that left us deep in debt.
We didn't mind the fighting job, but slogging through the rain.
Full many a bloke was starved to death along the Rhenish Plain.

After a number of similar verses detailing the failure of the Third Army's pay and ration systems, Rice concluded with this:

The starving soldier faltered in the Third Army Zone,
His eyes put on a dying look—He had not strength to groan;
His comrade bent to lift him, as he murmured softly—Tell
That Quartermaster when he comes I'll meet him down in hell.[48]

Rice spent fourteen months in the US Army, splitting most of the time between France and Germany. He returned to the *New York Tribune* in 1919.[49] In addition to his focus on baseball, Rice also covered other sports, such as football, tennis, and golf. Rice was a member of the Baseball Writers of America Association and later the Baseball Hall of Fame Old Timer's Committee. In 1922, Rice called the first-ever play by play for a World Series live on radio as the principal announcer. After that experience Rice quickly decided that he was meant to be a sports writer, not a sports announcer.[50] Rice continued to write about sports until his death in 1954. In 1966, Henry Grantland Rice was posthumously awarded the prestigious J. G. Taylor Spink Award by the Baseball Hall of Fame, given annually "for meritorious contributions to baseball writing."[51]

Wesley Branch Rickey
(20 December 1881–9 December 1965)

Branch Rickey was born in Stockdale, Ohio, and was a catcher, left fielder, and first basemen in his short-lived professional career. He played for the St. Louis Browns and the New York Highlanders from 1905 to 1907. With a career batting average of only .239, he soon realized his playing days were going to be coming to a quick end. He left the major leagues and became the coach of the University of Michigan baseball team while pursuing a law degree there. In 1914, Rickey received the opportunity to return to professional baseball as the manager of his former team, the St. Louis Browns. His managing career was interrupted when he entered the Army in 1918. Rickey was commissioned as a major in the newly created Chemical Warfare Service and was sent to France. He participated in the St. Mihiel and Meuse-Argonne Offensives.[52]

A number of familiar baseball names served in his unit, including three future Hall of Fame players: George Sisler, Christy Mathewson, and Ty Cobb.[53] After the war Rickey returned to the States and moved across town to manage the St. Louis Cardinals starting in 1919. Seven lackluster seasons led to his release as manager of the Cardinals in 1925. He remained with the organization and was selected to be their general manager. Rickey had found his niche. He was the first to establish a "farm system, " with minor-league teams being associated with a major-league club; the rest of professional baseball soon followed that pattern. Rickey would eventually leave the Cardinals to move to the Brooklyn Dodgers, the Pittsburgh Pirates, and then back to the Cardinals. With all the many other accomplishments and the occasional missteps that Branch Rickey made in his long career, he is probably best known for his work with the Brooklyn Dodgers and his signing of Jackie Robinson to break the color barrier of baseball. Even before that great accomplishment, Rickey had developed a loyal following of players and fans. Al Bridwell, a well-known shortstop during the early days of the twentieth century, said, "I don't think the greatest man in baseball was Cobb or Ruth or Wagner. I think it was Branch Rickey. I think he's done more for baseball than any man who ever lived."[54] Others saw him in a less glamorous light:

> He had a reputation for being parsimonious. . . . He could be devious. He could make you suspicious. He was unashamed for respecting baseball for exactly what it was—a business. He never hesitated to peddle a star player for all the cash he could get, one of his most famous credos being, "Better a year too early than a year too late."[55]

In retrospect, his foresight in devising a viable minor-league farm system for big-league clubs and his boldness and single-handed determination to bring African American ballplayers into the major leagues certainly outweighed his faults. Branch Rickey was inducted into the Baseball Hall of Fame in 1967, two years after his death.

Taken during Branch Rickey's short playing career in the major leagues, this photograph shows him in the uniform of the St. Louis Browns. In addition to his many baseball accomplishments, Rickey is also known for convincing Christy Mathewson, Ty Cobb, and George Sisler to serve with him in the Army's Chemical Warfare Service. *Courtesy of Library of Congress*

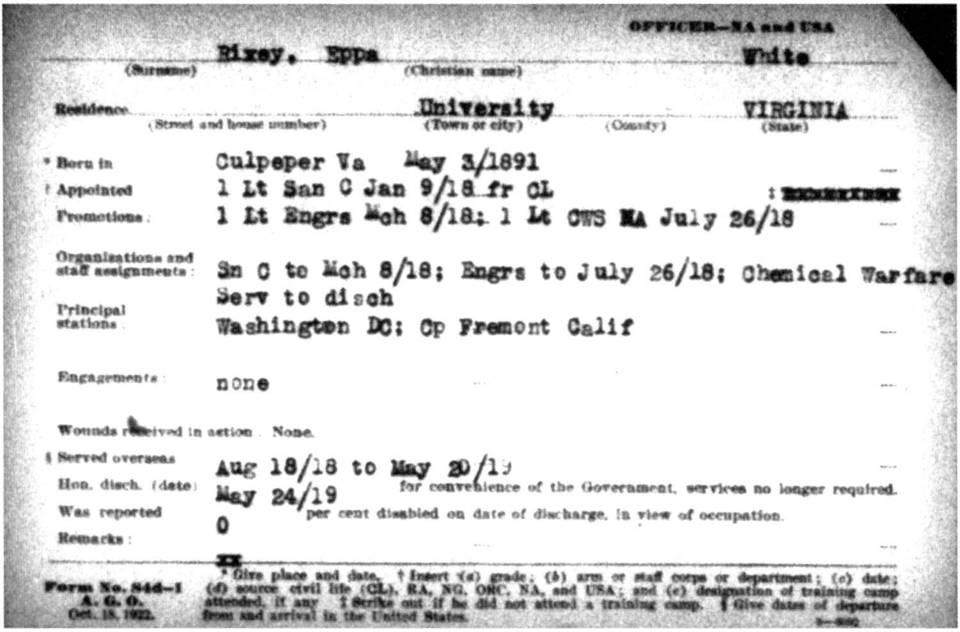

OFFICER—NA and USA

Rixey, Eppa (Surname) (Christian name) White

Residence (Street and house number) University (Town or city) (County) VIRGINIA (State)

* Born in: Culpeper Va May 3/1891

† Appointed: 1 Lt San C Jan 9/18 fr CL

Promotions: 1 Lt Engrs Mch 8/18; 1 Lt CWS NA July 26/18

Organizations and staff assignments: Sn C to Mch 8/18; Engrs to July 26/18; Chemical Warfare Serv to disch

Principal stations: Washington DC; Cp Fremont Calif

Engagements: none

Wounds received in action: None.

§ Served overseas: Aug 18/18 to May 20/19

Hon. disch. (date): May 24/19 for convenience of the Government, services no longer required.

Was reported 0 per cent disabled on date of discharge, in view of occupation.

Remarks:

Form No. 84d-1 A. G. O. Oct. 18, 1922.

* Give place and date. † Insert (a) grade; (b) arm or staff corps or department; (c) date; (d) source civil life (CL), RA, NG, ORC, NA, and USA; and (e) designation of training camp attended, if any. ‡ Strike out if he did not attend a training camp. § Give dates of departure from and arrival in the United States.

The wartime service card for Hall of Fame pitcher Eppa Rixey, showing his assignment as a lieutenant in the US Army Chemical Warfare Service. Rixey had first been appointed an officer in the Army Sanitary Corps with duty at Camp Fremont, California, before being sent to France in August 1918. Rixey's 266 victories were the record for most wins by a National League left-handed pitcher for many years. *Courtesy of Library of Virginia*

Eppa "Jeptha" Rixey
(3 May 1891–28 February 1963)

Eppa Rixey was born in Culpeper, Virginia, but spent most of his early years in Charlottesville, Virginia. Unlike many of the ballplayers of his era, Rixey attended college and showcased his pitching skills for the University of Virginia team. As a result he never played in the minor leagues. Rixey signed with the Philadelphia Phillies in 1912. During his career Rixey was a contradictory figure. He hated losing so much that he was known to sulk or destroy locker rooms after losing a game, yet he often spent his off seasons patiently teaching Latin to high school students. In January 1918, he parlayed his college education into a lieutenant commission in the US Army Sanitary Corps, a branch of the

Medical Corps. Shortly after that he was transferred to the Engineer Corps, then into the Chemical Warfare Service. He served in France from August 1918 to May 1919.[56] On returning to the major leagues, Rixey struggled at first to regain his pitching form. After being traded to the Cincinnati Reds, he started to reestablish his skills and pitched for them for twelve years until 1933. He amassed a final record of 266 wins and 251 losses—both records for his era by a left-handed National League pitcher. He was elected to the Hall of Fame in 1963 but died before his induction ceremony.[57]

Ralph Edward Sharman (11 April 1895–24 May 1918)

Sharman was born in Cleveland, Ohio. After bouncing around in the low minor leagues beginning in 1915, Sharman made his big-league debut with the Philadelphia Athletics in September 1917. In thirteen games Sharman batted .297, a respectable start indeed. With the season over and the United States at war, Sharman enlisted in the 3rd Field Artillery Regiment, Ohio National Guard, at Fort Thomas, Kentucky, on 7 November 1917. Sharman's regiment was soon redesignated as Battery F, 136th Field Artillery Regiment, 37th Division, and was composed of Ohio National Guard soldiers. On 24 May 1918, Cpl. Sharman drowned in the Alabama River near Camp Sheridan during a training exercise. After a parade of honor through Montgomery, Alabama, Sharman's body was returned to Cleveland for burial.[58]

George Harold "Gorgeous George" Sisler (24 March 1893–26 March 1973)

George Sisler was born in Manchester, Ohio, and is known as one of the greatest first basemen to ever play the game. He started with the St. Louis Browns after graduating college in 1915. After the 1918 season was shortened because of the war, Sisler went to work at the Lebanon Steel Plant to perform "war essential" work. Shortly after he started there, he was convinced by his former University of Michigan baseball coach and St. Louis Browns manager, Branch Rickey, to join the Army's Chemical Warfare Service. Sisler was commissioned a second lieutenant and was stationed at Camp Humphreys, Virginia. His unit was preparing to deploy to France when the Armistice was signed on 11 November 1918. Returning to major-league baseball, he continued his all-star-quality play for the St. Louis Browns, Washington Senators, and the Boston Braves. In 1920, he set the record for hits during a season with 257, a record not broken until 2004. He had a career batting average of .340 with 2, 812 career hits. He hit over .400 twice and over .300 thirteen times in his fifteen-year career. He was inducted into the Baseball Hall of Fame in 1939.[59]

Charles Phelps Taft II

(20 September 1897–24 June 1983)

Charles P. Taft II was born in Cincinnati, Ohio. He was the son of the twenty-seventh president and tenth chief justice of the Supreme Court, William Howard Taft. Charles studied law at Yale until he left school to enlist with a Regular Army field artillery unit. He worked his way from the rank of private up to sergeant major. On 10 January 1918, Taft was sent to France and served as an instructor.[60] After the Armistice was signed, he returned home and finished his law degree. Today, Taft is best known for serving as the mayor of Cincinnati from 1955 to 1957 and as being the Republican candidate for governor of Ohio in 1952. His influence and work with the community helped with the redevelopment of Cincinnati, and he served on the Cincinnati City Council for thirty-two years. Taft was a passionate Cincinnati Reds fan. Throughout his tenure as city councilman and mayor, he would often listen to Reds games with an earplug during meetings.[61] His enthusiasm for baseball and the Cincinnati Reds never dimmed. It led to him playing a key role in the planning and construction of Riverfront Stadium for the Cincinnati Bengals football team and his beloved Reds.[62] Taft died in June 1983, and his obituary noted that he was nicknamed "Mr. Cincinnati."[63] Fittingly, US Army field artillery soldiers, such as Taft had been, are nicknamed "red legs" because of the Civil War practice of wearing red stripes on their trousers, and Taft's favorite team was also known at times as the Cincinnati "Red Legs." It was a happy coincidence he probably enjoyed.

Former US president William H. Taft visits the Fort Myer, Virginia, Officers Training Camp and talks with his son, Charles P. Taft II. The younger Taft was attending the training camp in preparation for Army service. Charles, a rabid baseball fan, later served as the mayor of Cincinnati and played a major role in the construction of Riverfront Stadium for the Cincinnati Reds and Bengals. *Courtesy of Library of Congress*

Norman Triplett

(18 October 1893–20 October 1918)

Triplett was born in La Mott, Pennsylvania. He played catcher for the semipro La Mott Stars before joining the Negro Leagues as an outfielder for the Hilldale Athletic Club in 1917. Triplett made just two appearances with Hilldale before returning to the La Mott team in July 1917. On 4 August 1918, Triplett was inducted into the Army as a private in the 15th Provisional Company, Colored Detachment, 160th Depot Brigade at Camp Custer, Michigan. On 23 August, Triplett was transferred to Company M, 803rd Pioneer Infantry Regiment; nine days later he was promoted to private first class. On 17 September, Triplett sailed with his unit aboard the *Teiresias*, bound for France. On 20 October, Triplett succumbed to "measles and pneumonia, " probably as a result of contact with influenza.

In 1920, Triplett's brother, Armstead, applied for and received the Victory Medal with "France" service clasp. Fourteen years later, four of Triplett's brothers—Armstead, Wallace, Mahlon, and Frank (both Wallace and Frank were World War I combat veterans of the 368th Infantry Regiment)—applied for a Pennsylvania veteran's bonus on behalf of Norman. For some reason the application took almost three years to adjudicate; the sad result was disapproval, although the grounds for the negative response are not specified. Interestingly, the Tripletts' application was notarized by James L. Moore, adjutant of Moore-Triplett American Legion Post 451; this post was most likely named partly in honor of Norman Triplett, the young former ballplayer who gave his live in the service of his country.[64]

Another victim of the Spanish flu, Norman Triplett was an outfielder in the Negro Leagues before being drafted. Again, the orange color AGO Form 724 reflects that Triplett died while serving in France with the 803rd Pioneer Infantry. *Courtesy of Pennsylvania, WWI Veterans Service and Compensation Files, via Ancestry.com*

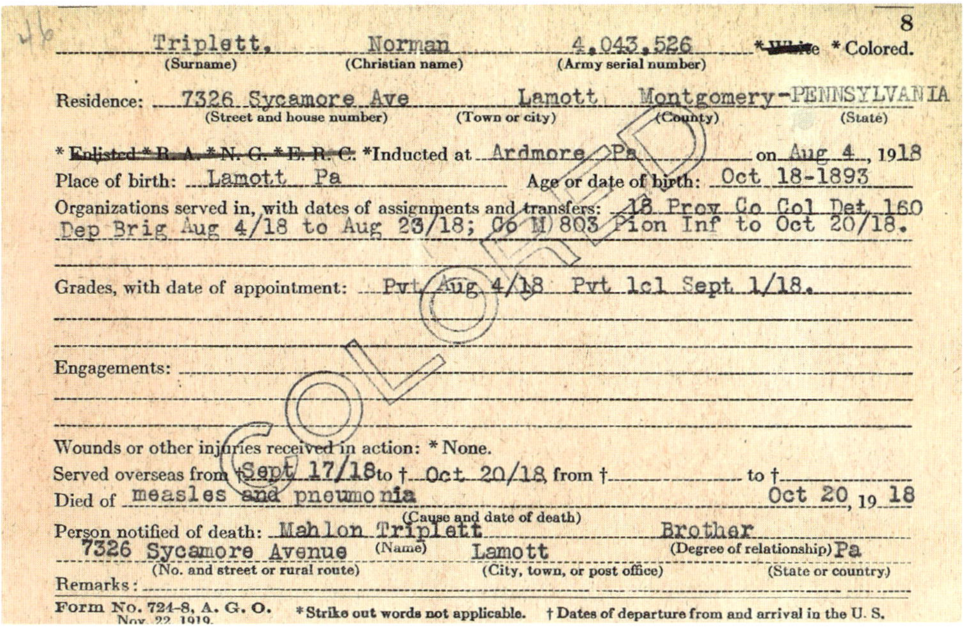

8

Triplett. (Surname) Norman (Christian name) 4.043.526 (Army serial number) ~~White~~ * Colored.

Residence: 7326 Sycamore Ave (Street and house number) Lamott (Town or city) Montgomery (County) PENNSYLVANIA (State)

* ~~Enlisted * R. A. * N. G. * E. R. C.~~ *Inducted at Ardmore Pa on Aug 4, 1918

Place of birth: Lamott Pa Age or date of birth: Oct 18-1893

Organizations served in, with dates of assignments and transfers: 18 Prov Co Col Det 160 Dep Brig Aug 4/18 to Aug 23/18; Co M 803 Pion Inf to Oct 20/18.

Grades, with date of appointment: Pvt Aug 4/18 Pvt 1cl Sept 1/18.

Engagements:

Wounds or other injuries received in action: * None.

Served overseas from † Sept 17/18 to † Oct 20/18 from † to †

Died of measles and pneumonia (Cause and date of death) Oct 20, 19 18

Person notified of death: Mahlon Triplett (Name) Brother (Degree of relationship)

7326 Sycamore Avenue (No. and street or rural route) Lamott (City, town, or post office) Pa (State or country)

Remarks:

Form No. 724-8, A. G. O. Nov. 22, 1919. *Strike out words not applicable. † Dates of departure from and arrival in the U. S.

Robert Gustave "Bun" Troy (27 August 1888–7 October 1918)

"Bun" Troy was born in Wurzach, Germany, and grew up near Pittsburgh, Pennsylvania. A pitcher, he played baseball in the low minors before being called up by the Detroit Tigers in September 1912. His only big-league appearance was on 15 September, when he went up against the great Walter Johnson of the Washington Senators. He pitched well, holding the Senators to a shutout until the seventh inning. Troy and reliever Ed Willett gave up six runs—some of them due to fielding errors—and the Tigers lost the game six to three when it was called before the ninth inning due to darkness. Disgusted, Troy abandoned the Tigers and moved back to Pennsylvania; he played in the low minors for the next few years before entering the Army on 18 September 1917.

He was assigned to Company G, 319th Infantry Regiment, in the 80th Division. Troy was promoted to corporal on 8 October 1917, and he went overseas with his unit in May 1918. Promoted to sergeant on 7 August, Troy was killed in action while fighting against men from his native country in the Meuse-Argonne Offensive on 7 October 1918.[65]

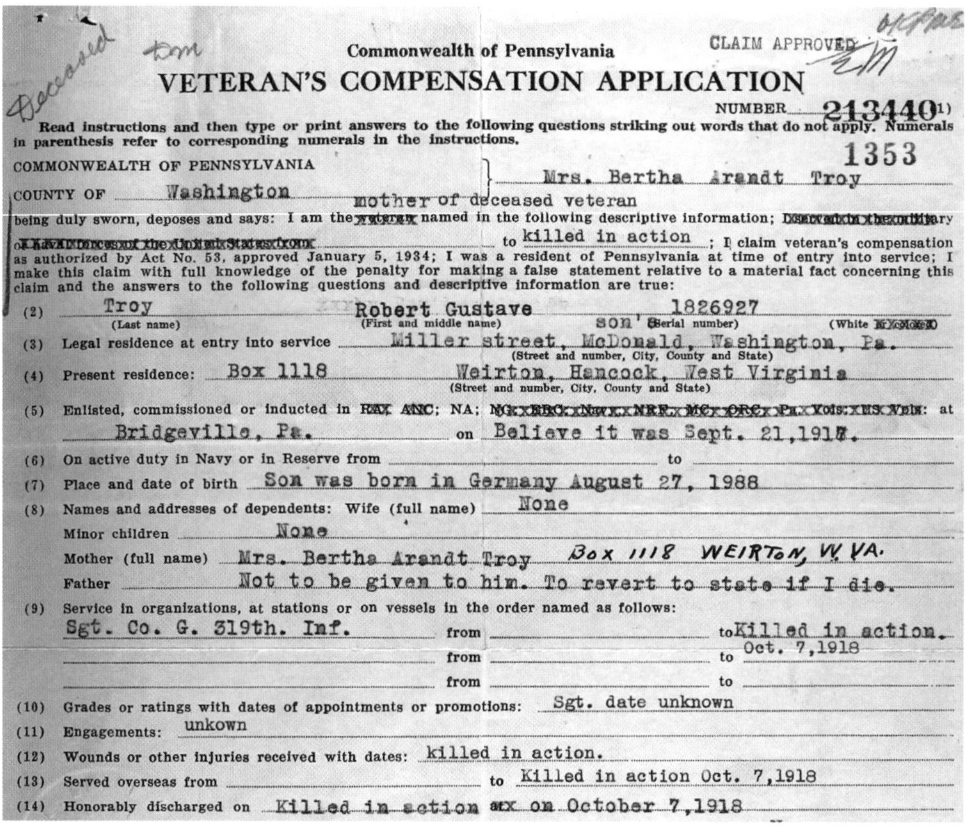

Deceased

Commonwealth of Pennsylvania

CLAIM APPROVED

VETERAN'S COMPENSATION APPLICATION

NUMBER 213440 (1)

1353

Read instructions and then type or print answers to the following questions striking out words that do not apply. Numerals in parenthesis refer to corresponding numerals in the instructions.

COMMONWEALTH OF PENNSYLVANIA
COUNTY OF Washington } Mrs. Bertha Arandt Troy mother of deceased veteran

being duly sworn, deposes and says: I am the ~~veteran~~ named in the following descriptive information; ... to killed in action; I claim veteran's compensation as authorized by Act No. 53, approved January 5, 1934; I was a resident of Pennsylvania at time of entry into service; I make this claim with full knowledge of the penalty for making a false statement relative to a material fact concerning this claim and the answers to the following questions and descriptive information are true:

(2) Troy (Last name) Robert Gustave (First and middle name) son's Serial number 1826927 (White)

(3) Legal residence at entry into service Miller street, McDonald, Washington, Pa. (Street and number, City, County and State)

(4) Present residence: Box 1118 Weirton, Hancock, West Virginia (Street and number, City, County and State)

(5) Enlisted, commissioned or inducted in ~~RA~~ ANC; NA; ... at Bridgeville, Pa. on Believe it was Sept. 21,1917.

(6) On active duty in Navy or in Reserve from ... to ...

(7) Place and date of birth Son was born in Germany August 27, 1888

(8) Names and addresses of dependents: Wife (full name) None
Minor children None
Mother (full name) Mrs. Bertha Arandt Troy BOX 1118 WEIRTON, W. VA.
Father Not to be given to him. To revert to state if I die.

(9) Service in organizations, at stations or on vessels in the order named as follows:
Sgt. Co. G. 319th. Inf. from ... to Killed in action. Oct. 7,1918
from ... to ...
from ... to ...

(10) Grades or ratings with dates of appointments or promotions: Sgt. date unknown

(11) Engagements: unkown

(12) Wounds or other injuries received with dates: killed in action.

(13) Served overseas from ... to Killed in action Oct. 7,1918

(14) Honorably discharged on Killed in action ~~at~~ on October 7,1918

The Pennsylvania Veteran's Compensation Application filed by Robert "Bun" Troy's mother in February 1934. Troy had pitched for the Detroit Tigers in his one major-league game. Serving with the 80th Division in the Meuse-Argonne Offensive, Troy was killed in action on 7 October 1918. His mother's application was approved and she was awarded $200.00 for his service. *Courtesy of Pennsylvania, WWI Veterans Service and Compensation Files, via Ancestry.com*

A detail from Sgt. Bun Troy's headstone in Robinson Run Cemetery in Allegheny County, Pennsylvania. *Courtesy of Findagrave via Ancestry.com*

Pearl "Specks" Webster (8 July 1889–16 November 1918)

"Specks" Webster was born in Wayland, Missouri. In 1911, Webster, a speedster who could play catcher, first base, and the outfield all equally well, began his career as a catcher on the Chicago Leland Giants. From 1912 to 1916, Webster played for the Brooklyn Royal Giants. During the winter seasons he traveled to the South, where he played in the Florida Coconut League, "a circuit of teams made up of hotel-run clubs from Miami and Palm Beach." During the 1917 regular season Webster played for the Hilldale Daisies; the next year found him with the Grand Central Terminal Red Caps. Inducted into the Army the same day as his teammate Ted Kimbro, Webster played ball on one of Camp Dix's teams until he was assigned to Company F, 807th Pioneer Infantry Regiment, on 30 August 1918. Just five days later, Webster sailed for France with his unit aboard the SS *Maui*. The 807th saw action during the Meuse-Argonne Offensive, and Webster was promoted to corporal. After having lived through combat, Webster became ill with influenza, which was working its deadly way through all armies in autumn 1918. On 16 November—just five days after the Armistice—Corporal Webster succumbed to lobar pneumonia.[66]

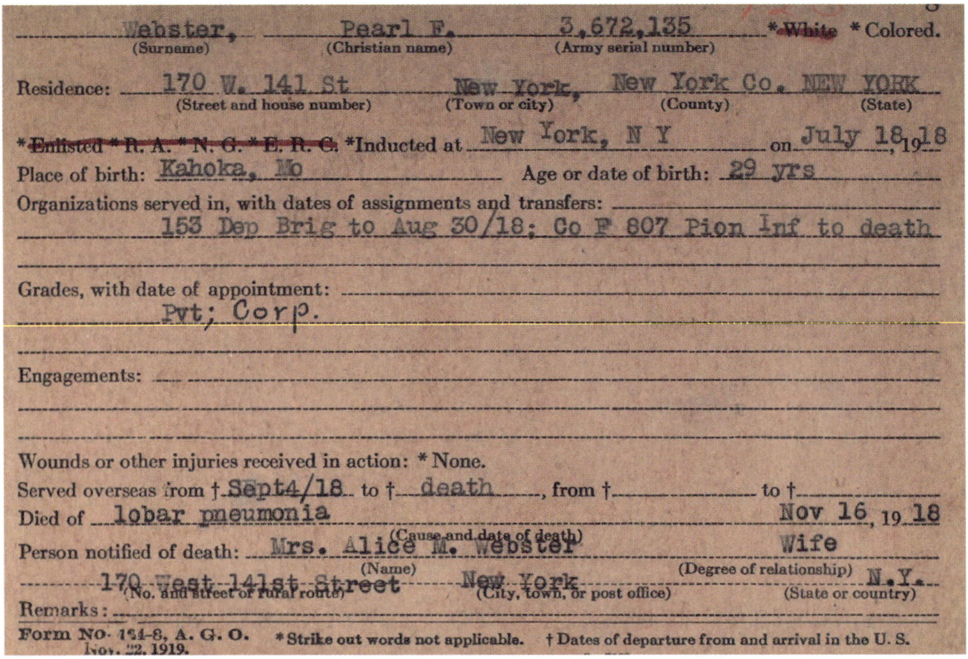

Webster, (Surname) Pearl F. (Christian name) 3,672,135 (Army serial number) *~~White~~ *Colored.

Residence: 170 W. 141 St (Street and house number) New York, (Town or city) New York Co. (County) NEW YORK (State)

*~~Enlisted *R. A. *N. G. *E. R. C.~~ *Inducted at New York, N Y on July 18, 1918

Place of birth: Kahoka, Mo Age or date of birth: 29 yrs

Organizations served in, with dates of assignments and transfers: 153 Dep Brig to Aug 30/18; Co F 807 Pion Inf to death

Grades, with date of appointment: Pvt; Corp.

Engagements:

Wounds or other injuries received in action: * None.

Served overseas from † Sept4/18 to † death, from † to †

Died of lobar pneumonia Nov 16, 1918 (Cause and date of death)

Person notified of death: Mrs. Alice M. Webster (Name) Wife (Degree of relationship)

170 West 141st Street (No. and street or rural route) New York (City, town, or post office) N.Y. (State or country)

Remarks:

Form No. 1[illegible]-8, A. G. O. Nov. 22, 1919. * Strike out words not applicable. † Dates of departure from and arrival in the U. S.

Pearl "Specs" Webster was a highly regarded ballplayer in the Negro Leagues before he was drafted on the same day as his friend and teammate Ted Kimbro. Webster was assigned to the 807th Pioneer Infantry Regiment—an African American unit—and survived the Meuse-Argonne Offensive, only to succumb a short while later to the Spanish flu. *Courtesy of New York, Abstracts of World War I Military Service, via Ancestry.com*

8th Inning
A Perfect Game? Strange Events and Occurrences

The history of the United States military, like the history of baseball, is a fascinating topic. Both are defined by a strict set of rules, yet within the confines of those rules, there is enough leeway to allow for unique individuals and unusual occurrences to sometimes take center stage. What follows are some of those instances that do not fit easily into a tidy box score or a military unit's morning report.

There's Baseball, and Then There's Everything Else . . .

The men of Company I, 51st Pioneer Infantry Regiment, were in training at Camp Wadsworth, South Carolina, in spring 1918. They were anxious to find opponents for their baseball team. To that end, team manager Sgt. Fritz placed a notice in a camp magazine that they "would like to book games with any company or regimental team in camp, on Thursday and Sunday afternoons." According to Fritz, the company "has strengthened her team this year and expects to put up as good a showing as last fall, when they met and defeated all teams played."[1] Given the enthusiasm of the Doughboys for the game, Company I no doubt found many worthy opponents.

The 51st remained enthused about their baseball team throughout the war and into their tour of duty with the Army of Occupation of Germany in 1919. News of their skill spread to almost the highest levels. Members of the 51st were attached to the United States IV Corps during the occupation for special duty; when their duty was finished, they expected to return to their home regiment. Knowing that some members

The British ship *Oronsa* was one of many that fell victim to German U-boats. Her sinking in April 1918 was particularly notable to baseball fans in the AEF because she was carrying $30,000 worth of donated baseball equipment for the troops.

A group of 51st Pioneer Infantry Regiment soldiers take a break from work to pose for a picture and enjoy some of the local German beer. Some of their comrades in the 51st were such valuable baseball players for the IV Corps team that it was requested that they remain with the Corps even after their unit's mission was completed. *Courtesy of NYDMNA*

of the 51st were successfully representing the IV Corps in baseball and track-and-field teams and were reluctant to lose them, the commander of IV Corps sought the retention of these men on Corps duty.

On 12 May 1919, Acting Chief of Staff of IV Corps Col. (later Gen.) Walter Krueger wrote a letter to the commander of the Third Army. Col. Krueger requested that Gen. Dickman intervene to ensure star baseball players on the 51st be retained on detached duty with the Corps. According to Krueger, "their relief would seriously impair the chances of the IV Corps in the Baseball League." Even worse, without the 51st men on detached duty, the IV Corps baseball team would be disbanded. The request to keep the men was very specific, naming individual soldiers. The 51st Pioneer Infantry Regiment baseball players mentioned in the letter were: 1st Lt. William J. Starr, Co. D; Lt. McLeod; Pvt. Edward Lewis, Co. I; PFC Charles A. Wagner, Co. E; PFC Frank Fountain, Co. I; Cpl. John H. Simmons, Co. I; Cpl. Valentine Melvin, Co. C; Mech. Edward Martin, Co. C; Sgt. William E. Parks, Co. L; and Cpl. James DeMotta, Co. I.[2]

An interesting group of Service of Supply (SOS) and 84th Division Doughboys pose while showing off a French helmet, a German helmet, a rifle, and, most importantly, their baseball bat.

Georgia Peach Slated For a New Berth

Ty Cobb, considered the cream of Major league outfielders, is being mentioned in several probable trades back in the States. It is doubtful if Hughey Jennings will let the Georgia Peach slide from his clutches unless some real money or stars is offered for him. Cobb has been up there with the best of them for several years and, while he is not getting

"TY" COBB

younger, his work last year was up to the standard.

Cobb was over here in France as a captain in the Chemical Service and for a time held out on his contract, probably on the grounds that being a member of the A. E. F. he would be more of a drawing card than ever. Yes, if he was up there in the lines using that wonderful right arm of his guiding the destinies of his charges or throwing hand grenades at the Boches we would think he should, We are not condemning him for accepting a position in the branch he was best fitted, but after receiving the best of it over here why use that as a means of obtaining more money at his profession?

Another clipping from a Doughboy newspaper of the period. Written after Capt. Ty Cobb of the Chemical Warfare Service had returned to the States, this column chides him for not serving in one of the combat arms branches, such as infantry or field artillery. What the paper does not mention is that Cobb became violently ill after accidental exposure to mustard gas. *Courtesy of the* Stars and Stripes

Occupation? Ballplayer

Most National Guard units were meant to reflect their community of origin, but by the time the Army personnel system had finished shuffling soldiers between units to prepare them for deployment to France, much of the local flavor was gone. The 112th Machine Gun Battalion, although originally raised from Maryland and Virginia units, had soldiers from thirty-three different states, the District of Columbia, and two other countries: Canada and Russia. Occupations represented among the 112th's machine gunners were everything from farmers and clerks to street car conductors, and, most significantly, a "ball player."[3]

The First Baseball Team in the AEF?

American Base Hospital Number 5 was organized in February 1916 at Harvard University, before war was declared. It was mobilized in May 1917, and by that summer the hospital unit was attached to the British Expeditionary Forces (BEF). It set up operation in the area between the towns of Dannes and Camiers, close to the English Channel. As a result of its proximity to the front lines, it was attacked several times by German aircraft and suffered some of the first casualties by US Army units. Two officers and three enlisted men were killed, and three officers (including a nurse) and five enlisted were wounded during these attacks. One of the surgeons who served in Number 5 while it was supporting the British was an American, Dr. Harvey Cushing. As American soldiers began to show up as patients in his hospital, Cushing was unpleasantly surprised to find how many men unfit for service had been transported across the ocean. In addition to some with chronic heart disease and tuberculosis, Harvey found one soldier suffering from mitral stenosis to the point that he could neither run nor climb stairs.[4]

In contrast to the weakness of some of their patients, the medical and support staff appears to have been fairly robust. They can lay claim to having fielded one of the first baseball teams in the AEF. Almost immediately after arrival in France on 30 May 1917, they moved to their designated site at Camiers. Shortly thereafter they fielded a team. All that is known is that the battery (pitcher and catcher) was Sgt. First Class Edwin Cook of Boston and Pvt. First Class Herman E. Bartlett of Berea, Kentucky. A series of games were played against teams from Canadian hospital unit numbers 1 and 3, and the "Chicago Unit" (probably US Army Base Hospital Number 12, formed from the staff of Northwestern University Medical Department in Chicago and also supporting the BEF in the area near Camiers). Sadly, no other information is available.[5]

Other base hospitals quickly followed suit. Interestingly enough, while most units suffered from a lack of good baseball equipment, Base Hospital Number 9 (originating from New York Hospital in New York City) noted the large quantity of baseball supplies sent to it by the Red Cross: "We have received almost enough baseball equipment to start a World Series while even into such diverse things as quoits and bicycles we have not been neglected."[6]

Base Hospital Number 46, raised from the staff of the Medical Department of the University of Oregon in Portland, Oregon, fielded a team of which they were quite proud. The full team consisted of Sgt. Elmer R. Bashor (catcher), Pvt. First Class Harry Kackley (pitcher), Cpl. Charles B. Osborne (pitcher), Pvt. First Class Richard B. Stinson (first base), Pvt. First Class Andrew G. Miller (second base), Sgt. Gordon S. Brown (shortstop), Pvt. First Class Clifford R. Harlow (third base), Pvt. First Class Roy E. Briggs, Pvt. First Class Edwin Morene, Pvt. First Class George W. Miller, Pvt. Roy Mitchell (outfield), Sgt. Garret Stelsel (manager), and Lt. Dorwin L. Palmer (director of athletics). The team had to wait until it received a shipment of baseball equipment from the Red Cross on 1 February 1919, "a trifle late for the season of 1918." Despite the late start, the team got into shape quickly enough for a game on 4 July, at which they defeated a team from Base Hospital Number 116. The Base Hospital Number 46 team was successful that season, being beaten only by a team fielded by a "Mobile Operating unit that had the good fortune of having several ex-professionals in its line-up." Hospital Number 46's pitcher Harry Kackley, "with his long right arm, shattered the fond hopes of many a slugger, for he had plenty of curves, a good 'fast' one, and fair control." What more could one ask for in an amateur soldier hurler?

The hospital's catcher, Elmer Bashor, had "all kinds of fight and a cool head, " and he caught many men attempting to steal second base. At first base, "speed demon" Richard Stinson "never failed on a ground ball." And the daring base runners George Miller and Andrew Miller executed a squeeze play that won a game one to zero for the team. The team had great support from the officers, men, and nurses of the unit, and this accounted in part for their success.[7]

Closest Game to the Front Lines?

The men played baseball when in rear areas while training or reorganizing. Such activity helped alleviate the boredom and tediousness of training, or time spent waiting to be part of an operation. But the ever-resourceful Doughboy players were not content to confine their ball playing to "down time" in rear areas. Veteran Lafayette Schank later claimed to have played in baseball games nearer to the front than any other games during the war. In summer 1918, "behind the Alsatian front near the American railhead which was located just east of Fontaine, " members of Salvage Squad No. 6 formed a team that played pickup games against other teams in the area. Opponents included teams from "a rolling canteen unit . . . the Engineer personnel of the railhead, and members of either the 32nd or 29th Division on detached service there." The names of only three of the players on the Salvage Squad team were reported: Clyde Crooks (Waterloo, Indiana), Victor E. Swithenbank (Marysville, California), and Raymond H. Rhodes (Toledo, Ohio).

Some of the games were played while the guns of the American 1st Anti-Aircraft Battalion "were banging away at enemy airplanes flying overhead." The players were not immune from danger on such occasions, as pieces of steel casings from the munitions "fell just as hard as though labeled 'Made in Germany.'"[8]

Baseball at Belleau Wood? (June 1918)

The YMCA received a lot of criticism from the Doughboys for some of its policies, and the fact that many believed a good number of the "Y" workers were in the age group that should have been carrying a rifle and wearing an Army uniform. It was also embroiled in a never-ending controversy about selling "donated" cigarettes to the Doughboys. Nevertheless, there was little doubt that the YMCA provided a much-needed service for the soldiers, and many of its personnel showed their courage in the front lines. Among the bravest was chief athletic director of the YMCA in France, Elwood Brown. Brown obviously was a firm believer that sporting equipment was a key morale factor in maintaining the soldiers' fighting spirit, but he needed an opportunity to prove its value. That opportunity was not long in coming.

In June 1918, after hearing that the AEF was involved in some heavy fighting in the area around Chateau-Thierry, Brown loaded his automobile with baseball and boxing equipment and headed out to find the battle. Among the first Army leaders he encountered was Brig. Gen. James Harbord, the Army officer commanding the Marine 4th Brigade, which recently fought its way into Belleau Wood and was holding as best it could under German pressure. Brown quickly explained to Harbord what he had in his vehicle and said that although he did not want to get in the way, he believed the Marines on the front lines could use the morale boost he could provide with sports equipment. Harbord considered the offer and said:

> You fellows can go just as far as you've the guts to go. Of course you won't organize a ball game on the battle-field. But go ahead. I leave it to you to work out.[9]

Following further discussions with 2nd Division Chief of Staff (and later division commander) Maj. Gen. Omar Bundy, Brown went forward to where the troops were waiting for the next German attack or artillery barrage. As he got closer to the front lines, he encountered "sometimes officers who welcomed him, or again others who enthusiastically cast him out."[10] Whenever he reached the waiting troops he handed out baseballs, baseball gloves, boxing gloves, and exercise pamphlets. All were gratefully received by the Marines. When he had distributed most of the equipment, he turned his vehicle around and was heading back when he came across a US Army field artillery battery firing the famous French 75s. He stopped and introduced himself to the first sergeant he found. At first, the sergeant was upset that Brown had no cigarettes to hand out to the artillerymen, but his mood changed when the YMCA representative handed him a brand new baseball. In short order the artillerymen were playing "pitch and catch" in the area between the cannons. At least they were until the battery commander showed up and asked what was going on. After the sergeant explained that Elwood Brown had brought the baseballs the men were throwing around, the captain nodded his understanding. He then ordered the men to move farther away from the 75s and into an area covered by a tree line if they were going to continue playing. Once the men had moved, the captain told Brown:

> I want to tell you it's one good job, your bringing things like this up here to us. Take these fellows of mine, they don't even have the relief of seeing the fight. One half of them is always in rest, the other at the guns. So then, what has the resting crew got to do? Why, it sits around idle, waits and fusses and worries and swears. This ball stunt of yours is a wonder. Bring us anything more you can, whenever you can find us.[11]

It's a Simple Game If You Have the Equipment (June 1918)

As bad as the baseball equipment shortage was in training camps back in the United States, it was worse in France. Cargo space in ships sailing from US East Coast ports was jealously guarded and fought over for transporting more-essential war equipment. Even such basic items as mess kits were being manufactured in France to save cargo room. Army engineers had figured out how to ship more locomotive engines and trucks; they shipped them partially disassembled and let the Services of Supply soldiers in French ports and reception camps reassemble them. The AEF published ordinances and regulations forbidding units from bringing from the States anything that did not apply directly to a unit's combat mission, but exceptions were made. An appeal directly to Gen. Pershing gave cargo space for books being shipped by the American Library Association for distribution to the Doughboys. In April 1918, the British cargo ship *Oronsa* was transporting about $30, 000 worth of donated baseball equipment to the AEF. Unfortunately for Doughboy morale, a German U-boat torpedoed and sank the *Oronsa* on 28 April off the coast of Wales, almost at the end of its voyage. In addition to the three crewmen who were killed in the attack, the Doughboys' baseball equipment was lost.

Recognizing the importance of the national pastime to the soldiers and needing to keep them busy during their few hours away from their daily efforts, the Army recruited the YMCA to help obtain equipment. "Y" representatives soon found a French leather goods manufacturer who was willing to attempt making a baseball glove to US specifications, and in a short while the sample was ready for inspection. Although the pocket between the thumb and forefinger was laced with a sturdy twine instead of leather, the glove appeared to meet the need.[12]

With the baseball mitt situation apparently solved, the next item was the bat. Just as they would have back home, soldiers used any suitable piece of wood they could find, including wagon wheel spokes and tree limbs. The *Stars and Stripes* noted that in any unit "lucky enough to have a real bat, it is screwed together and tied together and clamped together every time it threatens to crack."[13] Realizing the importance of the quest for bats, the Doughboys' favorite newspaper even posted a message to "any French wood turner." They were encouraged to apply to the *Stars and Stripes* for a lucrative, long-term contract to make bats for the AEF.[14] The paper also noted the irony that should the containers of bats sunk with the *Oronsa* ever float ashore, the people finding them and noting the US Army address would be surprised at the primitive weapons apparently being used by the Doughboys.

Meanwhile, at the World Series (September 1918)

As noted, a number of Doughboys who were wounded in action attended the 1918 World Series between the Chicago Cubs and the Boston Red Sox. As part of the plan to shorten the season, the series started on 5 September instead of its usual time in late September or early October. The presence of the wounded soldiers in the stands seemed to have inspired patriotism in all present at one game. When it came time for the seventh-inning stretch, the band played the "Star Spangled Banner." Soon the entire audience was singing—a triumph for patriotism. Unfortunately, the level of patriotism did not reach down into the clubhouses of the participating teams. Low attendance at games had caused a drop in ticket prices throughout the year, and the World Series was no different. Now, with a good portion of the gate receipts being promised to various war charities, each player's share would be only about $1, 000. As a result, the players from both teams threatened to quit before game 5 of the Series. It appears that a strike was avoided only after a "florid clubhouse speech" by American League president Ban Johnson, who "managed to bully and cajole the two teams into continuing the Series."[15] After nearly an hour's delay in starting, the players finally appeared on the field and began the game. Harry Hooper, right fielder for the Sox, was the first player to take the field, and it was left to him to make a public statement:

> "We will play, " he said, speaking for both teams, "not because we think we are getting a fair deal, because we are not. But we'll play for the sake of the game, for the sake of the public which has always given us its loyal support, and for the sake of the wounded soldiers and sailors who are in the grandstand waiting for us."[16]

Fair deal or not, the game went on, and the Cubs managed to avoid World Series defeat by winning the game three to zero. Ultimately, on 11 September, the Red Sox won game 6 and the 1918 World Series. Unfortunately, the bad blood and mistrust between ballplayers and owners would be manifested even more the following year and was one of the significant underlying causes of the 1919 "Black Sox" scandal.

A Bad Month for Baseball (October 1918)

The Meuse-Argonne Offensive—the largest land battle in American history—began on 26 September 1918. The US First Army, with 1.2 million Doughboys either preparing to attack or in tactical reserve, had the task of breaking the Hindenburg Line at some of its most heavily defended areas. Another 600, 000 Doughboys were on hand to provide logistical support for the attacking soldiers.

Leading one of the attacking companies of the 307th Infantry Regiment, 77th Division, was former major leaguer Capt. Edward Grant. Grant had attended a civilian readiness training camp before the war, and the Army quickly recognized his leadership skills. During his baseball career, Grant had played in more than 1, 000 major-league games and had compiled a career batting average of .249. None of that mattered on 5 October, as Grant led his company forward trying to pierce the German defenses and rescue the famed "Lost Battalion, " a unit from his own division. Grant was killed by German artillery fire as he led his men. He was the first major-league ballplayer to be killed in action during the war. The New York Giants erected a monument in his honor at their Polo Grounds stadium, but unfortunately it was demolished along with the stadium in 1964. Grant continues to be honored by the Edward L. Grant Highway, which remains in use today in the Bronx, not far from Yankee Stadium.[17]

Just a few days after Grant's death, and close to where he was killed, two former minor leaguers and battery mates, Cpl. Bernard Leo Dolan and Sgt. Matthew S. Lanigan, were serving with the 78th Division. On 16 October, both men were killed in action while attacking German positions near the Aire River. Lanigan's hometown newspaper later reported their deaths and wrote that the two were "inseparable pals. In the army they were allotted places in ranks side by side and thus they went into the battles in France."[18] Like Eddie Grant, they too now rest in the Meuse-Argonne American Cemetery.

Although not taking part in the offensive, Lt. Alexander Thomson "Tom" Burr, a former Yankee outfielder, was undergoing gunnery training as a pilot in the 31st Aero Squadron in France. On 12 October, his aircraft collided with another aircraft and Burr was killed. The same day Harry M. Glenn, a former catcher with the St Louis Cardinals, died of the Spanish flu while in training to be an Army aircraft mechanic in Minnesota. In all, it had been a bad month for baseball.

Eddie Grant, seen here in a Cincinnati Reds uniform, was the first, and most prominent, former major-league ballplayer to be killed in action during the war. Grant had already retired from baseball when war was declared. Because of his previous attendance at an officer-training camp, Grant was inducted into the Army as an infantry captain in the 307th Infantry Regiment. *Courtesy of Library of Congress*

This version of Form AGO 84-C records the facts of Capt. Edward Grant's service in the Army and his death in combat during the Meuse-Argonne Offensive in October 1918. Note that Grant's date of death is listed as 9 October. Most other sources, including his grave stone in the Meuse-Argonne cemetery, list his death date as 5 October. *Courtesy of New York, Abstracts of World War I Military Service, via Ancestry.com*

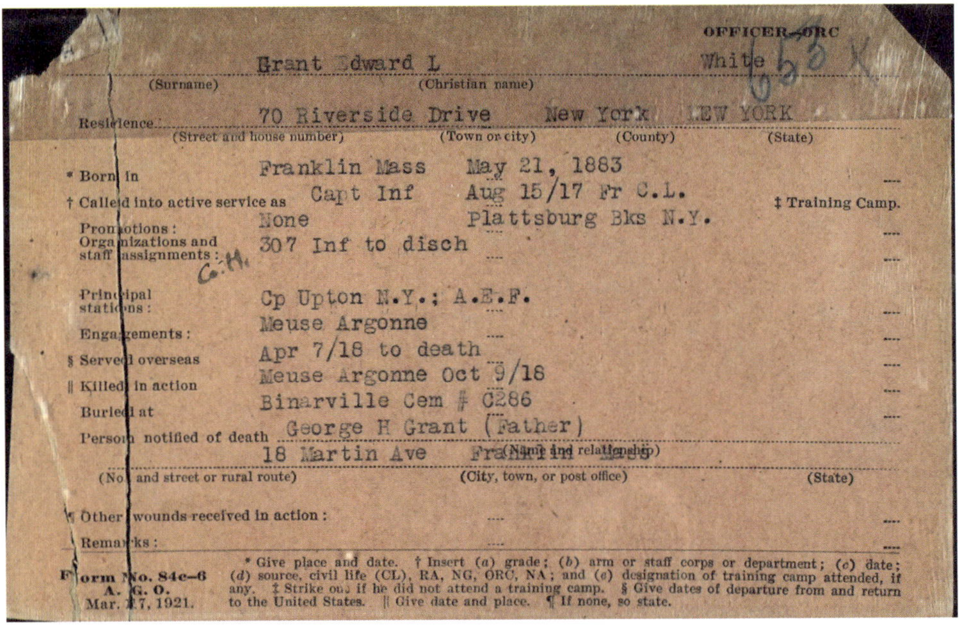

OFFICER—ORC

Grant Edward L (Surname) (Christian name) White

Residence: 70 Riverside Drive (Street and house number) New York (Town or city) (County) NEW YORK (State)

* Born in: Franklin Mass May 21, 1883

† Called into active service as: Capt Inf Aug 15/17 Fr C.L. ‡ Training Camp. Plattsburg Bks N.Y.

Promotions: None

Organizations and staff assignments: 307 Inf to disch

Principal stations: Cp Upton N.Y.; A.E.F.

Engagements: Meuse Argonne

§ Served overseas: Apr 7/18 to death

‖ Killed in action: Meuse Argonne Oct 9/18

Buried at: Binarville Cem # C286

Person notified of death: George H Grant (Father) (Name and relationship)

18 Martin Ave (No. and street or rural route) Franklin Mass (City, town, or post office) (State)

¶ Other wounds received in action:

Remarks:

Form No. 84c–6 A. G. O. Mar. 17, 1921.

* Give place and date. † Insert (*a*) grade; (*b*) arm or staff corps or department; (*c*) date; (*d*) source, civil life (CL), RA, NG, ORC, NA; and (*e*) designation of training camp attended, if any. ‡ Strike out if he did not attend a training camp. § Give dates of departure from and return to the United States. ‖ Give date and place. ¶ If none, so state.

Gas!

Perhaps among the most-terrible aspects of the Great War—and there were many—was the advent of gas warfare. The battlefields of northern Europe were particularly well suited for the use of gas. The various forms of the deadly weapon, such as chlorine, phosgene, and mustard gas, were heavier than air, and after being dispersed across enemy lines, the gases tended to remain in low-lying areas, such as trenches and shell holes, much longer than anticipated. The inclement weather in late 1918 also contributed to keeping the gases at ground level where the troops were. As a result, many Doughboys encountered heavier concentrations of the gases than their training or rudimentary protective equipment could handle. It was estimated that over 72, 000 Doughboys were wounded in gas attacks by Germans or through accidental exposure. Included in that total were a number of ballplayers: former Washington

Senators pitcher Charlie Becker, former Pirates infielder Oran Dodd, New York Giants and Hall of Fame pitcher Christy Mathewson, Philadelphia Athletics pitcher Marsh Williams, Negro League pitcher Tony Mahoney, and Red Ormsby, a former pitcher who would later become an American League umpire. Although none of these men were killed directly by their exposure to gas attacks, almost all died within ten years of the end of the war from the lingering effects of gas.[19]

Christopher "Christy" Mathewson had finished his playing days and was managing the Cincinnati Reds in 1918, when he decided to join the Army. Perhaps among the three most famous major leaguers to be in the AEF in France, Christy Mathewson served in a Chemical Warfare Service unit with Ty Cobb and Branch Rickey. *Courtesy of Library of Congress*

Certainly an unusual sight for baseball fans of the period, Capt. Christy Mathewson is seen here in his US Army uniform instead of a more familiar New York Giants uniform. *Courtesy of US Army*

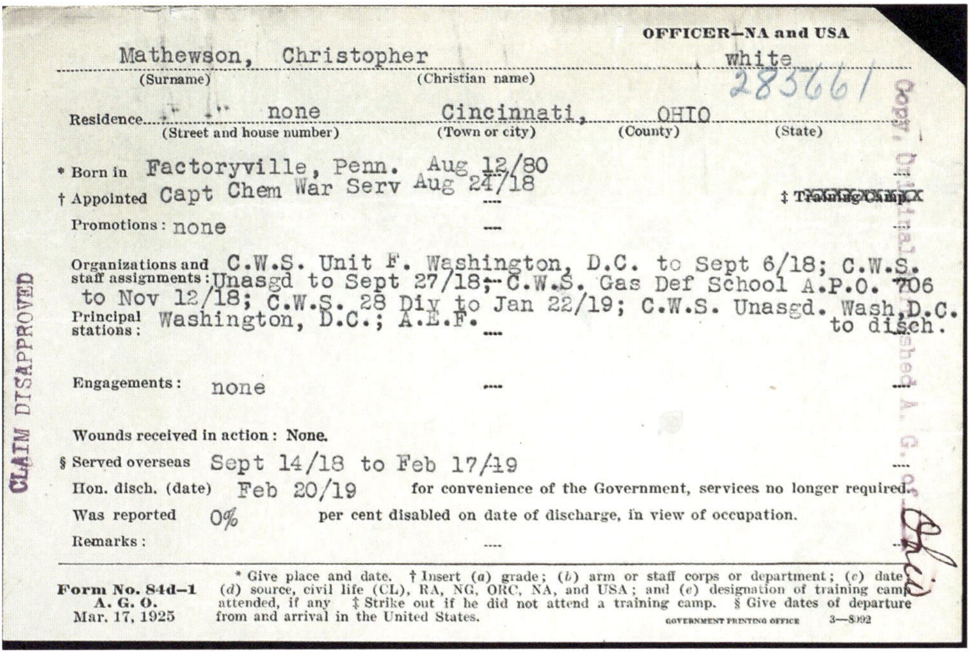

OFFICER—NA and USA

Mathewson, Christopher — white
(Surname) (Christian name)

283661

Residence ... none — Cincinnati, — OHIO
(Street and house number) (Town or city) (County) (State)

* Born in Factoryville, Penn. Aug 12/80

† Appointed Capt Chem War Serv Aug 24/18

‡ ~~Training Camp~~ XXXXXXXXX

Promotions: none

Organizations and staff assignments: C.W.S. Unit F. Washington, D.C. to Sept 6/18; C.W.S. Unasgd to Sept 27/18; C.W.S. Gas Def School A.P.O. 706 to Nov 12/18; C.W.S. 28 Div to Jan 22/19; C.W.S. Unasgd. Wash,D.C. to disch.

Principal stations: Washington, D.C.; A.E.F.

Engagements: none

Wounds received in action: None.

§ Served overseas Sept 14/18 to Feb 17/19

Hon. disch. (date) Feb 20/19 for convenience of the Government, services no longer required.

Was reported 0% per cent disabled on date of discharge, in view of occupation.

Remarks:

CLAIM DISAPPROVED

Copy, Original Furnished A. G. O.

Form No. 84d–1
A. G. O.
Mar. 17, 1925

* Give place and date. † Insert (a) grade; (b) arm or staff corps or department; (c) date; (d) source, civil life (CL), RA, NG, ORC, NA, and USA; and (e) designation of training camp attended, if any ‡ Strike out if he did not attend a training camp. § Give dates of departure from and arrival in the United States.

GOVERNMENT PRINTING OFFICE 3—8992

The war service card for Christy Mathewson. While this card lists all of Mathewson's different assignments in the Chemical Warfare Service (CWS), it fails to mention that he was accidentally exposed to mustard gas. He would suffer severely from that exposure the remainder of his life. *Courtesy* of *Pennsylvania, WWI Veterans Service and Compensation Files, via Ancestry.com*

A typical uniform and collar insignia for an officer serving in the US Army Chemical Warfare Service in France in 1918. Because of Branch Rickey's influence, at least four other future Baseball Hall of Famers—Ty Cobb, Christy Mathewson, Eppa Rixey, and George Sisler—served in that branch of the Army during the war.

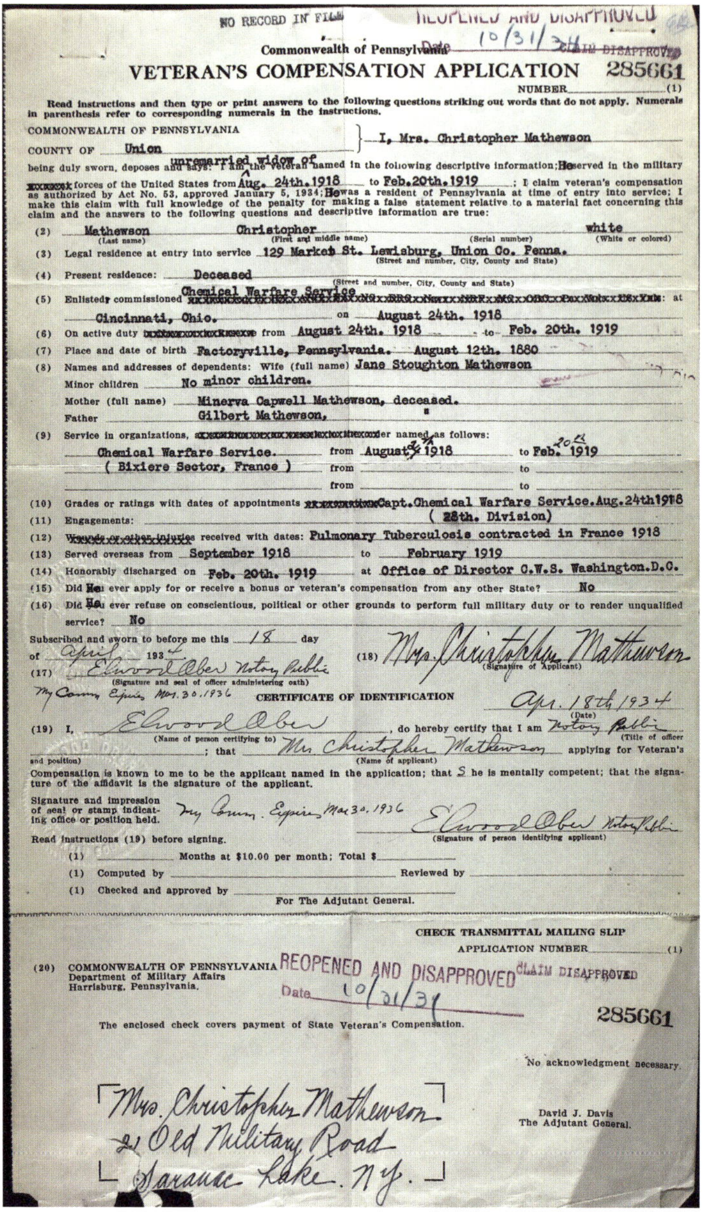

NO RECORD IN FILE — REOPENED AND DISAPPROVED — Date 10/31/34 — CLAIM DISAPPROVED

Commonwealth of Pennsylvania

VETERAN'S COMPENSATION APPLICATION 285661

NUMBER (1)

Read instructions and then type or print answers to the following questions striking out words that do not apply. Numerals in parenthesis refer to corresponding numerals in the instructions.

COMMONWEALTH OF PENNSYLVANIA
COUNTY OF Union } I, Mrs. Christopher Mathewson

being duly sworn, deposes and says: unremarried widow of the veteran named in the following descriptive information; He served in the military forces of the United States from Aug. 24th. 1918 to Feb. 20th. 1919; I claim veteran's compensation as authorized by Act No. 53, approved January 5, 1934; He was a resident of Pennsylvania at time of entry into service; I make this claim with full knowledge of the penalty for making a false statement relative to a material fact concerning this claim and the answers to the following questions and descriptive information are true:

(2) Mathewson (Last name) Christopher (First and middle name) (Serial number) white (White or colored)

(3) Legal residence at entry into service 129 Market St. Lewisburg, Union Co. Penna. (Street and number, City, County and State)

(4) Present residence: Deceased (Street and number, City, County and State)

(5) Enlisted commissioned Chemical Warfare Service at Cincinnati, Ohio. on August 24th. 1918

(6) On active duty from August 24th. 1918 to Feb. 20th. 1919

(7) Place and date of birth Factoryville, Pennsylvania. August 12th. 1880

(8) Names and addresses of dependents: Wife (full name) Jane Stoughton Mathewson
Minor children No minor children.
Mother (full name) Minerva Capwell Mathewson, deceased.
Father Gilbert Mathewson,

(9) Service in organizations, under named as follows:
Chemical Warfare Service. from August 24 1918 to Feb. 20 1919
(Bixiere Sector, France) from to
from to

(10) Grades or ratings with dates of appointments Capt. Chemical Warfare Service. Aug. 24th 1918

(11) Engagements: (28th. Division)

(12) Wounds or other injuries received with dates: Pulmonary Tuberculosis contracted in France 1918

(13) Served overseas from September 1918 to February 1919

(14) Honorably discharged on Feb. 20th. 1919 at Office of Director C.W.S. Washington. D.C.

(15) Did He ever apply for or receive a bonus or veteran's compensation from any other State? No

(16) Did He ever refuse on conscientious, political or other grounds to perform full military duty or to render unqualified service? No

Subscribed and sworn to before me this 18 day of April 1934

(17) Elwood Ober Notary Public (Signature and seal of officer administering oath)
My Comm. Expires Mar. 30. 1936

(18) Mrs. Christopher Mathewson (Signature of Applicant)

CERTIFICATE OF IDENTIFICATION Apr. 18th 1934 (Date)

(19) I, Elwood Ober (Name of person certifying to), do hereby certify that I am Notary Public (Title of officer and position); that Mrs. Christopher Mathewson (Name of applicant) applying for Veteran's Compensation is known to me to be the applicant named in the application; that She is mentally competent; that the signature of the affidavit is the signature of the applicant.

Signature and impression of seal or stamp indicating office or position held. My Comm. Expires Mar 30. 1936 Elwood Ober Notary Public (Signature of person identifying applicant)

Read instructions (19) before signing.

(1) Months at $10.00 per month; Total $
(1) Computed by Reviewed by
(1) Checked and approved by
For The Adjutant General.

CHECK TRANSMITTAL MAILING SLIP
APPLICATION NUMBER (1)

(20) COMMONWEALTH OF PENNSYLVANIA
Department of Military Affairs
Harrisburg, Pennsylvania.

REOPENED AND DISAPPROVED CLAIM DISAPPROVED
Date 10/31/34

285661

The enclosed check covers payment of State Veteran's Compensation.

No acknowledgment necessary.

Mrs. Christopher Mathewson
21 Old Military Road
Saranac Lake. N.Y.

David J. Davis
The Adjutant General.

Although Christy Mathewson did not die from his exposure to gas, his life was no doubt shortened by it, and he passed away in 1925. In 1934, his widow filed a claim for Veterans Compensation with the state of Pennsylvania. The usual compensation was ten dollars for each month served; with Mathewson's eight months of service in the United States and France, his widow should have received eighty dollars. For some undisclosed reason her claim for the money was denied. *Courtesy of Pennsylvania, WWI Veterans Service and Compensation Files, via Ancestry.com*

The Spanish Flu

The world of 1917 and 1918 was a dangerous place, even discounting the inherent danger from being killed or wounded in combat. There were other ways besides being wounded in action in which a Doughboy could end up requiring hospitalization, including such things as work-related or training accidents, exposure to a venereal disease, or exposure to other contagious diseases such as meningitis, the mumps, the flu, and pneumonia. This last category—contagious nonvenereal diseases—was by far the largest and affected the most Doughboys. Flu and associated pneumonia proved as deadly as German gunfire. What made this version of the flu and subsequent pneumonia so deadly in comparison to earlier flu epidemics was that it appeared to specifically target healthy young adults. Most previous flu epidemics were deadliest for infants and those over sixty-five; this strain was particularly lethal for those in the twenty to thirty-five age group. This was the exact group that most heavily populated the Army, Navy, and Marine Corps in the United States and France.

In September 1918, the new strain of flu hit the East Coast training camps of Devens, Dix, Meade, Humphreys, and Lee, then migrated to Grant, Sherman, Riley, and Pike while moving westward and southward. This version was dramatically much more fatal than the version that arrived earlier in the year. By the end of September, the situation was bad and getting worse. On 24 September 1918, twenty-five of the training sites across the United States reported having flu patients. Just three days later, Army Chief of Staff Gen. Peyton March ordered the delay of draftee call-ups who were scheduled for October. It was simply too dangerous to send men to the camps where they might become infected, and conversely, it would be imprudent to send potentially infected men to training sites not yet affected.

As a result of the epidemic during October 1918, it seemed that Doughboys in France fighting in the Meuse-Argonne had a better chance of surviving the war than the soldiers training in the East Coast or midwestern camps. Overcrowding in these camps exacerbated the problem as the epidemic swept through the eastern half of the United States and into the heart of the country. Among the thousands of soldiers who died in training camps during the pandemic were a number of professional ballplayers, including former St. Louis Cardinal catcher Harry Glenn and former Chicago White Sox and Boston Braves outfielder La Verne Ashford "Larry" Chappell, who died just three days before the Armistice was signed. Negro League star third baseman Arthur Kimbro and three minor-league players—Ralph Worrell (International League), Harry Acton (Central League), and John Inglis (New York State League)—also died from the disease.[20] As we have seen, even the mighty Babe Ruth was not immune. While en route to his war service job he became sick after exposure to the flu but fortunately survived the encounter.

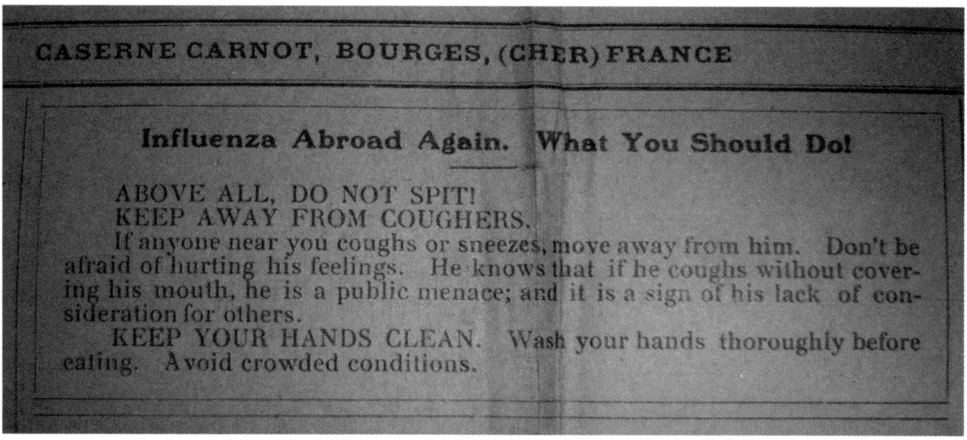

CASERNE CARNOT, BOURGES, (CHER) FRANCE

Influenza Abroad Again. What You Should Do!

ABOVE ALL, DO NOT SPIT!
KEEP AWAY FROM COUGHERS.
If anyone near you coughs or sneezes, move away from him. Don't be afraid of hurting his feelings. He knows that if he coughs without covering his mouth, he is a public menace; and it is a sign of his lack of consideration for others.
KEEP YOUR HANDS CLEAN. Wash your hands thoroughly before eating. Avoid crowded conditions.

With the shooting war ending in France, another dangerous enemy was making an appearance in all the Army camps and bases: the Spanish flu. The instructions are clear and definitive—stay away from anyone who might infect you with the deadly disease. More American soldiers would die from the flu pandemic than from German gunfire.

The Marine Corps: "First to Fight" and a Baseball Powerhouse?

The United States Marine Corps has long enjoyed its reputation as a fighting force to be wary of crossing. Its performance in combat at Belleau Wood, at Blanc Mont, and in the Argonne did much to cement that reputation in US military history. What is less well known is that the Marine Corps also fielded some impressive baseball teams during the Great War. Perhaps the most illustrious of these teams is the one that was put together by Brig. Gen. Smedley Butler while he was serving as commandant at Quantico. Among the players on the Marine team were such well-known pitchers as Emmett "Red" Ormsby, a highly regarded minor-league hurler; Michael "Mike" Cantwell of the New York Yankees; William I. "Billy" Burke of the Boston Braves; and a crafty little left-hander, Earl Hamilton, from the Pittsburgh Pirates. Battery mate for this imposing staff of pitchers was Jay "Nig" Clarke, a renowned catcher and a formidable hitter from the Cleveland Indians. The infield and outfield consisted of a number of former minor leaguers and college ballplayers. Among the college players was a power-hitting first baseman from Villanova named Pasquarella who earlier helped the Marines beat the Philadelphia Athletics in an exhibition game by hitting two home runs. The Marine Corps team was captained by longtime St. Louis Cardinal second baseman John "Dots" Miller. Miller had also made an impression on his Marine Corps comrades by qualifying as an expert marksman while training at Parris Island.[21]

The Quantico team became so well known that in June 1918, they were challenged to play a double header against two different handpicked Navy teams in Washington, DC. Also on hand for the games was the Marine Corps band, and it was expected that a company of Marines would also entertain the crowd with a close-order-drill exhibition.[22] While the results of those games are lost to history, what is known is that the majority of the Marine team would shortly thereafter be serving in the 5th Marine Brigade in France. One member of the team, Red Ormsby, would be exposed to gas while there. The long-term effects of this exposure effectively ended his pitching career and put him on the path to becoming an American League umpire for almost twenty years.[23]

Not wanting to be outdone by Quantico, the Marine Corps Recruit Depot at Mare Island, California, also put together a ball club of minor-league and college players. Topping off their undefeated season, they defeated the highly regarded team from the University of California by a score of four to three.[24]

The Eternal Triangle—Baseball Style

Sometimes the smooth, orderly flow of a ball game could be rudely interrupted. This happened in the middle of a game in Trier, Germany, in May 1919. As one of the soldiers was preparing to bat, an angry German man accosted him. As the local man berated the soldier in German, it soon became obvious to all witnesses that the soldier had won the affections of the German man's girlfriend. Making matters worse, she was among the crowd watching the game. After a short period of listening to the abusive language, the Doughboy practiced his swing and connected with the angry man's head, knocking him to the ground. Fortunately no serious damage was done, and a local medic also present at the game managed to bandage the German boyfriend's head. The vivid lesson for the local citizenry was not to confront a soldier while he was awaiting his turn to bat. The *AMAROC News* later wrote:

> It is to be hoped in the interest of peace and good feeling, that *frauleins*, when attending ball games in the future will . . . make their eyes behave . . . because it leads to a great waste of batting energy which could be more profitably applied to the game. The swing which landed in this instance would have easily sent the ball out of the grounds.[25]

Even Army Aviators Have a Sense of Humor

As part of the war reparations under the 11 November 1918 Armistice, the Germans were required to hand over a number of their aircraft to each of the Allied armies. During the first months of occupation duty, whenever there was good flying weather the pilots of the Army Air Service enjoyed "test flying" these enemy planes, as well as putting their own aircraft on display. As a result, the Doughboys were used to seeing aircraft performing stunts over the Rhine River and nearby US airfields. It even became fairly commonplace to see airplanes flying under the Pfaffendorf Bridge just south of Coblenz. Unfortunately, there were a large number of fatal and near-fatal crashes as a result of these impromptu air shows.

In July 1919, during a baseball game at the 1st Division's Rhinebrohl diamond on the east side of the Rhine River, an airplane flew over the field. The few soldiers who bothered to look up were shocked to see a man fall out of the plane and hurtle toward the ground. The spectators hurried to the area where it appeared the unfortunate man would land, but were surprised to discover that the falling figure was really just a dummy. The pilot then circled the field and came in to a short landing. He picked up his dummy and stuffed him back into the plane. With no explanation, he "thanked everybody for their kind attention" and took off again, leaving the ballplayers in wonder.[26]

Baseball Can Be Hazardous to Your Health

The 23 May 1919 edition of the *AMAROC News* reported that "for the fourth time in the last three weeks, an American soldier" had suffered a broken arm from playing baseball. Referring to the four soldiers as the "S.O.L. squad" (short for "shit out of luck, " a popular Doughboy phrase of the period), the newspaper identified the most recent sufferer as Pvt. Allen Spears of the 1st Division. The paper also laid the blame for the increased injuries on comments by Bill "Rowdy Bill" Coughlin, a former major-league baseball player who was serving in the occupation of Germany, employed by the Knights of Columbus to teach umpiring to the soldiers of the Third Army.

Coughlin reportedly said that "a lot of the Yanks over here [in Germany] were going to break into the big leagues if they kept in shape and continued to show the same baseball at home as they did over here."[27] The newspaper offered the opinion that the injury problem stemmed therefore from Army ballplayers trying so hard to improve their skills that they were hurting themselves. The paper also ventured the opinion that soldiers had been using their "imagination and figured that the ball was a grenade and the catcher was a German with a bayonet, " and so were overextending themselves by throwing too hard. Whether or not Rowdy Bill's encouraging words were responsible for the injuries was never proven. One thing is obvious: he knew baseball. By 1920, Coughlin was head coach of the baseball team at Lafayette College in Pennsylvania, a position he held for the next twenty-three years. During that period the team suffered only one losing season. There is no record of any of his players breaking their arms by throwing too hard.

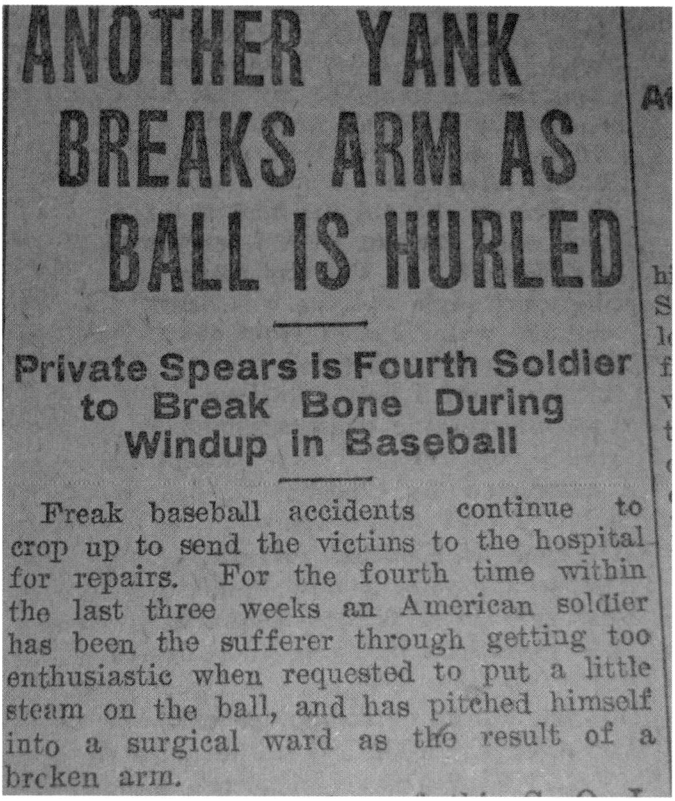

ANOTHER YANK BREAKS ARM AS BALL IS HURLED

Private Spears is Fourth Soldier to Break Bone During Windup in Baseball

Freak baseball accidents continue to crop up to send the victims to the hospital for repairs. For the fourth time within the last three weeks an American soldier has been the sufferer through getting too enthusiastic when requested to put a little steam on the ball, and has pitched himself into a surgical ward as the result of a broken arm.

Baseball, the way Doughboys played it, was a very physically demanding game. This clipping from the 1 July 1919 edition of the *AMAROC News* shows that baseball-related injuries were becoming a common occurrence in the Army of Occupation.

Baseball Player and Medal of Honor Recipient

Arthur J. Forrest was born in St. Louis, Missouri, in May 1895, although some sources give a birth year of 1896 or 1897. In 1917, Forrest played for the Hannibal (Missouri) Mules and the Quincy (Illinois) Gems, both teams in the Triple-I League. Forrest was living in Hannibal when he was drafted in September 1917. He reported as ordered to Camp Funston and was assigned to Company D, 354th Infantry Regiment, 89th Division. By the time Forrest went overseas with his regiment in June 1918, he had been promoted to sergeant. During the vicious fighting in the Meuse-Argonne Offensive, Forrest earned the Medal of Honor. His Medal of Honor citation reads in part:

> When the advance of his company was stopped by bursts of fire from a nest of 6 enemy machine guns, without being discovered, he worked his way single-handed to a point within 50 yards of the machine gun nest. Charging, single-handed, he drove out the enemy in disorder, thereby protecting the advance platoon from annihilating fire, and permitting the resumption of the advance of this company.[28]

He was also awarded the Montenegrin Bravery Medal and the French *Croix de Guerre*. With the Armistice signed, his division became part of the Army of Occupation in the German Rhineland.[29] After the war, Forrest played as a catcher for ten seasons on various minor-league teams; he never rose higher than Class AA. When he finally gave up his baseball career, he went to work for the Veterans Administration. Forrest died in November 1964.

9th Inning

Home Field at Last

With the signing of the Armistice on 11 November 1918, the guns fell silent on the western front after more than four years of fighting. The war had been fought on land, in the air, and at sea. In the four-hundred-mile-long trench lines stretching from the Swiss border to the Belgian coast, every possible combination of Allied forces fought the Central Forces. Men from North Africa, Cambodia, and Canada fought Austro-Hungarians from Croatia and Galatia. French, Australian, New Zealand, and British soldiers had fought Germans and Turks in the Dardanelles. Working together, British and Japanese soldiers had captured the German territory of Kiautschou in China. Italians fought Austrians and Germans in the mountains of the Alps so many times they began to give the campaigns numbers. British, French, and Belgian soldiers fought the Germans in West Africa and seized their colonies in Togo and the Cameroons. Portuguese, British, and Indian soldiers fought Germans and their African colonial soldiers throughout East Africa. The British navy had sunk a German warship in the Rufiji River in Africa. The German navy and the British navy battled to a draw at Jutland.

Even after the Armistice the fighting continued in some places. Red Russians fought White Russians and their British, French, Japanese, Chinese, and American allies along the rail lines of Siberia. Americans, British, French, Canadian, and Italian soldiers fought Bolsheviks in northern Russia. Red Russians invaded Poland and fought the Poles' newly formed army consisting of ethnic Poles and some American supporters. Inside the vast spaces of Russia, a desperate force known as the Czech Legion fought the Germans, Russians, and anyone else in their way as they moved eastward, looking for a way to return to their homes. The list of the combatants could extend much longer, but for the purpose of our story, this is certainly enough. Most importantly, having done exactly what President Wilson had asked of them—beat the Germans and make the "world safe for Democracy"—the Doughboys just wanted to go home. For them, it was time to enjoy being the victors in the greatest war in history.

Notably, and to their surprise, the United States had changed in their absence. Prohibition would soon become the law of the land, and the Doughboys' newly acquired thirst for French *vin* and German *bier* would go unquenched. They would also soon discover that their heroic deeds at Belleau Wood, along the Marne, and in the Meuse-Argonne were of little interest to a country that was now moving quickly into the "Roaring '20s." Some African American and foreign-born Doughboys would find that wearing a United States Army or Navy uniform was

Using team names such as "Gassers" and "Shell Shockers," these Doughboys are playing baseball as part of their convalescent program. The umpire in this January 1919 photograph is a Red Cross officer standing behind the pitcher. Although there are very few spectators, they have managed to attract the attention of two Red Cross nurses and what appears to be a work party on the far side of the fence. *Courtesy of National Archives*

no shield against prejudice. Even that last bastion of stability and tradition, big-league baseball, would be shaken to its core with the taint of gambling, fixed games, and the "Black Sox Scandal."

Ironically, some of the root causes for the scandal lay in the Great War. Shortening the 1918 major-league baseball season had cost many players money because the team owners had shortened their paychecks an equal amount. Some members of the Chicago White Sox were angered and disgusted with this loss of pay. The Sox players were further agitated when team owner Charles Comiskey

> publicly embarrassed players who sought war-related work instead of enlisting in the armed forces. Repeatedly, he called such men "slackers" and questioned their manhood. . . . Comiskey reviled his players not only in private conversations but sought the newspapers to air his opinions.[1]

Some of these pay-shortened and insulted players later became involved in the conspiracy to throw the World Series. Another potential contributor to the scandal also had Great War roots: the closing of racetracks as a war-related measure. Sporting events have always been a favorite of gamblers, and now one of their most favorite venues, the racetrack, was closed to them. As a result, it did not take long for baseball to become an even-bigger target than previously for professional betting.[2]

But the baseball scandal, like Prohibition, still lay ahead for the Doughboys who were anxiously awaiting their return to the United States. In November 1918, there were more than two million soldiers in the AEF in France. There were another two million in training camps in the United States, either finishing their training or waiting for transportation to France. Even with a quarter million of his soldiers taking part in the occupation of the German Rhineland, Gen. Pershing still had a significantly large force that needed to be sent back to the Unites States for demobilization. The AEF was a money-consuming machine. Every day it remained in France meant more mouths to be fed and more salaries to be paid by American taxpayers. It had taken seventeen months to transport the AEF to France. Now, most Americans wondered how long it would take to bring all of them home. Of course, for the individual Doughboy, the question was much more personal: "When do I get to go home?" The answer they all received was the same: "Soon, but not yet."

First, the soldiers still in stateside training camps or at transit camps on the East Coast had to be demobilized to make room for returning AEF soldiers. Some of the stateside men had been in training for over a year, while others had been in camp less than a week. Regardless of their time in training, they all needed to be given a physical, a final tally of pay they were owed, and then transportation home.

Army Chief of Staff Gen. Peyton March moved quickly. On 11 November 1918, he halted the ongoing mobilization process, which was still bringing men into the Army. He also canceled all further draft calls. Just five days later, he ordered the immediate discharge of 98, 189 men in the seventy-one

More Doughboy humor, this cartoon from the *Stars and Stripes* shows the one athletic event all the soldiers would like to take part in: the long jump that will bring them home again.

development battalions in camps scattered around the country. These development battalions had been organized at every major training site to serve as home units for men who required additional help or training before they could be assigned to an actual unit.

Next in line for disbandment were the 30, 000 soldiers assigned to lumber units in the Northwest who were milling materials for aircraft. Another 30, 000 "light duty" soldiers in the US guards battalions were also discharged. Altogether these orders quickly resulted in the discharge of almost 200, 000 men, but there still remained many thousands more in the training camps.

As this was taking place, March ordered Pershing to send home those units in France that were "no longer needed" as soon as "transportation could be secured."[3] Every available ship that could be found was pressed into service to bring the Doughboys home. Even US Navy cruisers and battleships were outfitted with rows of bunks and used as troop transports. Helping out to some degree by making the voyages home shorter was the fact the ships did not have to take antisubmarine measures this time and could sail directly to their designated ports of debarkation.

Those training and transit camps that were now designated to serve as demobilization centers also received guidance to establish their own demobilization operation, and they were to use personnel already serving at their sites. In spite of criticism both in the press and Congress about the slowness and problems of the demobilization, March remained convinced he was on the right track. He replied to his critics that "I wish to make it clear that demobilization is not proceeding haphazardly, but in accordance with a very definite and considered policy."[4] He also pointed out that the United States had demobilized 732, 766 men during the 11 November 1918–4 January 1919 period. This was more than twice the number for Great Britain in the same period. By 1 May 1919, the US demobilization figure stood at nearly two million. Just five months later, that number would be nearly doubled. By then AEF no longer existed, except for 20, 000 soldiers in Germany, 6, 000 soldiers still in North Russia and Siberia, and several hundred officers and enlisted men working in France. This last group of soldiers was needed to handle burials, graves registration, and the various administrative

While all the Doughboys were happy to be headed home to return to civilian life, it is important to remember that there were still US military personnel on duty in foreign countries around the world, including this Marine Corps baseball team in the Dominican Republic.

duties involved in selling off excess materiel no longer needed by the Army. The last of the AEF Doughboys from France returned to the United States in January 1920.

And what did the Doughboys leave behind? Much of the military equipment such as trucks, railcars, and tools that either had been purchased in Europe or transported from the US was sold to European nations. The nations were in desperate need of such items to rebuild their war-shattered economies and infrastructure. The trains and tracks of the French rail system were barely functioning in 1919 due to years of overuse and undermaintenance. Particularly important to France were the locomotives, rail cars, and track repair equipment from the US Army railway engineer and transportation units. Other industries in Europe desperately needed lumber and sawmill tools from the US Army forestry units. Thousands of motor vehicles of all types were also sold to local businesses to reduce the amount of material being sent back to America.

Mrs. Edith Bolling Wilson, President Woodrow Wilson, Secretary of War Newton Baker, and an unidentified US Army officer stand for the National Anthem at an Army-Navy baseball game in Washington in 1919. This would be one of the few relaxing moments in 1919 for the president, as he would spend a great deal of time and effort personally attempting to convince the US Congress and the American people that the Treaty of Versailles was a good and fair document. Both his health and his reputation would suffer as a result. *Courtesy of Library of Congress*

Two other interesting "leave behinds" from the American presence in France were jazz and "draw poker, " both now very popular in Europe and distinctly American inventions. Along with those two cultural gifts, some Doughboys introduced another old American tradition to Europe: train robbery. In September 1919, two Doughboys who were absent without leave (AWOL) went on a crime spree that included robbing passenger trains and shooting to death a Luxembourg man who tried to intervene. Dressed unimaginatively in army uniforms and wearing masks, they robbed two trains near the Luxembourg-German border before being caught and returned to the US Army for punishment.[5]

Drawing as much attention as President Warren G. Harding, Gen. Pershing shakes hands with the president at a baseball game in the early 1920s. By this time Pershing was serving as the Army chief of staff and had been promoted to a rank developed specifically for him: General of the Armies. *Courtesy of Library of Congress*

But what of baseball? One US Army unit history declared, "During the war more men in this country and in France were playing baseball than ever before in history—or since."[6] As we have seen, almost the first thing to be done by the AEF whenever establishing an Army camp was to lay out a baseball diamond. Even the *New York Times* reported that "Diamonds now abound where American Soldiers have passed." The *Times* writer then let his wishful thinking guide his next words:

> When the last of the American Doughboys leave the fields of France, Belgium, Luxembourg, and Germany for home, behind them will be hundreds of baseball diamonds cut in the countryside of these lands, and a host of people from all the nations intensely interested in a game that before the war was foreign and strange to them.[7]

He was wrong. Except for the small enclave of baseball fanaticism along the banks of the Rhine River, where the AFG remained until January 1923, the crack of the bat, stealing of bases, and calling of balls and strikes disappeared from Europe. What had been baseball diamonds and football gridirons were either abandoned or quickly converted to soccer fields and rugby pitches.

In an attempt to repair some of its damaged image, Major League Baseball declared that any soldier or sailor in US military hospitals would be given free admission to all games.[8] Professional ballplayers released from their military units or their war-related service quickly rejoined their clubs to prepare for the 1919 season.

Fortunately for all concerned, the late 1918 wave of Spanish flu that had devastated the civilian populations of New York, Baltimore, Philadelphia, Boston, and other large East Coast cities and towns moved westward across the country and had lessened in intensity the farther it went. Other successive waves of flu, while still deadly to some of those affected, were nowhere near as widespread. It was finally safe to return to baseball stadiums without too-much fear of contagion.

With war over, for the vast majority of Americans who did not suffer its lingering effects, as had Grover Cleveland Alexander and Christy Mathewson, things were looking up. As Donald Honig wrote in *Baseball America*:

> Nothing, it seemed, could stop or divert the old ball game, that pampered, nonideological American institution with its millions of custodians and defenders. The most a world war had done was snip a few games from the schedule and borrow some of its players for a while. And the immediate aftermath of [the Black Sox] scandal saw the game go rollicking into its gaudiest, most prosperous decade because the Black Sox scandal had proved that the game—the thing, the idea, the dream, and the vision—was near spiritual in this country.[9]

Although there was a 1919 baseball season, it was still playing catch-up, and the teams were trying to put their players back into baseball uniforms instead of US Army khaki or US Navy blue. The 1920 baseball season could therefore be considered the first true postwar season. By then, almost all the ballplayers who had been in the military were back with their teams and in better playing shape. Despite the 1921 trial of the Black Sox conspirators, baseball helped ease Americans back onto a peacetime footing. Still to come for baseball fans, including those thousands of baseball-crazy veterans, were the on-field heroics of Babe Ruth, Lou Gehrig, and the 1920s and 1930s Yankees. These great players were joined on the field by Hall of Fame-worthy exploits of Bill Terry, Mel Ott, Rogers Hornsby, Dizzy Dean, Hack Wilson, the Waner brothers, and a host of other great stars.

Baseball had limped along during the Great War, and it suffered a black eye with the Black Sox scandal, but in the end, it remained what it had always been: America's favorite game. No doubt many Doughboys, when they remembered their time in service, had better memories of the baseball field than the battlefield.

Although he did not serve in the US military during the war, choosing instead war service work, Babe Ruth belatedly joined the New York National Guard and posed in a borrowed uniform for this photograph with Gen. Pershing in 1921. *Courtesy of Library of Congress*

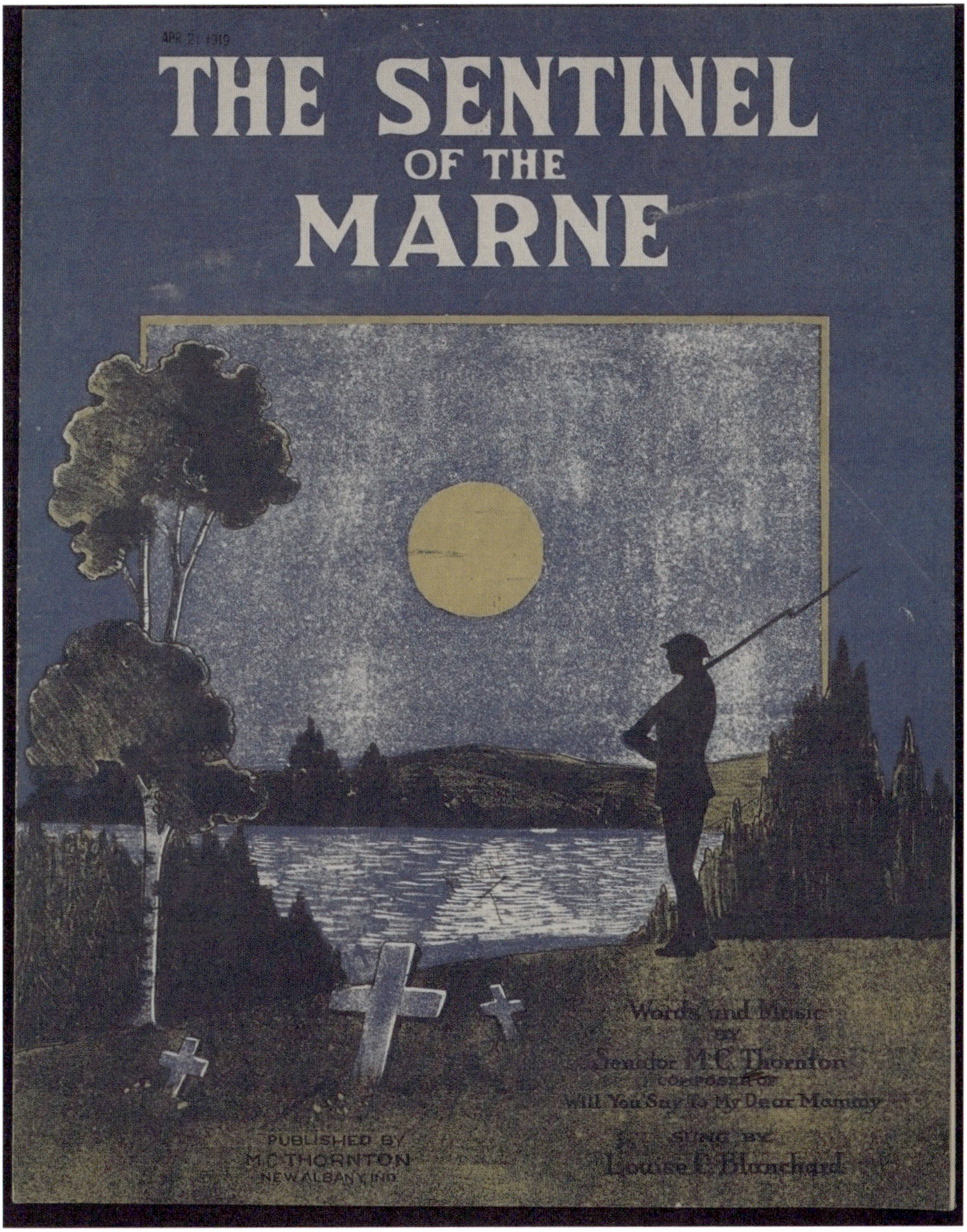

The postwar song "Sentinel of the Marne" was written to extoll the virtues of the American soldiers in France, but the rather melancholy words and cover art provide a poignant reminder that many US soldiers and Marines were in cemeteries in France, "sleeping in God's blessed keeping." *Courtesy of Library of Congress*

Home again, with the war and the Spanish flu epidemic behind them, the Doughboys turned their thoughts to baseball and the importance of a "squeeze play." Ironically, since baseball in the "twenties" featured a much-livelier ball, and batting averages and home-run production soared, tactics such as squeeze plays and bunts all but disappeared from the game for most of the decade.

A solemn reminder that not all the soldiers made the long jump home under their own power. These Doughboys are among the 200,000 soldiers who were wounded in action and now must play baseball with the assistance of hospital workers. *Courtesy of Library of Congress*

Notes

The Casey Stengel quote used in the dedication is from *Stengel: His Life and Times* by Robert W. Creamer, p. 166.

Foreword

1. *The CRO*, 16 April 1919.

2. Ibid.

1st Inning

1. Kal Wagenheim, *Babe Ruth: His Life and Legend* (New York: Praeger, 1974), 7.

2. Lawrence S. Ritter, *The Glory of Their Times* (New York: William Morrow, 1984), 33.

3. Ibid., 227.

4. Donald Honig, *Baseball America* (New York: Macmillan, 1985), 77.

5. Ritter, *The Glory*, 34.

6. Ibid., 186.

7. Ibid., 92.

8. Ibid., 66–67.

9. Honig, *Baseball America*, 78.

10. "Black Baseball's Negro Baseball Leagues, " blackbaseball.com.

11. Gerald F. Jacobsen, *History of the 107th Infantry* (New York: Seventh Regiment Armory, 1920), 3.

12. Daniel R. Beaver, *Newton D. Baker and the American War Effort, 1917–1919* (Lincoln: University of Nebraska Press, 1966), 30–31, referencing "The Papers of Tasker H. Bliss, " Library of Congress.

13. Leonard P. Ayers, *Source Records of the Great War*, ed. Charles F. Horne (New York: National Alumni, 1923), 14.

14. For more on foreign-born soldiers in the US military during World War I, see Alexander F. Barnes and Peter L. Belmonte, *Forgotten Soldiers of World War I: America's Immigrant Doughboys* (Atglen, PA: Schiffer, 2018).

15. John P. Cooper Jr., *The History of the 110th Field Artillery with Sketches of Related Units* (Baltimore: War Records Division, Maryland Historical Society, 1953), 43.

2nd Inning

1. "Sussex Incident, " www.britannica.com/event/Sussex-Incident#ref100986.

2. "The Zimmermann Telegram, " www.archives.gov/education/lessons/zimmermann.

3. "World War I Draft Registration Cards, " www.archives.gov/research/military/ww1/draft-registration.

4. Selective Service Act p. 3, 19 August 1918.

5. "The 1917 Season, " *New York Times*, 8 September 1912; National Pastime Museum. David Fultz was a multitalented individual who had starred on the Brown University baseball and football teams while earning a law degree. He played in the major leagues for the Philadelphia Phillies, the Philadelphia Athletics, and the New York Yankees (Highlanders). When the US entered the war, Fultz shut down his law business and joined the military to serve as a US Army officer.

6. "Year in Review: 1917 American League, " Baseball Almanac, www.baseball-almanac.com/yearly/yr1917a.shtml.

7. Ibid.

8. Peter L. Belmonte, review of Jim Leeke, *From Dugouts to the Trenches: Baseball During the Great War* (Lincoln: University of Nebraska Press, 2017); Roads to the Great War Blog, 4 July 2017, http://roadstothegreatwar-ww1.blogspot.com/2017/07/from-dugouts-to-trenches-baseball.html.

9. "On Account of War, " https://baseballhall.org/discover/short-stops/1918-world-war-i-baseball.

10. "1918: All Work or Fight and No Play, " www.thisgreatgame.com/1918-baseball-history.html.

11. US Provost Marshal General, *Final Report of the Provost General to the Secretary of War on the Operations of the Selective Service System to July 15, 1919* (Washington, DC: US Government Printing Office, 1920), 9.

12. *Stars and Stripes*, 28 June 1918.

13. *Stars and Stripes*, 19 July 1918.

14. *Stars and Stripes*, 13 June 1918.

15. "1918: All Work or Fight and No Play, " www.thisgreatgame.com/1918-baseball-history.html.

16. Brian McKenna, "Bethlehem Steel League, " https://sabr.org/bioproj/topic/bethlehem-steel-league.

17. Brig. Gen. Kenneth R. Wiggins Jr., *Delaware in World War I* (Charleston, SC: History Press, 2015), 54–55.

18. Ibid.

19. Ritter, *The Glory*, 291.

20. McKenna, "Bethlehem Steel League."

21. Wagenheim, *Babe Ruth*, 44–45.

3rd Inning

1. Ralph D. Cole and W. C. Howells, *The Thirty-Seventh Division in the World War, 1917–1918* (Columbus, OH: Thirty-Seventh Division Veterans Association, 1926), 258.

2. Raymond D. Fosdick and Edward F. Allen, *Keeping Our Fighters Fit for War and After* (Washington, DC: Commission on Training Camp Activities, 1918), 4–5.

3. Beaver, *Newton D. Baker*, 290.

4. American Library Association home page.

5. Fosdick and Allen, *Keeping Our Fighters Fit*, 8.

6. Ibid., 24.

7. Chaplain F. C. Reynolds and Chaplain William F. McLaughlin, *115th Infantry U.S.A. in the World War* (Baltimore: Read-Taylor, 1920), 53.

8. Fosdick and Allen, *Keeping Our Fighters Fit*, 51.

9. Ibid.

10. Reynolds and McLaughlin, *115th Infantry U.S.A.*, 55.

11. Cole and Howells, *Thirty-Seventh Division*, 259–260.

12. *Gas Attack of the New York Division* 1, no. 22 (20 April 1918): 10.

13. *Stars and Stripes*, 4 April 1918.

14. *Stars and Stripes*, 3 July 1918, and SABR website.

15. *Stars and Stripes*, 4 April 1918.

16. Ibid.

17. *Gas Attack of the New York Division* 1, no. 22 (20 April 1918): 10.

18. Arthur E. Barbeau and Florette Henri, *The Unknown Soldiers: Black American Troops in World War I* (Philadelphia: Temple University Press, 1974), 26–31.

19. George Wythe, *A History of the 90th Division* (New York: 90th Division Association, 1920), 7–9.

20. Fosdick and Allen, *Keeping Our Fighters Fit*, 54–55.

21. US War Department, *Commission on Training Camp Activities Report* (Washington, DC: US War Department, 1918), 11–13.

22. States Publication Society, *The Official History of the Eighty-Sixth Division* (Chicago: States Publication Society, 1921), 44.

23. *Stars and Stripes*, 23 June 1918.

24. Brian McKenna, *Early Exits* (Lanham, MD: Scarecrow, 2007), 18–19.

25. *Stars and Stripes*, 3 May 1918.

26. *New York Times*, 26 March 1918.

27. Robert W. Creamer, *Stengel: His Life and Times* (New York: Simon and Schuster, 1984), 125.

28. Edgar S. Gorrell, "History, Construction Co. No. 11, " Gorrell's History of the American Expeditionary Force Air Service, 1917–1919, US National Archives and Records Administration, RG120, Roll 0021, Series E, Vol. 25, Squadron Histories, 2.

29. Harold H. Burton, *600 Days' Service: A History of the 361st Infantry Regiment of the United States Army* (Portland, OR: James, Kerns & Abbott, 1921), 19.

4th Inning

1. John A. Cutchins, *An Amateur Diplomat in the World War* (Richmond, VA: American Legion, Commanders Committee, 1938), 68.

2. *New York Times*, 28 August 1919.

3. Ibid., 28 Aug 1919.

4. *Stars and Stripes*, 28 June 1918.

5. Col. Joseph H. Ford, *The Medical Department of the United States Army in the World War*, vol. 2 (Washington, DC: US Government Printing Office, 1927), 611–612.

6. James G. Harbord, *The American Army in France, 1917–1919* (Boston: Little, Brown, 1936), 475.

7. Harry S. Truman, *Autobiography of Harry S. Truman*, ed. Robert H. Ferrell (Columbia: University of Missouri Press, 2002), 50–51.

8. John A. Cutchins, *History of the Twenty-Ninth Division, "Blue and Gray," 1917–1919* (Philadelphia: Press of MacCalla, 1921), 247.

9. Chester E. Baker, *Doughboy's Diary* (Shippensburg, PA: Burd Street Press, 1998), 120.

10. Barbeau and Henri, *The Unknown Soldiers*, 164.

11. Cutchins, *Twenty-Ninth Division*, 24.

12. Frank B. Tiebout, *A History of the 305th Infantry* (New York: Wynkoop Hallenbeck Crawford, 1919), 205–206.

13. Commanding General 88th Division, *The 88th Division in the World War of 1914–1918* (New York: Wynkoop Hallenbeck Crawford, 1919), 83–84.

14. *The CRO*, 15 February 1919.

15. Ibid., 22 February 1919.

16. McKenna, *Early Exits*, 83.

17. *The CRO*, 6 April 1919.

18. Ibid.

19. James G. Adams, *Review of the American Forces in Germany* (Coblenz, Germany: Adams, 1921), 351–352; *The CRO*, 3 May 1919.

20. *The CRO*, 8 June 1919.

21. Ibid.

5th Inning

1. Commanding General, *The 88th Division*, 79.

2. *Stars and Stripes*, 21 March 1919.

3. Ibid., 8 February 1919.

4. Christian A. Bach and Henry Noble Hall, *The Fourth Division in the World War* (Garden City, NY: Fourth Division, 1920), 236.

5. Cutchins, *Twenty-Ninth Division*, 251–252.

6. *Stars and Stripes*, 28 March 1919.

7. Ibid., 4 April 1919.

8. Fosdick and Allen, *Keeping Our Fighters Fit*, 29–30.

9. States Publication Society, *Official History of the 86th Division*, 43–44.

10. *The CRO*, 21 May 1919.

11. *AMAROC News*, 23 April 1919.

12. Ibid., 5 July 1919.

13. Burton, *600 Days' Service*, 179.

14. Alfred E. Cornebise, *The AMAROC News: The Daily Newspaper of the American Forces in Germany, 1919–1923* (Carbondale: Southern Illinois University Press, 1981), 148.

15. Ibid.

16. Maj. Gen. Johnson Hagood, *Caissons Go Rolling Along*, ed. Larry A. Grant (Columbia: University of South Carolina Press, 2010), 77.

17. Camp Lee Base Hospital, "Sports Update, " in *Lest We Forget*, ed. Harry M. Baker (Camp Lee, VA: Camp Lee Base Hospital, 1919), 228–230.

18. Cole and Howells, *Thirty-Seventh Division*, 263.

19. Adams, *Review of the American Forces in Germany*, 137.

20. Cornebise, *The AMAROC News*, 170.

6th Inning

1. *Die Wacht am Rhein*, 1 April 1919.

2. *Stars and Stripes*, 4 April 1919.

3. American Expeditionary Forces, General Staff, General Headquarters, *Candid Comment on the American Soldier of 1917–1918 and Kindred Topics by the Germans* (Chaumont, France: American Expeditionary Forces, 1919), 19.

4. US Department of the Army, *American Representation in Occupied Germany, 1920–1921*, vol. 1 (compiled by the Assistant Chief of Staff, G-2, American Forces in Germany, 1921), 180.

5. Adams, *Review of the American Forces in Germany*, 352–353.

6. *Fourth Corps Flare*, 12 April 1918.

7. Ibid.

8. *The Barrage*, 9 May 1919.

9. Francis X. Rogers and Homer C. Looze, *417th Motor Supply Train (M.T.C.)* (Coblenz, Germany: Görres-Druckerei, 1919), 15.

10. William J. Sponsler, *A Brief History of the Unit 310, Motor Transport Corps, 1918–1919* (Coblenz, Germany: Görres-Druckerei, 1919), 53–59; *AMAROC News*, 20 July 1919.

11. *AMAROC News*, 31 July 1919.

12. Ibid., 27 May 1919.

13. *The Indian*, 3 June 1919, 14.

14. Ibid., undated, 12.

15. *AMAROC News*, 5 July 1919.

16. Ibid., 4 July 1919.

17. Ibid., 5 July 1919.

18. John Veneziano, *National Baseball Hall of Fame and Museum 2015 Yearbook* (Lynn, MA: H. O. Zimman, 2015), 123.

19. *AMAROC News*, 2 August 1919.

20. *New York Times*, 15 and 28 August 1919.

21. Moses N. Thisted, *Pershing's Pioneer Infantry of World War I* (Hemet, CA: Alphabet, 1981), 312.

22. *AMAROC News*, 29 July 1919.

23. Adams, *Review of the American Forces in Germany*, 354.

24. Cornebise, *The AMAROC News*, 142, citing *AMAROC News* issue of 20 May 1920.

25. Adams, *Review of the American Forces in Germany*, 360.

26. Ibid., 360–361.

27. *New York Times*, 15 November 1920.

28. Adams, *Review of the American Forces in Germany*, 351.

7th Inning

1. National Baseball Hall of Fame and Museum website; Honig, *Baseball America*, 88.

2. Honig, *Baseball America*, 92.

3. Robert Watson Chubb, *Regimental History, 342nd Field Artillery, 89th Division* (New York: 89th Division, Regimental Historian, 1921), 13–14; Honig, *Baseball America*, 92–93.

4. Donald Dewey and Nicholas Acocella, *The New Biographical History of Baseball* (Chicago: Triumph Books, 2002), 5.

5. Society for American Baseball Research website.

6. Dewey and Acocella, *New Biographical History of Baseball*, 5–6; and Creamer, *Stengel*, 271.

7. Baseball's Greatest Sacrifice website: Calvin Bryant.

8. Ibid., Alexander T. "Tom" Burr.

9. Ibid., Harry E. Chapman.

10. Ibid., LaVerne "Larry" Chappell.

11. Dewey and Acocella, *New Biographical History of Baseball*, 73–76.

12. Richard Gurtowski, "Remembering Baseball Hall of Famers Who Served in the Chemical Corps, " *Army Chemical Review*, July–December 2005, 52–54.

13. Baseball in Wartime website.

14. Gurtowski, "Remembering Baseball Hall of Famers, " 52–54.

15. *New York Times*, 28 August 1919.

16. Baseball's Greatest Sacrifice website: Nicles (Nick) DiGiacomo. This site errs in giving an immigration year of 1907, and a birthplace of Caserta, Italy. DiGiacomo's naturalization paperwork gives a date of entry into the US of 28 April 1912, and a birthplace of Monteodorisio (as does his draft registration card). DiGiacomo signed his name as "Nicles, " but his Italian given name was probably Nicola. For naturalization and military service information, see Ancestry.com, *Maryland in the World War: Military and Naval Service Records*, vols. I and II.

17. Dewey and Acocella, *New Biographical History of Baseball*, 121–122.

18. Jim Leeke, "Caseys at the Bat, " Knights of Columbus website, 1 July 2017, www.kofc.org/en/columbia/detail/caseys-at-the-bat.html.

19. "K of C Service in the Great War, " Knights of Columbus website.

20. Society for American Baseball Research website.

21. Baseball Reference website.

22. *New York Times*, 8 September 1912; National Pastime Museum website; and Ancestry.com, *New York Abstracts of World War I Military Service*.

23. Baseball's Greatest Sacrifice website: Harry M. Glenn.

24. Baseball Almanac, *Professional Baseball Players, 1876–2004*, on Ancestry.com.

25. Richard A. Rinaldi, *The United States Army in World War I: Orders of Battle; Ground Units, 1917–1919* (Takoma Park, MD: Tiger Lily, 2005), 45.

26. Baseball Almanac, *Professional Baseball Players*.

27. National Pastime Museum website: Hank Gowdy.

28. Fort Benning Environmental Management Division, *Historic Fort Benning through Art*, Cultural Resources Management Program, 2007, www.benning.army.mil., 6–7.

29. Baseball's Greatest Sacrifice website: Edward L. "Eddie" Grant; Dewey and Acocella, *New Biographical History of Baseball*, 161.

30. Ancestry.com, *World War I Naval Deaths, 1917–1919*; Baseball's Greatest Sacrifice website: Newton "Newt" Halliday.

31. Ancestry.com; Baseball's Greatest Sacrifice website: Ted Kimbro.

32. Dewey and Acocella, *New Biographical History of Baseball*, 236–238.

33. States Publication Society, *Official History of the Eighty-Sixth Division*, 76.

34. Honig, *Baseball America*, 115.

35. Dewey and Acocella, *New Biographical History of Baseball*, 236–238 and 369–372.

36. Ibid., 269–270.

37. Gurtowski, "Remembering Baseball Hall of Famers, " with note from Ty Cobb's *My Life in Baseball*, 52–54.

38. Dewey and Acocella, *New Biographical History of Baseball*, 269–270.

39. Gurtowski, "Remembering Baseball Hall of Famers, " 52–54.

40. Honig, *Baseball America*, 153; Dewey and Acocella, *New Biographical History of Baseball*, 269–270.

41. Ancestry.com, *Pennsylvania, WWI Veterans Service and Compensation Files*.

42. Dewey and Acocella, *New Biographical History of Baseball*, 324–325.

43. New York Community Trust website.

44. Baseball Reference website.

45. Ibid.

46. New York Community Trust website.

47. National Pastime Museum website: "Grantland Rice, Our Grand Old Game and Everything Else."

48. *Die Wacht am Rhine* 1, no. 3 (1 April 1919).

49. Lee Congdon, *Legendary Sports Writers of the Golden Age: Grantland Rice, Red Smith, Shirley Povich, and W. C. Heinz* (Lanham, MD: Rowman & Littlefield, 2017), 2.

50. *New World Encyclopedia* website: Grantland Rice.

51. Baseball Reference website.

52. Missouri History Museum website.

53. Gurtowski, "Remembering Baseball Hall of Famers, " 52–54.

54. Ritter, *The Glory*, 124–125; Dewey and Acocella, *New Biographical History of Baseball*, 348–352.

55. Honig, *Baseball America*, 251.

56. Virginia War Service records, Rixey AGO Form 844-Officer.

57. Dewey and Acocella, *New Biographical History of Baseball*, 354.

58. Baseball's Greatest Sacrifice website: Ralph E. Sharman; Ancestry.com, *Ohio Soldiers in World War I, 1917–1918*.

59. Dewey and Acocella, *New Biographical History of Baseball*, 388–389.

60. Henry F. Pringle, *The Life and Times of William Howard Taft*, vol. 2 (Norwalk, CT: Easton, 1986), 906; *Yale Alumni Weekly*, 11 October 1918: 84.

61. Howard Wilkinson, "Charlie Taft: City Hall Legend and Reds Fan for the Ages, " WVXU 91.7 FM Radio website.

62. Ball Parks of Baseball website: Riverfront Stadium.

63. *New York Times*, July 25 1983.

64. Baseball's Greatest Sacrifice website: Norman Triplett.

65. Baseball's Greatest Sacrifice website: Robert Gustave "Bun" Troy; Findagrave.com.

66. Ancestry.com for transport manifest; Baseball's Greatest Sacrifice website: Pearl "Specks" Webster.

8th Inning

1. *Gas Attack of the New York Division* 1, no. 20 (6 April 1918): 22.

2. Cpl. James DeMotta's actual surname was D'Amato; see Ancestry.com, Army transport manifest, SS *Kroonland*, 26 July 1918. For the letter about retaining 51st men on duty with the IV Corps, see National Archives and Records Administration, RG 165. Thanks to Dr. Margaret McMahon—author, historian, and genealogist—for calling these to our attention.

3. Cutchins, *Twenty-Ninth Division*, 313–315.

4. Lyn MacDonald, *The Roses of No Man's Land* (New York: Macmillan, 1980), 261–262.

5. Anonymous, *The Story of U.S. Base Hospital No. 5*, written by a member of the unit (Cambridge, UK: Cambridge University Press, 1919).

6. Anonymous, *Base Hospital No. 9, A. E. F.: A History of the Work of the New York Hospital Unit during Two Years of Active Service*, written by the Padre (New York: n.p., 1920), 109.

7. Anonymous, *On Active Service with Base Hospital 46, U.S.A., Mar. 20, 1918, to May 25, 1919* (N.p., n.d.), 159–160.

8. Company Clerk, "Then and Now, " *American Legion Monthly* 4, no. 3 (March 1928): 39.

9. Katherine Mayo, *That Damn Y: A Record of Overseas Service* (Boston: Riverside Press Cambridge, 1920), 237.

10. Ibid., 238.

11. Ibid., 240.

12. *Stars and Stripes*, 7 June 1918.

13. Ibid.

14. Ibid.

15. Wagenheim, *Babe Ruth*, 44.

16. Meredith Goad, "In 1918, Different Time, Same Outcome, " *Portland Press Herald*, 28 October 2004, A-1.

17. Dewey and Acocella, *New Biographical History of Baseball*, 161.

18. American Battle Monuments Commission website: Bernard L. Dolan and Matthew S. Lanigan files.

19. McKenna, *Early Exits*, 85–88.

20. Ibid., 85–86.

21. *The Leatherneck*, 10 February 1923, 2; *National Army News* 1, no. 9 (20 May 1918): 14.

22. *Washington Post*, 9 June 1918.

23. McKenna, *Early Exits*, 88.

24. *The Leatherneck*, 10 February 1923, 2.

25. *AMAROC News*, 27 May 1919.

26. Ibid., 4 June 1919.

27. Ibid., 23 July 1919.

28. George H. English, *History of the 89th Division U.S.A.* (Denver, CO: War Society of the 89th Division, 1920), 386.

29. Ibid., 390–393.

9th Inning

1. McKenna, *Early Exits*, 5–6.

2. Ibid.

3. Gen. Peyton C. March, *The Nation at War* (Garden City, NY: Doubleday, Doran, 1932), 318.

4. Ibid., 327.

5. *New York Times*, 17 September 1919.

6. Cole and Howells, *Thirty-Seventh Division*, 259.

7. *New York Times*, 26 August 1919.

8. *AMAROC News*, 21 April 1919.

9. Honig, *Baseball America*, 182.

Bibliography

Adams, James G. *Review of the American Forces in Germany*. Coblenz, Germany: Adams, 1921.

Allen, Henry T. *My Rhineland Journal*. Boston and New York: Houghton Mifflin, 1923.

American Expeditionary Forces, General Staff, General Headquarters. *Candid Comment on the American Soldier of 1917–1918 and Kindred Topics by the Germans*. Chaumont, France: American Expeditionary Forces, 1919.

Anonymous. "Historic Fort Benning through Art." Accessed through www.benning.army.mil.

Anonymous. *On Active Service with Base Hospital 46, U.S.A., Mar. 20, 1918, to May 25, 1919*. N.p., n.d. Accessed through https://archive.org/stream/14230710R.nlm.nih.gov/14230710R#page/n7/mode/2up.

Anonymous. *The Story of U.S. Base Hospital No. 5*. Written by a member of the unit. Cambridge, UK: Cambridge University Press, 1919. Accessed through https://ia600703.us.archive.org/26/items/39002011122562.med.yale.edu/39002011122562.med.yale.edu.pdf.

Anonymous. *Base Hospital No. 9, A. E. F.: A History of the Work of the New York Hospital Unit during Two Years of Active Service*. Written by the Padre. New York: n.p., 1920. Accessed through https://archive.org /stream/14230580R.nlm.nih.gov/14230580R#page/n5/mode/2up.

Ayers, Leonard P. *Source Records of the Great War*. Edited by Charles F. Horne. New York: National Alumni, 1923.

Bach, Christian A., and Henry Noble Hall. *The Fourth Division, Its Services and Achievements in the World War*. Garden City, NY: Fourth Division, 1920.

Baker, Chester E. *Doughboy's Diary*. Shippensburg, PA: Burd Street Press, 1998.

Ballew, Bill. "The Great Flood, Baseball's Fastest Game Highlight Tourist's 1916 Season." *Tourists* 2 (2016), Asheville Tourists Gameday Program.

Barbeau, Arthur E., and Florette Henri. *The Unknown Soldiers: Black American Troops in World War I*. Philadelphia: Temple University Press, 1974.

Barnes, Alexander F., and Peter L. Belmonte. *Forgotten Soldiers of World War I: America's Immigrant Doughboys*. Atglen, PA: Schiffer, 2018.

Beaver, Daniel R. *Newton D. Baker and the American War Effort, 1917–1919*. Lincoln: University of Nebraska Press, 1966.

Burton, Harold H. *600 Days' Service: A History of the 361st Infantry Regiment of the United States Army*. Portland, OR: James, Kerns & Abbott, 1921.

Camp Lee Base Hospital. "Sports Update." In *Lest We Forget*. Edited by Henry M. Baker. Camp Lee, VA: Camp Lee Base Hospital, 1919.

Center of Military History. *Order of Battle of the United States Land Forces in the World War*. Vol. 3, Pt. 2, *Zone of the Interior: Territorial Departments Tactical Divisions Organized in 1918 Posts, Camps, and Stations*. Washington, DC: Center of Military History, United States Army, 1988.

Ceresi, Frank. "The Little Known Service of Branch Rickey, Ty Cobb and the Great Matty." Accessed through http://baseballinwartime.com.

Chafets, Zev. *Cooperstown Confidential*. New York: Bloomsbury, 2009.

Chubb, Robert Watson. *Regimental History, 342nd Field Artillery, 89th Division*. New York: 89th Division, Regimental Historian, 1921.

Cole, Ralph D., and W. C. Howells. *The Thirty-Seventh Division in the World War, 1917–1918*. Columbus, OH: Thirty-Seventh Division Veterans Association, 1926.

Commanding General 88th Division. *The 88th Division in the World*

War of 1914–1918. New York: Wynkoop Hallenbeck Crawford, 1919.

Company Clerk. "Then and Now." *American Legion Monthly* 4, no. 3 (March 1928).

Congdon, Lee. *Legendary Sports Writers of the Golden Age: Grantland Rice, Red Smith, Shirley Povich, and W. C. Heinz*. Lanham, MD: Rowman & Littlefield, 2017.

Cooper, John P., Jr. *The History of the 110th Field Artillery with Sketches of Related Units*. Baltimore: War Records Division, Maryland Historical Society, 1953.

Cornebise, Alfred E. *The AMAROC News: The Daily Newspaper of the American Forces in Germany, 1919–1923*. Carbondale: Southern Illinois University Press, 1981.

Creamer, Robert W. *Stengel: His Life and Times*. New York: Simon and Schuster, 1984.

Cutchins, John A. *History of the Twenty-Ninth Division, "Blue and Gray," 1917–1919*. Philadelphia: Press of MacCalla, 1921.

———. *An Amateur Diplomat in the World War*. Richmond, VA: American Legion, Commanders Committee, 1938.

Dewey, Donald, and Nicholas Acocella. *The New Biographical History of Baseball*. Chicago: Triumph Books, 2002.

English, George H. *History of the 89th Division U.S.A.* Denver, CO: War Society of the 89th Division. 1920.

Ford, Col. Joseph H. *The Medical Department of the United States Army in the World War*. Vol 2. Washington, DC: US Government Printing Office, 1927.

Fort Benning Environmental Management Division. *Historic Fort Benning through Art*. Cultural Resources Management Program, 2007, www.benning.army.mil.

Fortescue, Major Granville. "Training the New Armies of Liberty." *National Geographic Magazine* 32, nos. 5–6 (November–December 1917).

Fosdick, Raymond D., and Edward F. Allen. *Keeping Our Fighters Fit for War and After*. Washington, DC: Commission on Training Camp Activities, 1918.

Goad, Meredith. "In 1918, Different Time, Same Outcome." *Portland Press Herald*, 28 October 2004.

Gorrell, Edgar S. "History, Construction Co. No. 11." Gorrell's History of the American Expeditionary Force Air Service, 1917–1919. US National Archives and Records Administration, RG120, Roll 0021, Series E, Vol. 25, Squadron Histories.

Greenfield, Kent Roberts, Robert R. Palmer, and Bell I. Wiley. *United States Army in World War II, the Army Ground Forces: The Organization of Combat Ground Troops*. Washington, DC: Center of Military History, United States Army, 1987 (first printed in 1947).

Gurtowski, Richard. "Remembering Baseball Hall of Famers Who Served in the Chemical Corps." *Army Chemical Review*, July–December 2005, US Army Chemical, Biological, Radiological, and Nuclear School and the Maneuver Support Center of Excellence.

Hagood, Maj. Gen. Johnson. *Caissons Go Rolling Along*. Edited by Larry A. Grant. Columbia: University of South Carolina Press, 2010.

Harbord, James G. *The American Army in France 1917–1919*. Boston: Little, Brown, 1936.

Honig, Donald. *Baseball America*. New York: Macmillan, 1985.

Horsfall, G. Souvenir scrapbooks of the war and occupation, 1918–1919, 326th Field Signal Battalion. Private collection.

Jacobsen, Gerald F. *History of the 107th Infantry*. New York: Seventh Regiment Armory, 1920.

Keith, Wayne. Wartime diary of service in the States and in France with the 37th Division. Private collection.

Koehn, Robert. Collection of letters, 1918–1919, from the 83rd Division. Private collection.

Leeke, Jim. "Caseys at the Bat." Knights of Columbus website, 1 July 2017, www.kofc.org/cn/columbia/detail/caseys-at-the-bat.html.

MacDonald, Lyn. *The Roses of No Man's Land*. New York: Macmillan, 1980.

March, Gen. Peyton C. *The Nation at War*. Garden City, NY: Doubleday, Doran, 1932.

Mayo, Katherine. *That Damn Y: A Record of Overseas Service*. Boston: Riverside Press Cambridge, 1920.

McKenna, Brian. *Early Exits*. Lanham, MD: Scarecrow, 2007.

Ohio Adjutant General's Department. *The Official Roster of Ohio Soldiers, Sailors, and Marines in the World War, 1917–18*. 23 vols. Columbus, OH: F. J. Heer, 1926.

Pringle, Henry F. *The Life and Times of William Howard Taft*. Vol. 2. Norwalk, CT: Easton, 1986.

Pronchen, Joseph. "K of C Service in the Great War." Dated 1 May 2017, accessed through www.kofc.org/en/index.html.

Reynolds, Chaplain F. C., and Chaplain William F. McLaughlin. *115th Infantry U.S.A. in the World War*. Baltimore: Read-Taylor, 1920.

Rinaldi, Richard A. *The United States Army in World War I: Orders of Battle; Ground Units, 1917–1919*. Takoma Park, MD: Tiger Lily, 2005.

Ritter, Lawrence S. *The Glory of their Times*. New York: William Morrow, 1984.

Rogers, Francis X., and Homer C. Looze. *417th Motor Supply Train (M.T.C.)*. Coblenz, Germany: Gorres-Druckeri, 1919.

Scott, Emmett J. *The American Negro in the World War*. Chicago: Homewood, 1919.

Sponsler, William J. *A Brief History of the Unit 310, Motor Transport Corps, 1918–1919*. Coblenz, Germany: Gorres-Druckerei, 1919.

Stallings, Laurence T. *The Doughboys: The Story of the AEF, 1917–1918*. New York: Harper and Row, 1963.

States Publication Society. *The Official History of the Eighty-Sixth Division*. Chicago: States Publication Society, 1921.

Stewart, Richard W., ed. *American Military History*. Vol. 1, *The United States Army and the Forging of a Nation, 1775–1917*. Army Historical Series 1. Washington, DC: Center of Military History, United States Army, 2005.

Stewart, Richard W., ed. *American Military History*. Vol. 2, *The United States Army in a Global Era, 1917–2008*. Army Historical Series 2. Washington DC: Center of Military History, United States Army, 2010.

Thisted, Moses N. *Pershing's Pioneer Infantry of World War I*. Hemet, CA: Alphabet, 1981.

Tiebout, Frank B. *A History of the 305th Infantry*. New York: Wynkoop Hallenbeck Crawford, 1919.

Truman, Harry S. *The Autobiography of Harry S. Truman*. Edited by Robert H. Ferrell. Columbia: University of Missouri Press, 2002.

US Department of the Army. *American Representation in Occupied Germany, 1920–1921*. 2 vols. Compiled by the Assistant Chief of Staff, G-2, American Forces in Germany, 1921.

US Provost Marshal General. *Final Report of the Provost General to the Secretary of War on the Operations of the Selective Service System to July 15, 1919*. Washington, DC: US Government Printing Office, 1920.

US War Department. *Commission on Training Camp Activities Report*. Washington, DC: US War Department, 1918.

Veneziano, John. *National Baseball Hall of Fame and Museum 2015 Yearbook*. Lynn, MA: H. O. Zimman, 2015.

Wagenheim, Kal. *Babe Ruth: His Life and Legend*. New York: Praeger, 1974.

Wiggins, Brig. Gen. Kennard R., Jr. *Delaware in World War I*. Charleston, SC: History Press, 2015.

Wilkinson, Howard. "Charlie Taft: City Hall Legend and Reds Fan for the Ages." WVXU 91.7 FM Radio, 9 September 2017. Accessed through http://wvxu.org/post/charlie-taft-city-hall-legend-and-reds-fan-ages#stream/0.

Wythe, Maj. George. *A History of the 90th Division*. New York: 90th Division Association, 1920.

Newspapers/Unit Periodicals:

AMAROC News. The official newspaper of the American occupation of Germany, 1919–1922.

American Legion Monthly, March 1928.

The Barrage. The official newspaper of the 18th Field Artillery. 3rd Division. Published in Polch, Germany, in 1919.

Camp Dodger. The official newspaper of the 88th Division. Published at Camp Dodge, IA, in 1917–1918.

Camp Lee Bayonet. Published in Petersburg, VA, in 1918.

The CRO. The official newspaper of the Central Records Office. Published in Bourges, France, in 1919.

Die Wacht am Rhein: A Journal of Truth. The newspaper produced and printed by the G-2-C section of the Headquarters staff, US Third Army, in early 1919.

Fourth Corps Flare. The official newspaper of the units assigned to the US IV Corps. Published in Mayen, Germany, in 1919.

Gas Attack of the New York Division. The official magazine of the 27th Division, 1917–1919.

Gettysburg Times, 1918.

Hour Glass of the Seventh Division–United States Army. French edition 1919.

The Indian. The official news magazine of the 2nd Division. Published in Germany in 1919.

The Leatherneck, 1918–1928.

National Army News, 1917–1919.

New York Times, 1918–1922.

Portland Press Herald, 2004.

Star and Stripes. The official newspaper of the American Expeditionary Forces, 1918–1919.

Washington Post, 1918.

Yale Alumni Weekly, 1918.

"Take Me Out to the Ball Game, " credited to composer Albert Von Tilzer; lyricist: Jack Norworth.

Websites

Ancestry.com:

Baseball Almanac, *Professional Baseball Players, 1876–2004*

Maryland Military Men, 1917–1918

Maryland in the World War: Military and Naval Service Records, vols. I and II

New York, Abstracts of World War I Military Service, 1917–1919

Ohio Soldiers in World War I, 1917–1918

Pennsylvania, WWI Veterans Service and Compensation Files, 1917–1919, 1934–1948

US World War I Draft Registration Cards, 1917–1918.

World War I Naval Deaths, 1917–1919

Ball Parks of Baseball, www.ballparksofbaseball.com/ballparks/riverfront-stadium/

Baseball Reference, www.baseball-reference.com/bullpen/JG_Taylor_Spink_Award
Baseball in Wartime, www.baseballinwartime.com/chemical_warfare.html
Baseball's Greatest Sacrifice, www.baseballsgreatestsacrifice.com:
biographies/bryant_calvin.html
biographies/burr_alex.html
biographies/chapman_harry.html
biographies/chappell_larry.html
biographies/giacomo_jock.html
biographies/glenn_harry.html
biographies/grant_eddie.html
biographies/halliday_newt.html
biographies/kimbro_ted.html
biographies/sharman_ralph.html
biographies/triplett_norman.html
biographies/troy_robert.html
biographies/webster_specks.html
Find a Grave, www.Findagrave.com
Knights of Columbus, www.kofc.org/en/index.html
Missouri History Museum, "WWI Artifacts and Memories: Branch Rickey, " by Patrick Allie, WWI curator, www.historyhappenshere.org/node/7704
National Baseball Hall of Fame and Museum, https://baseballhall.org/
National Pastime Museum:
"Grantland Rice, Our Grand Old Game and Everything Else, " www.thenationalpastimemuseum.com/article/grantland-rice-our-grand-old-game-and-everything-else
"The 1917 Season, " www.thenationalpastimemuseum.com/article/1917-season
New World Encyclopedia, www.newworldencyclopedia.org/entry/Grantland_Rice
New York Community Trust, www.nycommunitytrust.org/Portals/0/Uploads/Documents/Grantland%20Rice.pdf
Society for American Baseball Research, http://sabr.org/
Sports Reference, www.baseball-reference.com/bullpen/Grantland_Rice

Index

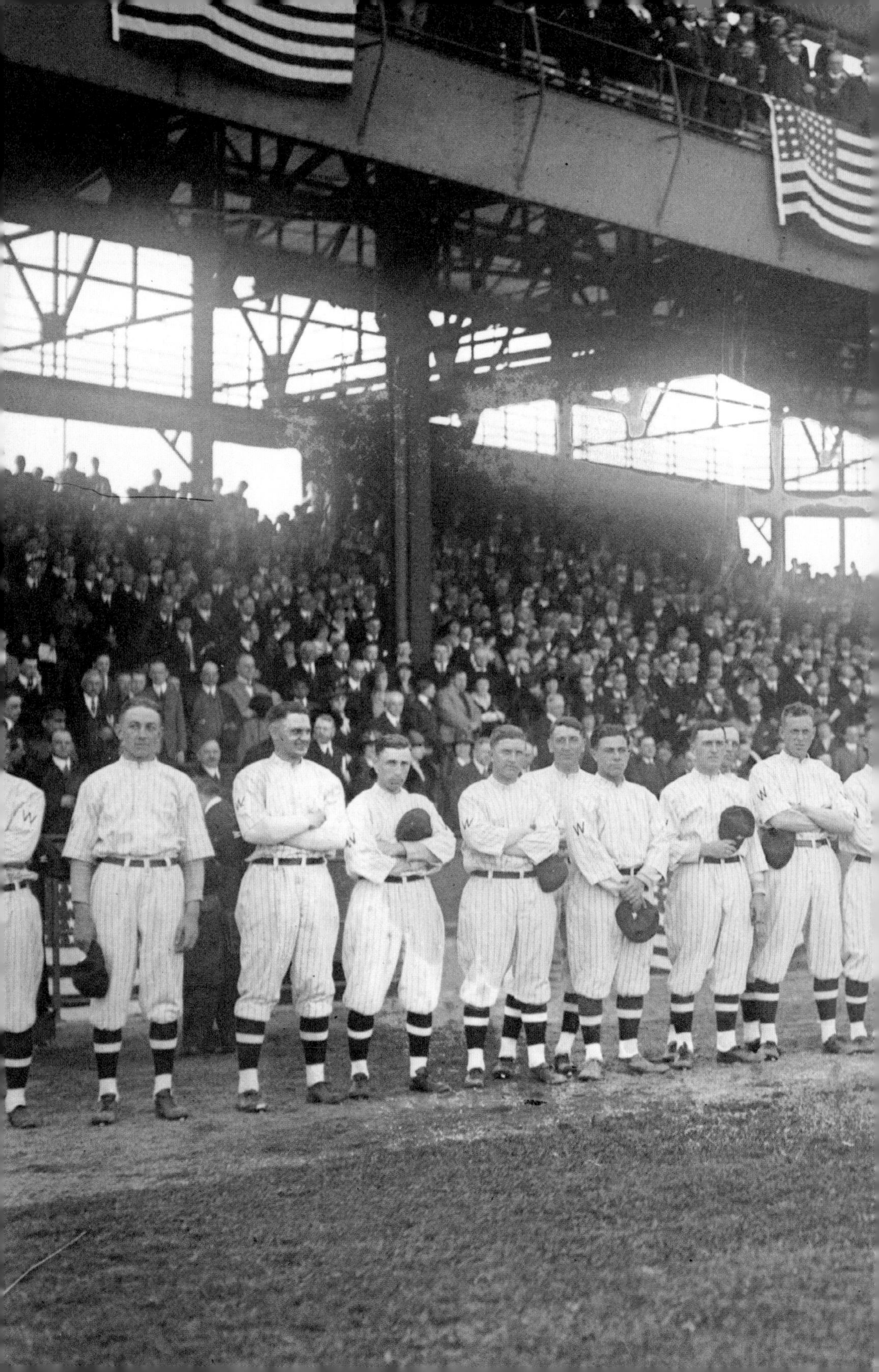